# Double Jeopardy

*A volume in the series*

## Adolescent Development and Legal Policy

EDITED BY FRANKLIN E. ZIMRING

Also in the series:

*An American Travesty: Legal Responses to Adolescent Sexual Offending*
by Franklin E. Zimring

# Double Jeopardy

*Adolescent Offenders with*
*Mental Disorders*

## Thomas Grisso

*Foreword by Franklin E. Zimring*

University of Chicago Press | *Chicago & London*

The University of Chicago Press, Chicago 60637
The University of Chicago Press, Ltd., London
© 2004 by The University of Chicago
All rights reserved. Published 2004
Paperback edition 2006
Printed in the United States of America
13  12  11  10  09  08  07  06      2  3  4  5

ISBN: 0-226-30914-2 (cloth)
ISBN: 0-226-30929-0 (paper)

Library of Congress Cataloging-in-Publication Data

Grisso, Thomas.
    Double jeopardy : adolescent offenders with mental
    disorders / Thomas Grisso.
        p.    cm.—(Adolescent development and legal policy)
    Includes bibliographical references and index.
    ISBN: 0-226-30914-2 (Cloth : alk. paper)
    1.  Juvenile delinquents—Mental health—United States.
        2.  Juvenile delinquents—Rehabilitation—United States.
        3.  Juvenile delinquents—Mental health services—United
        States.    I. Title.    II. Series.

    RJ506.J88  G75    2004
    364.36—dc22
                                          2003018271

# Contents

# Foreword

At some point during adolescence, millions of young persons will be arrested by police or otherwise referred to the agencies of juvenile justice in the United States. Hundreds of thousands of young persons will suffer from serious emotional disorders during the transition to adulthood. The sheer arithmetic of American adolescence would guarantee that many thousands of those who are processed and adjudicated by institutions of juvenile justice suffer from serious emotional disabilities as well—even if there were no tendency for emotional problems to predispose adolescents to conflict and visible vulnerability. These are the children and adolescents at double disadvantage who are the subject of Thomas Grisso's important new study.

The conditions of double jeopardy that this book describes are important challenges to the quality of American juvenile justice. Youths who have serious emotional problems are more likely to be charged with serious acts of delinquency than nonafflicted youth. Every reform that reduces the number of kids who are locked up by diverting lower risk youths out of the system will probably increase the proportion of the institutional population that is at double jeopardy. Often, the further one goes in the system, the larger the overlap between emotional problems and custodial status in juvenile justice.

This study is organized around the special complications that the double-jeopardy population raises for the system's responses to their needs while in custody, to their potential incapacities to participate in the processes of juvenile justice, and to the assessment of their potential risk of harm to the community. In addition to organizing the growing body of research on emotional disorders among juvenile justice populations, this book provides a comprehensive structure for thinking about the double-jeopardy population. It uses a developmental perspective to inform its policy analysis, combining a command of the theoretical literature with practical insight in a most refreshing fashion.

*Double Jeopardy* is the first of a series of studies on adolescent development and legal policy that is supported by the John D. and Catherine T. MacArthur Foundation Research Network on Adolescent Development and Juvenile Justice. Our hope in launching the series is to commission monographs on specific topics that can be organized and addressed in ways that help researchers and policymakers alike. The model for this project is the series of monographs commissioned by Saleem Shah at the National Institute of Mental Health from the mid-1960s to the early 1980s. The board of editors for this series considered the overlap of emotional disorders and the institutions of juvenile justice to be an exemplary first topic for the project, and Thomas Grisso of the University of Massachusetts Medical School was an obvious choice as the author of a book on this topic.

This book vindicates the judgment of the editorial board. What Grisso provides for this important topic is a conceptual organization that serves as a structure for examining existing studies and as a framework for future work. In the immediate future, this book will serve as an up-to-date assessment of all that has been written in the field. But fifteen or twenty years from now, even as the literature on the topic will have expanded, the framework for analysis that Professor Grisso creates here will continue to provide assistance to the scholar and the practitioner.

*Franklin E. Zimring*

# Acknowledgments

Writing this book required surveying the most recent works in a wide range of literature: developmental psychology, of course, but also child clinical psychology and psychiatry, developmental psychopathology, developmental criminology, juvenile justice policy, and mental health services research. Part of the journey took me to places I'd been before, but some expeditions led deep into unfamiliar territory. Finding the right information, assimilating it, and attempting synthesis across fields often proved perplexing.

It would have been a lonely trip indeed without friends, among whom I especially thank Elizabeth Cauffman, Dan Connor, Fran Lexcen, Bob Schwartz, Linda Teplin, and some of the best of colleagues associated with three organizations: members of the MacArthur Foundation Research Network on Adolescent Development and Juvenile Justice, faculty of the Center for Mental Health Services Research at the University of Massachusetts Medical School, and Joe Cocozza and Kathy Skowyra of the National Center for Mental Health and Juvenile Justice.

For stimulation of ideas during drafting and revision of the manuscript, I especially thank David Arredondo, Ed Mulvey, and Laurence Steinberg, as well as the Adolescent Development and Legal Policy series editor Frank Zimring—known affectionately during this process as "Sergeant Zimring of the Book Police"—who called almost weekly to ensure that I was neither delinquent in my duties nor without helpful encouragement to stay the course. Daily assistance in finding relevant texts was provided with resourceful efficiency by "Detective" Judith Quinlan. And thanks once again, Donna, for keeping the late-night coffeepot from running low.

*Part 1*

# Examining Realities

## Chapter 1

# Reasons for Concern about Mental Disorders of Adolescent Offenders

Many agencies and advocates recently have urged that greater attention be given to the mental health needs of youths in the juvenile justice system (e.g., after an early warning by Cocozza, 1992: American Bar Association, 2001; Office of Juvenile Justice and Delinquency Prevention, 2000; National Council of Juvenile and Family Court Judges, 2000; National Mental Health Association, 2000; U.S. Surgeon General, 1999). They have pointed with alarm at an apparent increase in the proportion of youths with mental disorders in detention centers and juvenile correctional facilities, pressing the juvenile justice system to meet its obligation to provide them treatment.

This volume explores the basis for our obligations to identify and respond to adolescent offenders' mental disorders, examines the state of our knowledge about youths' mental disorders and their consequences, and charts a rational course for the juvenile justice system's response to the mental health needs of those who are in its custody. To set the stage, this chapter identifies why the question regarding mental health needs of juvenile offenders has arisen in recent years, the scope of the problem, and a foundation for examining the juvenile justice system's obligation to respond to youths' mental disorders.

## How Delinquent Youths' Mental Disorders Got Our Attention

The juvenile justice system, now a little more than a century old, has weathered many storms in its first century. But it will probably require another two decades for it to recover from the tempests of the 1990s.

The barometer began to fall around 1987, when headlines and then

Justice Department statistics reported an increase in lethal violence by youth. The gathering clouds soon erupted and produced a growing flood of homicides and aggravated assaults committed by youths ages thirteen to seventeen, increasing year by year until the rates had more than doubled by 1994 (U.S. Department of Justice, 1980–1993, 1994, 1995–1996). Explanations ranged from notions that our country had spawned a generation of "super-predators" (DiIulio, 1995; Fox, 1996) to more reasonable interpretations of the confluence of changes in the drug market and the availability and use of guns by adolescents, especially in the cities (e.g., Blumstein, 1995; Zimring, 1998). Compounding the effect was an increase in school violence in suburbs and small towns nationwide, which, although contributing little to the crime rate, kindled intense public feelings of grief and vulnerability.

Out of the alarming words and images created by these events grew a "moral panic . . . an exaggerated perception of the seriousness of the threat and the number of offenders, and collective hostility toward the offenders, who [were] perceived as outsiders threatening the community" (Scott & Steinberg, 2003, p. 807). Reacting swiftly, legislators erected what were meant to be bulwarks against the rising flood of juvenile crime. Virtually every state modified its laws pertaining to juveniles in ways that resulted in more punitive sanctions for serious violent offenses by youths (U.S. General Accounting Office, 1995; Torbet et al., 1996; Snyder & Sickmund, 1999; Grisso, 1996). They lowered the age and broadened the offense criteria for trying adolescents in criminal court rather than juvenile court, more often required a transfer to criminal court for young people charged with serious offenses (reducing judicial discretion), and increased the penalties that were legally available or required for cases retained in juvenile court. Many states' legislatures made it clear that these changes constituted a fundamental reform in the purposes of the juvenile justice system, simultaneously revising the "purpose clause" of their juvenile codes to reflect a primary emphasis on public safety and only secondarily on rehabilitation (Grisso, 1996; Snyder & Sickmund, 1999). Momentum carried this trend in legal reform through the late 1990s, well beyond 1995 when Justice Department statistics began reporting a decrease in the volume of youths' violent offenses (Blumstein & Wallman, 2000). The bulwarks still stand; there has been little subsequent change to the more punitive sanctions that were put in place during those stormy years.

Concurrent with these events, juvenile justice personnel in the early 1990s began to report what they thought was an increasing proportion of youths with mental disorders entering the juvenile justice system

(Cocozza, 1992). In fact, reviews of epidemiologic studies seem to i̇
that rates of mental disorders among adolescents in general (in the United
States and European countries) were increasing during the past few
decades compared to the first three-quarters of the twentieth century
(e.g., Fombonne, 1998), possibly due to modern changes in the social
context of adolescent development (Rutter & Smith, 1995). If the rates
of mental disorder among youths in the juvenile justice system increased
beyond that already-heightened base rate, there are several plausible
explanations:

- The increase in youth violence itself produced traumatizing conditions
  in neighborhoods, elevating the prevalence of symptoms of mental disorders among youths in those neighborhoods.
- New laws reducing judicial discretion and assigning penalties based primarily on a youth's offense worked to decrease "screening" and "diversion" of mentally disordered youths from juvenile justice processing,
  allowing more of them to penetrate the juvenile justice system than had
  formerly been the case.
- Simultaneous with changes in crime rates and legal reforms, public mental health services for children were deteriorating in many states due to
  complex financial circumstances, creating a functional "diversion" of
  mentally disordered youths into juvenile justice facilities.

There is substantial evidence for the last of these explanations. During
the 1990s, state after state experienced the collapse of public mental health
services for children and adolescents (e.g., *New York Times*, 2001) and
the closing of many—in some states, all—of their residential facilities
for seriously disturbed youths (e.g., *Arizona Daily Star*, 2000; *Columbus
Dispatch*, 2001). The juvenile justice system soon became the primary
referral for youths with mental disorders. In California, the *Los Angeles
Times* (November 21, 2000) reported that "absent adequate mental health
services, the cop has become the clinician . . . the jail has become a crisis
center," and quoted the chief of correctional services of the Los Angeles
County Sheriff's Department as acknowledging that the Los Angeles
County Jail was now the largest *de facto* mental health facility in the nation. Cases mounted in which parents gave up custody of their children
to the juvenile justice system, or managed to have their children arrested,
in order to obtain mental health services that they could no longer find
in their communities (e.g., *Columbus Dispatch*, 2002; *Progressive*, 2001;
*Omaha World-Herald*, 2002).

As the storm clouds of juvenile violence began to clear late in the 1990s, some surveyors of the wreckage—cited at the beginning of this chapter—began to call attention to the problem. They pointed to what appeared to be an alarming number of adolescents with mental disorders in juvenile justice custody, and they asserted the juvenile justice system's responsibility to identify them and to provide appropriate treatment.

But how big is the problem today? What is the nature of mental disorders among delinquent youths, and of what relevance are they for our nation's objectives for the juvenile justice system? Can we identify the young people about whom we are concerned? And above all, what types of intervention are needed? Can we chart a rational course for responding to their needs? The first step in answering these questions is to take a closer look at the scope of the problem, as described in studies of the prevalence of mental disorders among adolescent offenders in juvenile justice custody.

## How Big Is the Problem?

We have no reliable data on the prevalence of mental disorders among juvenile justice youths prior to the 1990s (Otto et al., 1992). Therefore, an empirical estimate of the increase in prevalence does not exist. Nevertheless, the perception in the mid-1990s that the proportion was growing resulted in significant efforts by government agencies and social researchers to identify the prevalence of mental disorders among youths in juvenile detention and correction settings.

### Studies of Prevalence in Juvenile Justice Settings

Several studies have identified a significant overlap between the populations of youths served by community public health agencies and youths in contact with a community's juvenile court (e.g., Rosenblatt, Rosenblatt, & Biggs, 2000; Vander Stoep, Evans, & Taub, 1997; Westendorp et al., 1986). In addition, some studies indicate that the prevalence of mental disorders among juvenile justice youths is higher than that among youths in other public health or educational settings (Stiffman et al., 1997), but about the same as those found among adolescents receiving services in community mental health programs and lower than those found in inpatient clinical services for youths (Atkins, Pumariega, & Rogers, 1999).

The specific scope of the problem, however, has been difficult to discern because of wide variations in estimates from study to study. (For a review of all such studies reported through 2002, see Cocozza & Skowyra, in press.) Research during the 1990s reported prevalence estimates for mental disorders in delinquent samples that varied from 50 to 100 percent. For example, prevalence for mental disorders among juvenile justice youth was reported as 53 percent in Maryland (Faenza, Siegfried, & Wood, 2000), about 60–70 percent for youths in Chicago (Teplin et al., 2002), 61 percent for youths in Georgia (Marsteller et al., 1997), and 76 percent in Texas (Pliszka et al., 2000). At the highest end of the spectrum, the prevalence of mental disorders for juvenile justice samples was reported to be 85 percent in Mississippi (Robertson & Husain, 2001) and 100 percent for youths in Ohio's juvenile justice facilities (Timmons-Mitchell et al., 1997).

The variability among these studies is considerable, but it is especially marked when one examines their reported prevalence rates for specific disorders. For example, a number of studies reported a prevalence of psychotic-spectrum disorders (e.g., schizophrenia) ranging from about 1 percent (Teplin et al., 2002) to 16 percent (Timmons-Mitchell et al., 1997) to 45 percent (Atkins, Pumariega, & Rogers, 1999). Mood disorders were listed as 10 percent (Wasserman et al., 2002), about 20 percent (Teplin et al., 2002), and 72 percent (Timmons-Mitchell et al., 1997); and anxiety disorders at 8 percent (Garland et al., 2001), 19 percent (Wasserman et al., 2002), 20–30 percent (Teplin et al, 2002), and 52 percent (Timmons-Mitchell et al., 1997). Attention-deficit/hyperactivity disorder (ADHD) was reported as low as 2 percent (Wasserman et al., 2002) and 18 percent (Pliszka et al., 2000) and as high as 76 percent (Timmons-Mitchell et al., 1997).

This troublesome variability may be related to many potential differences among studies in terms of their scope, framework, and measurement parameters. Moreover, often it is difficult to identify some of these study characteristics from their published reports. Generally, variation among studies has been along the following lines:

- Which mental disorders were included
- How "disorder" was defined (e.g., presence of symptoms versus a combination of their presence and their severity)
- Time frame for the presence of symptoms associated with the diagnosis (e.g., current, or past six or twelve months, or life-time prevalence)
- General methods for measuring disorders (e.g., unstructured clinical interviews, structured diagnostic interviews, paper-and-pencil measures, self-report, or multiple external sources of data)

- Specific instruments
- Use of criteria requiring a particular severity of disorder in order to qualify as a positive case
- Quality of the measures used
- Sample sizes (some being small)
- Contexts of youths' self-reports of symptoms (e.g., whether in the context of clinical care, the legal process, or research anonymity—which might influence youths' expectancies regarding use of the information and, thus, their motivations for reporting or concealing their symptoms)
- Types of facilities surveyed and thus the nature of the sample (e.g., youths on probation, in pretrial detention centers, or in postadjudication correctional facilities)
- Communities' uses of juvenile justice facilities (e.g., greater or lesser police diversion)
- Population characteristics, especially age, gender, and cultural or ethnic characteristics

Given the many ways studies can vary, it is not possible to sort out whether the differences in their results are due to actual differences in youths' characteristics from one study to another or due to methodological variation. The best we can do at present is examine a smaller set of studies that did have several methodological factors in common.

## The DISC Studies

Three recent studies—Atkins, Pumariega, & Rogers (1999), Teplin et al. (2002), and Wasserman et al. (2002)—examined large samples of youths in secure juvenile justice facilities (with the proportions of youths by ethnicity being representative of the facilities) and used the Diagnostic Interview Schedule for Children (DISC) as their measure. As described in chapter 3, the DISC provides psychiatric diagnoses according to criteria established by the *Diagnostic and Statistical Manual of Mental Disorders* (DSM) (American Psychiatric Association, 1987, 1994). In addition, all three studies provided data for four major types of disorders, as well as overall prevalence (meeting criteria for one or more disorders). Prevalence was expressed two ways: youths meeting basic diagnostic criteria, and youths meeting those criteria as well as exceeding a level of impairment suggesting clinical significance. (This distinction is discussed in chapter 2.)

Table 1 compares the prevalence figures provided by these studies for boys (because not all studies included girls). The glass is half empty and

Table 1.  Percent of Boys Meeting DSM Criteria for Mental Disorder and Criteria for Mental Disorder Plus Significant Impairment

| | Disruptive Disorders | Substance Use Disorders | Mood Disorders | Anxiety Disorders | One or More Disorders |
|---|---|---|---|---|---|
| Wasserman et al. | | | | | |
|    Meets Criteria | 32 | 50 | 10 | 20 | 62 |
|    Plus Impairment | 25 | 30 | 2 | 12 | NR |
| Teplin et al. | | | | | |
|    Meets Criteria | 41 | 51 | 19 | 21 | 66* |
|    Plus Impairment | 31 | NR | 16 | 20 | 63 |
| Atkins et al. | | | | | |
|    Meets Criteria | 43 | 20 | 24 | 33 | 72 |
|    Plus Impairment | NR | NR | NR | NR | 53 |

Notes: Atkins et al. sample includes a small proportion of girls; data were not reported separately by gender. Teplin et al. provide separate figures for girls as well, but they are omitted here in order to simplify the comparison to Wasserman et al.'s all-boy sample. Studies are from Wasserman et al. 2002; Teplin et al. 2002; and Atkins et al. 1999.

NR = not reported

*This figure was 74 percent for girls.

half full; there are some differences between studies, but overall, there are remarkable general similarities. The Wasserman et al. figures for specific disorders are somewhat lower than those of Teplin et al., which in turn are somewhat lower than those of Atkins, Pumariega, & Rogers. Wasserman et al. (2002) made this same comparison, noting that some of the discrepancies may be due to methodological differences between the studies:

- Wasserman used a newer version of the DISC (the DISC-IV) with somewhat different criteria than the one used by Teplin and Atkins (DISC-2.3) (described in chapter 3), and youths responded to questions via computer in Wasserman's administration in contrast to Teplin's and Atkin's use of interviewers.
- Wasserman's youths were in secure correctional facilities, while Teplin's were in a pretrial detention center. One might expect greater symptom severity for some psychological conditions among youths recently admitted to detention centers than among youths who have had time to "adjust" to confinement. Differences between results in these settings are

also possible because of differences in their willingness to report symptoms depending on their expectancies about people's responses to them.

- Wasserman measured current symptoms within the past month, while Teplin and Atkins measured symptoms during the past six months.
- The three studies used somewhat different measures of degree of impairment.

Despite these methodological differences, one sees considerable agreement at the broadest level of analysis; all three studies produced figures for "One or More Disorders" in roughly the 60–70 percent range. The discrepancies are more marked for specific levels of diagnostic classes, and they magnify further when one reaches a level of specificity beyond the classes shown in table 1. For example, for specific disorders associated with disruptive and impulsive behaviors, Wasserman and Teplin (respectively) reported 2 percent and 16 percent for ADHD, 3 percent and 14 percent for Oppositional Defiant Disorder, and 32 percent and 38 percent for Conduct Disorder. For disorders of mood, they reported (respectively) 7 percent and 13 percent for Major Depression, and 1 percent and 12 percent for Dysthymia. As noted earlier, these may be real differences associated with the different types of juvenile justice settings involved, or they might be related to one or more of the other methodological differences between the studies.

Thus, our best data suggest that the prevalence of disorders among juvenile justice youths is indeed quite high, but that either (a) we are uncertain about prevalence for specific disorders or (b) we should not expect to see similarities in prevalence of specific disorders across studies that sample from different types of facilities representing different "levels" of processing in the juvenile justice system.

The prevalence rates for almost all types of mental disorder are as high for girls in the juvenile justice system as for boys, and typically they are somewhat higher for girls, according to Teplin et al. (2002) and almost all other studies that have addressed the question. Very few studies have reported overall prevalence of mental disorders by ethnicity for juvenile justice youths. Teplin et al. (2002), however, reported a substantially higher prevalence (82 percent) among non-Hispanic white youths than among Hispanic (70 percent) or African American (65 percent) youths. I discuss these differences in greater detail later, but for the moment it is enough to note that the high prevalence rates in recent studies cut across gender and racial groups.

One would like to discuss these figures in the light of prevalence rates among adults in jails and prisons, but a meaningful comparison is not possible. The best data for adults in jails (Teplin, 1990, 1994) used an earlier version of the Diagnostic Interview Schedule designed for use with adults, so it did not identify the same disorders as in the adolescent studies (e.g., did not include attention deficit and disruptive behavior disorders). Moreover, it identified criteria for individuals' mental disorders only within the most recent two weeks (compared to one month for Wasserman et al. and six months for Teplin et al.). Where disorders themselves were more or less directly comparable (apart from the time factor), prevalence tended to be lower for adults in jail than for adolescents in detention. For example, Teplin et al. (2002) found that about 13 percent of detention boys (22 percent of girls) manifested Major Depressive Disorder, compared to about 4 percent of men in jail (10 percent of women) (Teplin, 1990, 1994). In the same studies, Substance Use Disorders were found for about 50 percent of boys and 46 percent of girls, compared to about 30 percent of men and 50 percent of women in jail. Similarly, prevalence of "serious mental disorders" for males in prisons has been reported to be in the area of 10–20 percent (Jemelka, Rahman, & Trupin, 1993; Pinta, 1999), figures that seem much lower than those found by Wasserman et al. (2002) for youths in juvenile correctional facilities. But method and measurement differences do not allow one to make much of the comparison.

## Making a Best Estimate

Concluding just how high we believe the prevalence of mental disorder to be also requires taking into consideration choices in what we categorize as a mental disorder. Some choices would suggest adjustments downward from the figures in these studies, while others would suggest even higher rates.

For example, should we exclude Conduct Disorder from our definition of a "mental disorder," inasmuch as its diagnosis is based primarily on the presence of persistent delinquent behavior rather than symptoms of disturbed thought and emotion? While some might believe we should, others point to research that seems to identify neurological and psychological impairments of a "clinical" nature underlying the majority of cases of Conduct Disorder (see generally Barkley, 1996; Hinshaw & Anderson, 1996). Moreover, as we will see in later chapters, youths with Conduct

Disorder frequently meet criteria for one or more other mental disorders. In fact, Teplin et al. (2002) reported that excluding cases involving Conduct Disorder in the absence of any other disorder, the overall proportion of youths in their sample with mental disorders was reduced only from 66 to 61 percent for boys and from 74 to 70 percent for girls (with additional requirements for significant impairment: 59 percent for boys, 66 percent for girls). Thus excluding Conduct Disorder would only slightly lower our estimates of the proportion of youths with mental disorders.

We might say that our real concerns do not include all youths who can meet criteria for any mental disorder, but rather those who have serious and chronic mental disorders. "Seriously emotionally disturbed" or SED youths have chronic, persistent, and multiple disorders (Davis & Vander Stoep, 1997); and although they constitute a small proportion of adolescents meeting criteria for mental disorders, they consume an extraordinary proportion of mental health resources, and their mental health needs typically continue through their adolescent years into adulthood. Some efforts to estimate their numbers place the figure around 9–13 percent (e.g., Friedman et al., 1996), and one could presume that the figure might be twice as high among youths in the juvenile justice system (Cocozza & Skowyra, 2000). But we would not want to restrict the system's attention only to these youths without careful scrutiny, because it is not immediately apparent that other disorders of less severity or chronicity are irrelevant, and, as we shall see later, there are many ways to define the seriousness of mental disorders.

In contrast, there is a strong argument for raising the estimates above those provided by the studies we have been reviewing, because few of them examined the full range of disorders that we might choose to include. Most studies, for example, did not assess for Mental Retardation and other developmental disorders, and few examined Posttraumatic Stress Disorder. Including these might not greatly increase the general prevalence estimate (because many youths with such disorders might already have met criteria for other disorders within the existing studies), but it would certainly move the figure upward.

Where does this leave us? No study has ever reported prevalence rates in any juvenile justice sample that were similar to those reported for youths in the general population of the United States, usually estimated at 15–25 percent for six-month to one-year prevalence of mental disorders (Costello et al., 1996; Kazdin, 2000a; Roberts et al., 1998). At the level of secure pretrial detention or postadjudication secure corrections, the proportion of youths with mental disorders (although defined in diverse ways) is probably two to three times higher than the prevalence for youths in general in the community.

This estimate is believable on its face. If the prevalence estimate is 20 percent in the general population, it is likely to be higher than that for adolescents in the general population who live in lower socioeconomic communities in which some majority of delinquent youths reside. We may also assume that within that subsample, delinquent youths as a group are likely to be sufficiently *more* deviant (and disturbed) than their already high-risk peers in order to warrant referral to the juvenile justice system. Thus it is not surprising that they manifest substantially greater prevalence estimates of mental disorder than U.S. youths on average. Moreover, the figures provided in existing studies must be considered conservative estimates, because they typically do not include some disorders that are relevant for an analysis of youths' mental health needs, especially those related to mental retardation and a number of other developmental disorders that I identify later. This is enough to warrant our concern, even if we are uncertain where the prevalence figure falls in the 45–75 percent range.

## The Relevance of Prevalence

As noted earlier, results from studies like those reviewed above have been part of the motivation for recent, urgent calls for widespread mental health screening and assessment of youths in the juvenile justice system, as well as appeals to provide appropriate services to all adolescents in the system with mental health needs. There is no doubt that our current prevalence figures offer a strong justification for increased attention to the problem. But of what kind, and with what scope? Must the juvenile justice system become the nation's mental health system for troubled adolescents?

As this analysis unfolds, we will see that our figures regarding youths who meet diagnostic criteria for mental disorders do not define the scope or nature of our obligation to respond to the mental health needs of adolescent offenders. Not all youths who meet diagnostic criteria need treatment. Some who do *not* meet diagnostic criteria nevertheless *do* need treatment. Others meet diagnostic criteria for which there is no reasonable treatment. Still other youths have multiple disorders that make it difficult to determine what type of treatment they need. And some treatments that are traditionally provided to youths are not effective and should not be provided at all.

We will later encounter all of these complexities as we explore the nature of psychopathology in adolescent offenders as it relates to the problem of deciding how the juvenile justice system should respond to their disorders. But first we must address a more basic question: Why should we respond to adolescent offenders' mental health needs? The question may seem superficial in light of the ease with which one can justify society's general obligation to provide treatment for youths suffering from mental disorders. Here, however, I suggest a broader perspective. There are three principal reasons why we should be concerned about adolescent offenders' mental disorders, reasons that provide a central structure for my analysis throughout this book:

- *Custodial treatment obligations:* Public agencies have a legal and moral responsibility to respond to the mental health needs of adolescents in their custody.
- *Due process protection in adjudicative proceedings:* Adults with mental disorders are afforded certain due process protections as defendants accused of criminal acts, and adolescents with mental disorders who are charged with crimes or with delinquencies in juvenile court must be assured equal protection.
- *Public safety:* To the extent that there is a relation between youths' mental disorders and their likelihood of future violent behaviors, obligations associated with the justice system's mandate to protect the public may require special provisions for the identification, management, and treatment of adolescents who manifest mental disorders.

These three areas of concern provide *sociolegal contexts* for our responses to young offenders with mental disorders. The following review of each context reveals primary questions regarding decisions about policy and practice in the juvenile justice system. They form the basic terrain for the later analyses in this book.

## The Treatment Context: States' Obligations to Provide Mental Health Treatment for Adolescents in Justice System Custody

A moral argument can be made that individuals in the custody of criminal and juvenile justice systems are entitled to services that are designed to provide treatment for their mental disorders that result in significant distress or dysfunction. The rationale for this obligation resides in the condition of custody itself. Restrictions of liberty inherently reduce individuals' access to public health services ordinarily provided to individuals as a consequence of their eligibility as citizens. Confined persons in custody of the government should therefore be provided a way to obtain similar services. In the case of adolescents, an additional rationale is their dependence on adults for access to most health services (e.g., the need for parental or custodial consent to the treatment of children).

A full assessment of the degree to which this moral obligation is recognized in law would require reviewing federal and state statutes that define those obligations, case law in specific states, and federal or state regulations that have been developed to implement legal requirements—all of which are beyond the scope of the present work. Nevertheless, it is necessary to consider certain general features of this terrain if we are to understand the treatment context.

Courts have sometimes interpreted states' juvenile justice purpose clauses to require that juvenile justice systems have some degree of responsibility to identify, and provide treatment for, youths in juvenile justice custody who have special mental health problems (see, e.g., *State v. S.H.,* 877 P.2d 205 [Washington 1994]; *In re J.F.,* 787 P.2d 364 [Montana 1990]). Federal rules are consistent with this presumption. For example, section 223 of the Juvenile Justice and Delinquency Prevention Act, 42 U.S.C. § 5633, states with respect to state plans that "(a) . . . In accordance with regulations which the Administrator shall prescribe, such plans shall . . . (8)(D) contain . . . (i) an analysis of mental health services available to juveniles in the juvenile justice system . . . and (ii) a plan for providing needed mental health services to juveniles in the juvenile justice system."

What do regulations of this type mean when they refer to "mental health services"? Presumably they are not referring to the general rehabilitation efforts that apply to every youth in the juvenile justice system. For example, many detention or corrections facilities, as well as community probation services, operate on a day-to-day system of monitoring and correction, behavior modification principles, weekly individual and/or group counseling sessions involving discussions of problem behavior and problem solving, and special educational, occupational, and recreational activities. All of these are designed to "rehabilitate" youths, and sometimes they are even provided by mental health professionals. Yet, inasmuch as these types of general rehabilitative efforts are already provided in the majority of juvenile justice systems to some degree, exhortations and mandates for "mental health services" for youthful offenders must have some more specific meaning.

If we are not referring to routine "rehabilitation" services, and if "mental health services" are not defined simply by the profession of the person providing the services, what do we mean by "mental health services" in this context? Let us presume that our mandates refer to the need for special clinical services that are signaled in some way by the identification of certain underlying conditions that are considered to be "clinical" in nature. In that case, it is clear that a starting point for identifying the need for special mental health services beyond "routine" rehabilitative efforts would be signaled in part by the identification of youths who have diagnosable mental disorders that are frequently treated by psychiatric or psychological intervention. I review these disorders in chapter 2 in the course of examining the diagnostic categories within the DSM that are used by mental health professionals. Generally they include *anxiety, mood, attention deficit, psychotic, somatoform, dissociative, eating, sleeping,* and *substance use* disorders, as well as *disruptive behavior disorders (conduct disorder, oppositional defiant disorder).* These disorders are identified by strictly assessing the presence or absence of certain symptoms, on the basis of which adolescents are then classified as "having" one or more of these disorders. We could say that the mandates for mental health services call for the availability of interventions that are designed to treat those disorders.

This is a reasonable way to begin identifying young people who need treatment. As Jensen and Watanabe (1999) have observed, "few would dispute the necessity of (DSM) diagnostic labels. . . . For good or ill, [they] have become the benchmark by which the appropriateness of persons' access to services is judged" (p. 118). Obtaining third-party reimbursement that finances the provision of mental health services often requires the identification of "patients" according to their DSM diagnostic label. So DSM diagnosis must play a primary role in any effort to circumscribe the population of youths with which we are concerned.

But this does not mean that we should limit our notion of "disorder" to DSM diagnoses and our notion of treatment only to efforts to modify them. As we shall see in chapter 2, there are effective ways to identify the mental health needs of youths that do not involve diagnoses. And in chapter 4, I review some effective treatment approaches that do not base their definitions of success on the reduction of symptoms of DSM-diagnosed disorders. So we should not automatically restrict our definition of "mental health needs" to DSM-diagnosed disorders, or our definition of "mental health services" and "treatment" to interventions that define their success according to the remission of the disorders that DSM diagnoses represent.

Finally, no matter what system we use to identify the population of adolescent offenders who manifest mental disorder, having identified them will not necessarily define which of those youths are in need of special treatment. There are two reasons that we should resist the knee-jerk reaction to prescribe treatment for all youths manifesting a mental disorder.

First, enormous financial and professional resources would be required to identify each adolescent's mental disorder and to provide treatment for it. We would want to know what impact this would have on our financial ability to perform other important services that are expected of the juvenile justice system. A full analysis of this issue is far too complex to undertake here, but at least its dimensions will have to be explored. For example, do our mandates refer to every youth who comes into contact with the juvenile justice system, including those who are seen only momentarily before being diverted from the system? Or might our obligations vary with regard to youths who penetrate the juvenile justice system to various levels of case processing, and youths who manifest disorders of particular severity?

Second, beneficent interventions unrestrained can carry with them potential dangers to liberty and self-determination. Pleas for treatment of adolescent offenders' mental disorders have a laudable humanitarian intent, but history is replete with examples of beneficent public policies that have ended up serving less-than-beneficent ends. Current general appeals for mental health reforms in juvenile justice are rarely accompanied by careful analysis of the potential negative implications of the reforms that they propose. Among the dangers, discussed in greater detail in later chapters, are increases in delinquency referrals (e.g., by parents) merely in order to obtain mental health services, the potential overuse of medications to achieve behavioral control, increases in length of confinement for purposes of diagnosis and treatment, and the potential misuse of information gained in clinical diagnostic procedures (for instance, as evidence to secure convictions).

These practical considerations for placing some limiting constraints on our obligation to treat youthful offenders with mental disorders need not be seen as merely convenient ways to reduce our burden. Clinical treatment is not prescribed anywhere in the world of health care merely upon determining that a person has a diagnosable disorder. Some disorders are best left untreated, while others may or may not require treatment depending on the degree of severity of symptoms in a particular case and on what is known about the probable course of the disorder. For still other disorders there is no known treatment.

Refining our treatment obligation, therefore, requires consideration of the nature of psychopathology in adolescents, especially among youthful offenders. What is the state of the art in defining mental disorders of adolescence, their severity, and their effects on youths' functioning? Can they be defined discretely, and if so, can they be identified reliably, especially among adolescent offenders? Having been identified, what do we know about their course and their consequences that should inform our refinement of the mandate to provide treatment to young offenders with mental disorders? Do we even have treatments that will work, and if so, for what disorders? Subsequent chapters address these questions, examining definitions of mental disorders of adolescence, as well as our capacities to identify them, to anticipate their consequences, and to treat them. This will be necessary before we return (in chapter 5) to an analysis of how the juvenile justice system's mandate to provide treatment to young offenders can be interpreted and implemented.

## The Adjudicative Context: Due Process Obligations in Legal Proceedings

A second reason for our concern about mental disorders among adolescent offenders is the potential relevance of mental disorder for due process guarantees in the adjudication of youths. Criminal law has long recognized the need for special protections of persons from potentially unfair consequences of their mental disorders during the adjudicative process. Three areas in which due process may be jeopardized by defendants' mental disorders include the waiver of *Miranda* rights during police interrogation, defendants' competence to stand trial, and exculpation or mitigation in the adjudication of alleged offenses (e.g., "not guilty by reason of insanity").

The first of these, waiver of *Miranda* rights, arises when there are questions about the admissibility of a defendant's confession at trial. Confessions are admissible if they have been made "knowingly, intelligently and voluntarily" after the defendant was informed of the rights to avoid self-incrimination and to obtain prior assistance of counsel (*Fare v. Michael C.*, 442 U.S. 707 [1979]). Defendants' mental disorders alone do not preclude a valid waiver of these rights (*Colorado v. Connelly*, 479 U.S. 157 [1986]). Yet the potential effects of mental disorder have long been considered relevant factors for judicial consideration when weighing the admissibility of a confession.

The second due process issue, competence to stand trial, requires that defendants must not be put to trial if they lack requisite abilities to participate meaningfully in their defense. Those abilities were broadly outlined in *Dusky v. United States,* 362 U.S. 402 (1960): whether the defendant has the capacity to assist counsel "with a reasonable degree of rational understanding" and has a "factual as well as rational understanding of the nature of the proceedings against him." These phrases typically have been interpreted to require the capacity to understand the nature and process of one's trial, to assist and work with counsel in one's defense, and to make important decisions that involve the potential waiver of constitutional rights—for example, accepting or refusing a pleas agreement (*Godinez v. Moran,* 113 S. Ct. 2680 [1993]). Deficits in these abilities typically must be due to mental illness or mental retardation, although not all states narrow the antecedent conditions in this way.

The insanity defense is a special plea of "not guilty by reason of insanity." It asserts that at the time of the alleged offense, due to mental illness or mental retardation, the defendant lacked the capacity to appreciate the wrongfulness of his or her conduct or lacked the capacity to control his or her behavior. The precise standard governing an insanity defense can vary from state to state, and the differences have important implications for the deficits that must be shown (Borum, 2003b). But over one-half of the states use some variation of the above definition, which is taken from the American Law Institute model standard (1962). In general, all of the standards require a showing of the effects of mental illness on the defendant's cognitions, motivations, emotions, or behavior at the time of the offense, with the potential that the defendant receive a "not guilty by reason of insanity" verdict, avoiding the usual sentence that would accompany a guilty verdict.

Over time, the evolution of modern law has created a functional approach to all three of these issues of due process (Grisso, 2003). It is not the mere presence of mental disorder that creates conditions of invalid waiver of rights, incompetence to stand trial, or insanity. They require sufficient evidence that an individual's mental disorder actually impairs functioning in a way that is legally relevant (for competence, actually impairs one's ability to participate in a defense, or for insanity, impairs a person's ability to appreciate wrongfulness or to control one's behavior at the time of an offense). Thus, among defendants with serious mental disorders, some may be found competent and some incompetent, and some may be found fully culpable and others not. The consequence of the disorder in the individual case—whether and how it actually impaired one's functioning—is the fact that matters for deciding the legal issue. In addition, laws in this area typically exclude certain mental disorders (e.g., personality disorders and substance abuse/dependence disorders) from consideration as a basis for insanity (Melton et al., 1997). Laws pertaining to competence to stand trial generally have been less restrictive regarding the types of disorders that might form a basis for dysfunction related to participation in one's defense.

How do these laws apply to youths with mental disorders? Criminal law (pertaining to adolescents tried in criminal court), juvenile law, and social science treatises provide little guidance (Grisso, 1998; Woolard, Reppucci, & Redding, 1996). Even recent treatises on the application of *Miranda* waiver (Feld, 2000), competence to stand trial (Bonnie & Grisso, 2000), and culpability laws (Scott, 2000) in adolescent cases say little about their application to youths with mental disorders in either criminal or juvenile court, focusing their arguments instead on youths' immaturity. Similarly, there is little case law on the application of the insanity defense in juvenile court (Woolard et al., 1996), and few cases (and no research) have addressed the potential relevance of psychopathology for the insanity defense among adolescents tried in criminal court. Concerning youths' capacities to waive *Miranda* rights, the most comprehensive study (Grisso, 1981) did not examine their relation to youths' mental disorders.

Why is there so little information on the relevance of mental disorder among adolescents for their capacities associated with adjudicative matters? The reason in part is historical; not until recent decades have the issues of adolescents' due process rights been seriously tested in the law.

In *criminal* court, for example, the issue of youths' competence to stand trial was not raised with any frequency until the 1990s. Before then, most youths tried in criminal court were older adolescents, and most had arrived there through a screening process that depended on judicial discretion, retaining those with serious mental disorders for juvenile court adjudication. Changing laws in the 1990s, however, took this screening process away from judges by transferring youths to criminal court based on the nature of their offenses alone, increasing the likelihood that criminal courts would have to deal with mentally disordered adolescents.

In *juvenile* court, the legal concepts of "incompetence" and "insanity" were rarely applied in delinquency cases prior to the 1990s (Scott, 1992). The potential for their application was set in the 1960s when the U.S. Supreme Court established that many constitutional protections for defendants in criminal courts were to be afforded to youths in delinquency cases in juvenile court (*Kent v. United States,* 383 U.S. 541 [1966]; *In re Gault,* 387 U.S. 1 [1967]). Among these were the right to avoid self-incrimination, the right to representation by counsel, and the right to an adjudicative process that mirrored many of the due process protections of criminal court proceedings. Yet the concepts of incompetence to participate in one's defense and exculpation due to insanity were slow to evolve in juvenile courts, partly because of their "civil" history and their continued mandate to provide rehabilitation.

Legislative reforms of the 1990s, however, made the concept of competence to stand trial very much a part of the picture in juvenile courts (see generally Grisso & Schwartz, 2000). Among these changes were the recognition of public protection as the primary purpose of the juvenile court (relegating rehabilitation to a secondary purpose), an increase in penalties and determinate sentences, and dispositional schemes that allowed for corrections jurisdiction of the juvenile justice system to extend well into the adult years in some circumstances. These conditions greatly reduced the salience of a "best interest" rationale for avoiding a "strong" interpretation of the place of defendant's rights in juvenile court. Confessions by adolescents now had more long-ranging implications, and a fair trial seemed now to require a "competent" defendant. By the end of the 1990s, over one-half of the states formally recognized the application of the concept of competence to stand trial in juvenile courts (Redding & Frost, 2002). Similarly, the trend to hold youths responsible for their offenses in ways that created significant punitive consequences began to draw some attention to the need to scrutinize the potential effects of mental disorder on their offending, such that serious mental disorder might warrant exculpation for reasons of insanity as in criminal cases.

As these issues were raised more frequently for adolescents in both criminal and juvenile courts, there was a tendency toward simple downward extensions of relevant legal definitions and procedures that had evolved in criminal law. Little attention was given to potential difficulties in their application created by adolescents' developmental status and the nature of mental disorders in adolescence. For example, the majority of adults who are found incompetent to stand trial for reasons of mental illness carry diagnoses of serious mental disorders, usually schizophrenia (Nicholson & Kugler, 1991). The typical age of onset for a first psychotic episode of schizophrenia is in the early twenties (for men) to late twenties (for women) (American Psychiatric Association, 1994). Does this mean that adolescents could rarely be found incompetent to stand trial due to mental illness? Or is it possible that other disorders of childhood and adolescence, different in form or kind from those seen in adults, might create functional deficits amounting to incompetence to stand trial?

Further analysis of these due process issues requires an examination of what we know about adolescent psychopathology that might relate to capacities associated with trial participation and culpability of defendants. Given the types of abilities that are relevant for these legal concepts, what are the relations between mental disorders of adolescence and those abilities? And how well can we identify those conditions in individual cases in order to ensure equitable application of due process protections for youths with mental disorders? I undertake this examination in subsequent chapters.

## The Public Safety Context: The Obligation to Reduce the Risk of Harm to Others

A third reason for concern about mental disorders among adolescent offenders is the potential relation between mental disorders and aggressive, harmful behavior. Although the system's mandate to reduce aggression may be interpreted broadly to refer to all forms of aggression, harm to others (in contrast to harm to property) has been the primary focus of public concern. The justice system's mandate to reduce the likelihood of harm to others creates two types of obligations, pertaining to (a) assessment and security, and (b) treatment to reduce risk of violence.

Concerning assessment and security, the justice system has an obligation to identify youths in its custody who present increased potential for future physical harm to others (hereinafter, "risk of harm") and to take reasonable steps to reduce the likelihood of harm. This responsibility arises at various points in juvenile case processing. "Danger to others" is one of the legal criteria justifying secure pretrial detention (*Schall v. Martin,* 467 U.S. 253 [1984]). Criteria applied to the question of judicial transfer (waiver) of an adolescent for trial in criminal court often requires a finding that the youth presents too great a danger to the public to be dealt with in juvenile justice programs (Dawson, 2000; Grisso, Tomkins, & Casey, 1988). For youthful offenders who remain in juvenile court, risk of harm arises as an important consideration in arranging for dispositional placements (e.g., secure correctional options) that will ensure the protection of the public.

Not all risk-of-harm questions are the same (Grisso, 1998). Detention cases focus on imminent likelihood of harm, whereas courts weighing posttrial disposition options will want to consider the risk of potential harm over a longer period of time—for example, the next year or two. In a juvenile court hearing on the question of an adolescent's transfer to criminal court, inquiring about future risk of harm may require considering an even more distant future, asking whether the youth is likely to continue to be a threat to the community many years later in adulthood.

The second public safety obligation—treatment to reduce risk of harm—is related to the more general mandate for the juvenile justice system to "rehabilitate" young offenders. The purpose of justice system rehabilitation is to change behavior in order to reduce recidivism and maximize public safety. Virtually all delinquency cases involve a judgment (if not a formal assessment) regarding the rehabilitative option that is most likely to decrease recidivism and therefore best serve public safety (and the interests of the youth).

Like questions about risk of harm, questions concerning rehabilitative disposition occur throughout juvenile case processing. They arise informally at early stages of processing where diversion from the full adjudicative process may be considered by probation officers. They occur formally in relation to the question of transfer to criminal court, asking whether the youth is "unamenable to rehabilitation" in the juvenile justice system (that is, whether in light of the characteristics of the youth and the potential interventions available to the juvenile justice system, there is little or no prospect for rehabilitation prior to the end of juvenile court jurisdiction) (Dawson, 2000; Grisso, Tomkins & Casey, 1988). They arise again, of course, in all cases with a delinquency finding, requiring a dispositional decision by the court regarding placement or services that will best serve the public interest in safety and reduced recidivism.

Questions of risk of harm and rehabilitation potential are brought together when raised in transfer and disposition hearings. The higher the risk of harm, the more restricted the range of intervention options that can be considered for potential rehabilitation plans. And the more resistant to rehabilitation influence the youth is perceived to be, the greater the likelihood that he may present both a short-term and a long-term risk of harm.

In all such questions, personnel in the juvenile justice system—from intake probation officers to judges—endeavor to weigh a youth's likelihood of future aggressive or violent behavior. How do adolescents' mental disorders enter into these judgments? First, mental disorders can effect the likelihood that a youth will engage in aggressive behavior. Some disorders might increase the risk and others decrease it, though still others may have no relation to future violence. If such relationships exist, then mental disorders—their type, chronicity, and expected course—would be factors to consider in an assessment and judicial weighing of the risk of harm. Second, if mental disorders play a role in risk of harm or recidivism, then their treatment becomes part of the juvenile justice system's rehabilitative obligation to reduce that risk. The likelihood that treatment will help to reduce risk, however, may vary for different disorders. Thus the nature and relative effectiveness of treatments for relevant mental disorders among delinquent youths becomes important information in assessing future risk of harm as well as likelihood of rehabilitation success.

Therefore, to improve policy and practice in meeting public safety obligations in cases involving youths with mental disorders, it is necessary that we examine our knowledge about (a) the relation between mental disorder and violence among youthful offenders, (b) our capacities to assess the likelihood of future violence in individual cases, and (c) the effects of various treatments for reducing aggression associated with mental disorders.

Research on the risk of violence among adults with mental disorders has progressed remarkably in the past decade (e.g., Link & Steuve, 1994; Monahan et al., 2001; Quinsey et al., 1998; Steadman et al., 1998). The findings suggest that simply knowing that people have a mental disorder does not always tell us much about their likelihood of engaging in future violence. Some disorders have a substantial relation to future violence (e.g., psychopathy: e.g., Hare, 1999), others have no relations or small to modest relations to future violence, and still others have small *negative* relations to violence (e.g., schizophrenia: e.g., Steadman et al., 1998). All disorders present increased potential for violence in combination with substance abuse (e.g., Swanson et al., 1997; Steadman et al., 1998). Many of the studies cited above have developed relatively sophisticated assessment methods for identifying which adults, with and without mental disorders, are more or less likely to be violent in the future, over both the short and the long term.

Unfortunately, research on the relation of violence and mental disorders among adolescent offenders lags far behind these advances with regard to adult patients and offenders. In chapter 4 I review some of the progress that has been made in identifying the antecedents of future violence in adolescents generally, as well as advances in understanding aggression among youths with mental disorders. What is needed, however, is information on the relevance of mental disorders for future aggression specifically among young offenders, as well as reliable ways to assess both their disorders and their risk of future harm. Later I examine the state of our knowledge and art in this regard, in preparation for considering what is needed to fulfill the juvenile justice system's responsibilities for public safety in cases of adolescent offenders with mental disorders.

## Laying a Foundation

I have outlined three reasons for concern about justice system responses to young offenders with mental disorders: (a) the custodial obligation to provide for their treatment, (b) the obligation to provide due process that protects defendants from the consequences of their disorders at trial and in relation to culpability for their offenses, and (c) the systems' obligation to provide for public safety. These form three sociolegal contexts within which we must examine how best to fulfill our obligations to respond to the mental disorders of adolescent offenders.

The description of each of these contexts raised questions about the nature of youths' mental disorders, their identification, and their consequences, all of which must be answered before we can form a coherent set of policies and practices for meeting our obligations in these three contexts. The following three chapters review the state of our knowledge in those areas, as evidenced in the basic research and clinical literature on developmental psychopathology (chapter 2), the clinical assessment of adolescents (chapter 3), and the potential ways in which youths' mental disorders are related to the purposes embedded in each of our three sociolegal contexts (chapter 4). After laying this foundation regarding current knowledge in these areas, we can return to the three sociolegal contexts (chapters 5, 6, and 7), applying that information to determine what we can and cannot confidently conclude—and what more we need to know—in order to shape policy and practice in the interests of society and of adolescent offenders with mental disorders.

In order to get our bearings, here is a brief preview of the questions explored in subsequent chapters:

- Chapter 2: What conditions should be included under the category of "mental disorders" for purposes of identifying the prevalence of mental disorders among adolescent offenders and our appropriate legal responses to them? To what extent is mental disorder stable or transient during adolescence? To what extent is it predictive of mental disorder in adulthood? The answers to these questions will have a substantial impact on how we can fulfill our treatment, due process, and public safety obligations.
- Chapter 3: How reliably can we identify mental disorders and their

symptoms among adolescent offenders? The nature of mental disorders among adolescents presents special challenges for accurately measuring them. Youths' mental disorders often are fluid and confounded by general developmental processes, setting a sort of ceiling on the degree to which they can be identified clearly. Other limitations arise because of the state of the art in measurement technology, as well as difficulties in its application in the context of juvenile justice programs.

• Chapter 4: What do we know about the relation between adolescent offenders' mental disorders and the purposes for which we want to identify them? All of our sociolegal contexts require attention to the relation between mental disorders of youthful offenders and matters of practical future consequence. The treatment context raises questions about our knowledge of a youth's specific mental disorder as a guide to the selection of a specific treatment modality in the fulfillment of our treatment obligation. The due process context requires asking about the actual relations between youths' mental disorders and capacities related to competence to stand trial and criminal responsibility. And the public safety context requires knowing whether and how youths' mental disorders are related to risk of short-range and longer-range future offending, as well as the degree to which their treatment is likely to reduce that risk. Given the nature of mental disorders in adolescence, can we even expect to find consistent relations between disorders and future offending, or predictable outcomes of treatment to reduce risk of harm?

• Chapters 5–7: Having established those foundations, we use them to address each of the three sociolegal contexts themselves, forming tentative policy and practice recommendations where we can—and where we cannot, pointing out what types of reliable information are needed to improve policy and practice in the future.

*Chapter 2*

# Defining Mental Disorders in Adolescents

The first step in determining the juvenile justice system's obligations to respond to youths' mental disorders is to define "mental disorder." We must approach the definition in three ways, each of which is the subject of a section of this chapter.

First, how do clinicians and developmental psychopathologists define *types* of mental disorder? What is the predominant approach to the taxonomy of mental disorders among adolescents? How are they classified?

Second, how do we define the *severity* of mental disorders and their actual impact on youths' activities of daily living? Simply identifying a mental disorder does not tell us all we want to know in our search for adequate responses to adolescent's disorders. For reasons explained later, we also need to know the seriousness of the disorder as it arises in specific cases. What concepts are available to do that?

Third, how does juvenile justice system *context* influence what is defined as a mental disorder for purposes of fulfilling the three sociolegal obligations? What we call "mental disorder" for purposes of policy is not necessarily determined only by clinical condition or even clinical necessity. The relevance of a clinical condition for specific areas of policy will be determined in part by legal and social objectives. In fact, some conditions might be defined as mental disorders for purposes of one sociolegal objective and not another.

## Classification of Mental Disorder

As noted in chapter 1, laws and policies that call for responses to youths' mental disorders usually do not define the disorders to which they apply.

They defer to the experts, presuming that psychiatry and clinical psychology have a consensual definition of child and adolescent psychopathology. This suggests a sense of assurance that the clinical sciences classify and conceptualize adolescent disorders in relatively clear-cut ways, which can then be applied to questions of treatment obligations, due process concerns, and public safety issues.

Yet this is not the message to be gleaned in the current literature by experts in psychopathology of children and adolescents. They tell us that "there is little professional consensus on how to define psychopathology [in adolescence]" (Ingram & Price, 2001, p. 6). Mash and Dozois (1996) identify the situation well: "Although it may appear that efforts to categorize mental disorders [of children and adolescents] are carving 'nature at the joints,' whether or not such 'joints' actually exist is open to debate (p. 15) . . . any classification system represents a construction rather than a reality" (p. 32).

This is not good news, given that eventually, when we analyze our obligations to respond to the mental health needs of juvenile offenders, we will need a way to define and conceptualize those needs and distinguish their varieties. So it is important to understand the controversies and limitations associated with current definitions of adolescent psychopathology, and how they manifest themselves in several important categories of disorder among young offenders.

Until fairly recently, the study of psychopathology in adolescence was dominated by conceptual systems and logical assumptions borrowed from the study of adult psychopathology. This tradition, largely medical in origin, uses sets of symptoms as criteria for categories of psychopathology. It presumes that each category of disorder may lead to the discovery of common causes, is likely to have a predictable course, and will facilitate the choice of effective treatment. Proper diagnosis of people in order to place them within this conceptual and empirical field is achieved by applying objective rules for their classification, such as those described in the *Diagnostic and Statistical Manual of Mental Disorders* (DSM-IV) (American Psychiatric Association, 1994).

This classification tradition, developed in the context of clinical psychiatry as applied to adults, has long been—and is currently—our primary way of defining disorders of children and adolescents. It is not the only way, however. Psychological research on child psychopathology has provided alternatives that describe disorder on various conceptual dimensions using a continuum rather than all-or-none diagnostic categories. One of the most fruitful examples is the description of child psychopathology along dimensions of "externalizing" and "internalizing" symptoms (e.g., Achenbach & Edelbrock, 1989). I later return to this approach after examining the traditional psychiatric classification of disorders, which clearly predominates in all current discussions of policy regarding child and adolescent disorders.

## DSM-IV Disorders of Adolescence

The DSM-IV system deals with the classification of disorders of children and adolescents in two broad ways. First, it offers a number of "Disorders Usually First Diagnosed in Infancy, Childhood, or Adolescence," organized under the following categories:

- mental retardation
- learning, motor skill, and communication disorders
- pervasive developmental disorders
- attention-deficit and disruptive behavior disorders (including oppositional defiant and conduct disorders)
- feeding and eating, tic, and elimination disorders
- "other disorders of infancy, childhood and adolescence"

Second, the system offers hundreds of categories (diagnoses) for other conditions that do not have separate criteria for children, adolescents, and adults (with a few exceptions that are noted later). These are grouped in such a way that each contains a large number of specific categories or diagnoses (e.g., the substance-related disorders group alone has over a hundred specific diagnostic categories). A partial list of these groupings includes:

- delirium, dementia, and amnestic and other cognitive disorders
- substance-related disorders
- schizophrenia and other psychotic disorders
- mood disorders (e.g., depressive disorders, bipolar disorders)
- anxiety disorders
- somatoform disorders
- personality disorders (except for antisocial personality disorder, which cannot be employed as a diagnosis for youths under eighteen)

Successive versions of the DSM system have continuously sought to improve the application of the criteria to children and adolescents.

Nevertheless, mental health professionals and researchers who study, diag-nose, and treat children claim that the paradigmatic assumptions at the heart of the DSM classification system continue to bedevil its application to adolescents. The model is substantially a downward extension of disor-ders of adulthood, treating disorders of adolescents simply as pre-adult forms of disabilities—buds that will reach full flower in adulthood. In so doing, child specialists have claimed, the system fails to conceptualize and classify what they see in practice and in empirical studies of children's and adolescents' psychological problems.

These discontents have become increasingly more articulate since the evolution of a conceptual approach called "developmental psychopathol-ogy." This perspective crystallized in the 1980s (Cicchetti, 1984, 1990; Rutter & Garmezy, 1983; Sroufe & Rutter, 1984) and matured in the 1990s (Cicchetti & Cohen, 1995; Cicchetti & Rogosch, 2002). Developmental psychopathology is not merely the study of psychopathology in childhood and adolescence. It is the study of how psychopathology emerges and changes in a developmental context, structured and guided by what is known about normal biological, cognitive, emotional, and social develop-ment during childhood, adolescence, and adulthood. Pertaining to adoles-cence, the developmental psychopathology perspective is "a shift away from seeing psychological disturbance during adolescence as either the grown-up version of childhood disorder or the immature or prodromal counterpart of adult pathology . . . to *the study of clinical phenomena in the context of adolescence as a developmental period*" (Steinberg, 2002, p. 124).

This perspective provides some concepts and general empirical findings that help us understand why we will encounter problems when we try to apply our traditional diagnostic concepts to the three sociolegal contexts for responding to young offenders' mental health needs. They include issues of (a) age relativity, (b) discontinuity, (c) comorbidity, and (d) ra-cial, cultural, and gender-related factors.

## Age Relativity

Entering the first-grade classroom on the first day of school, the six-year-old begins to sob, lingers by the door, and will not come in without special encouragement from the teacher. We watch and smile, remember-ing our own first day in school. But when the twelve-year-old does the same on the first day of middle school, we wonder what is wrong.

The fourteen-year-old carefully arranges drawing materials in a neat row in preparation for an art assignment, and we are impressed. The four-year-old does the same, refusing to begin drawing until each crayon is perfectly aligned just above the top edge of the drawing paper, and we consider for a moment that this is odd and perhaps significant regarding some underlying insecurity.

Few specific behaviors or reported emotions can be considered "symptoms" of mental disorder across the developmental span. Virtually every observed behavior or emotion that can be called a "symptom" is seen in almost all children or adolescents sometime during their development, with or without psychopathology (Mash & Dozois, 1996). Behaviors that are adaptive and "normal" at one age may be maladaptive and "abnormal" at another. And, of course, some behaviors and emotional conditions that signal psychopathology in adulthood are relatively normal at various pre-adult ages or developmental stages. As a consequence, most developmental psychopathologists emphasize that behaviors can be considered "symptoms" of disorder only to the extent that they deviate from normative behavior of one's own developmental peers, and that they are maladaptive only within the context of one's developmental period (e.g., Cicchetti & Rogosch, 2002).

In contrast, the DSM-IV system for classifying mental disorders provides little to distinguish the developmental relevance of various criteria that define certain disorders. For example, the system provides one set of behavioral and emotional criteria for diagnosing Major Depressive Disorder and Dysthymia in children, adolescents, and adults alike, with only brief notations concerning possible additional considerations for pre-adults (e.g., that "depressed mood," one of nine symptoms to be considered, might be expressed in children and adolescents as "irritable mood").

Another example outside the DSM-IV system is provided by recent research efforts to discover psychopathy in children and adolescents (e.g., Forth, Hart, & Hare, 1990; Frick et al., 1994; Lynam, 1997). Psychopathy is a concept that has been well defined in adult research for many years as a personality disorder involving callous, antisocial behavior (Hart & Hare, 1997). Recently the construct and its diagnostic criteria have been extended downward by researchers and clinicians for application to children and adolescents (as I discuss in chapter 4). In doing so, researchers have made few or no adjustments in the personal characteristics that are used to define it. Yet several "psychopathic" characteristics (e.g., impulsiveness, egocentricity) are both theoretically and empirically common, if not normative, at various stages of child or adolescent development (e.g., Edens et al., 2001; Seagrave & Grisso, 2002).

The concept of "age relativity," therefore, warns us that *adolescents' behaviors that appear as "symptoms" of mental disorders in DSM-IV are not always symptoms of mental disorder.* As in the case of psychopathy, this increases the risk that we will label as "disordered" certain classes of youths whose "symptoms" may simply be normative behavior for certain developmental transitions of adolescence. This is important when we are trying to locate mental disorders, and youths who have them, for purposes of identifying the juvenile justice system's treatment obligations.

## Discontinuity

Upon reaching a diagnosis for a disordered youth, there is a tendency to presume that his or her disorder is likely to manifest itself across time, especially if it goes untreated. That assumption generally is true for adults. In contrast, clinical developmental researchers tell us that some disorders identified in adolescence will tend to persist into adulthood while others will not, and still others are quite variable.

Continuity is more predictable for some disorders of childhood than for others. For example, childhood mental retardation and disorders with a basis in brain dysfunction are likely to continue across the developmental life span, while disorders of mood (Hammen & Rudolph, 1996) and anxiety (Albano et al., 1995) are more variable. For most disorders involving behavioral dysfunction or emotional distress, merely obtaining a diagnosis for a particular disorder in adolescence may not tell us much about its development or implications for the adolescent's diagnostic condition later in adulthood.

Some principles based on empirical findings help us to deal with this question. For example, research concerning some disorders suggests that if they appear early in childhood they are more likely to persist to later developmental periods. Yet the picture is complicated by the fact that among children or adolescents who are symptomatic and who *continue* to be symptomatic into adolescence or adulthood, their subsequent disorder may not be the *same* as their earlier one (for reviews, see Kazdin & Johnson, 1994; Pennington & Ozonoff, 1991).

While investigating these variations, child psychopathology researchers have developed the concepts of "equifinality" (different paths to a single disorder) and "multifinality" (one disorder taking multiple paths to different disorders) to express the complex pathways they discover in search of patterns of disorder (and remission) among children and adolescents (e.g., Loeber, 1991). There may be *general* consistencies behind these processes; for example, youths who have developed an inhibited, introversive personality style early in life may progress to certain types of disorders during their developmental life span that are less aggressive than for youths who are generally less inhibited (Kagan et al., 1984). But youths with either personality style may manifest a variety of disorders compatible with it.

As a consequence, it is difficult to infer cause or course of a youth's condition based simply on a diagnosis at a particular point during the youth's adolescence. There will be greater variability among adolescents than among adults in the projected meaning of the diagnosis for the future. Among youths given that diagnosis, some will not persist in the disorder while others will, and still others may follow a course to a different disorder. This warns us that we must be less confident about the long-range consequences of many disorders in adolescents, a fact that will be important later in deciding whether and how we should respond to young offenders' mental disorders.

## Comorbidity

A good auto mechanic knows that one problem in an automotive system often coexists with another. A worn set of spark plugs used too long will eventually result in damage elsewhere in the system, so that replacing the plugs will only partly solve the problem.

In addition to finding that two-thirds of the youths in Cook County's detention center met criteria for mental disorders, Teplin et al. (in press) discovered that about one-half of the youths met criteria for *two or more* mental disorders. (See also Marstellar et al., 1997: 44 percent.) Clinicians sometimes refer to the *presence* of two or more disorders as "comorbidity." But the term is often used by researchers to refer to a *relationship* between two or more disorders, such that across cases they tend to occur together at a greater-than-chance expectancy (Achenbach, 1995; Caron & Rutter, 1991), suggesting that they may have some causal relation.

Comorbidity is found among various disorders in persons across the developmental life span, but it is especially evident among children and adolescents. For purposes of our later discussions, some of the most important disorders for which comorbidity is high among adolescents are disorders of mood (e.g., Major Depression and Dysthymia), anxiety, attention-deficit/hyperactivity, disruptive behavior (e.g., Conduct Disorder), and substance use.

Examples are numerous. One review found that the presence of depression among community youths increased the likelihood of receiving some additional diagnosis by twenty times (Angold & Costello, 1993), and another found comorbidity rates of depression with anxiety disorders in the range of 30–75 percent (Kovacs, 1990). Depression and disruptive disorders have high comorbidity among adolescents (see Hammen & Rudolph, 1996, for a review). About 30–50 percent of adolescents with Attention-Deficit/Hyperactivity Disorder (ADHD) meet criteria for Oppositional Defiant or Conduct Disorder in adolescence (Barkley, 1990), and as many as 40–50 percent meet criteria for a mood disorder at some time in childhood or adolescence (Biederman, Newcorn, & Sprich, 1991). Finally, disruptive, anxiety, and depressive disorders have been found in increased proportions among delinquent youths with substance abuse diagnoses (e.g., Neighbors, Kempton, & Forehand, 1992; Richards, 1996). Teplin et al. (in press) found that about one-third of boys and girls in juvenile detention met criteria for both a substance use disorder and a disruptive behavior disorder or ADHD. Moreover, about half of the youths with that comorbid combination also met criteria for an anxiety disorder, an affective disorder, or both.

In policy or clinical discussions, one sometimes hears the claim that young offenders do not have "real" mental disorders, but are "mostly just conduct disordered" and therefore in need of offender rehabilitative services other than mental health interventions. (I discuss this assumption in greater detail at the end of this chapter.) Current data suggest that this view is usually wrong. Teplin et al. (in press) did not report separate figures for Conduct Disorder in their article on comorbidity, but they can be extrapolated from their original report of prevalence (Teplin et al., 2002). There they noted that 66 percent of their boys in detention ($n = 1,170$) met criteria for some mental disorder, and that the exclusion of Conduct Disorder reduced that figure only to 61 percent. In other words, only 5 percent of the male sample manifested Conduct Disorder alone. Those 5 percent constituted 13 percent of the boys diagnosed with Conduct Disorder, with 87 percent of boys with Conduct Disorder meeting criteria for at least one other psychiatric disorder. This finding is not unique. In an earlier review of the literature, Offord, Alder, and Boyle (1986) concluded that a majority of youths diagnosed with Conduct Disorder meet criteria for one or more additional diagnostic categories, and more recent studies continue to find the same (e.g., Angold, Costello, & Erkanli, 1999; Lambert et al., 2001). In light of these findings, when a clinician informs the court that a particular youth meets criteria for Conduct Disorder, the court routinely ought to reply, "And what else?"

Why is comorbidity so high among adolescents? One possible reason is that the development of symptoms of mental disorder, like the development of other cognitive and emotional conditions, tends to proceed during child-hood and adolescence from global to more differentiated forms. Thus children and adolescents might manifest distinct and separate forms of disorder less often than is seen in adults. For example, among adults, the concepts of "depression" and "anxiety" are sufficiently different from each other to be of value in defining distinct emotional experiences. In contrast, developmental psychopathologists are not sure that depression and anxiety represent entirely separate conditions in children or adolescents (Hinden et al., 1997). They overlap so greatly in measures of adolescent dysfunction that often test developers have combined them in one "anxious-depressed" scale (e.g., Achenbach, 1991b; Grisso & Barnum, 2003). Similarly, some theorists have proposed that the overlap between conduct problems and attention-deficit/ hyperactivity is so great that it questions the existence of separate entities (Hinshaw & Anderson, 1996).

High comorbidity rates among youth have led some theorists to propose that symptoms manifested in children and adolescents may reflect a "general psychopathology," consistent with immature development and consequent lack of differentiation of disorder into discrete categories (e.g., Lilienfeld, Waldman, & Israel, 1994; Rutter, 1994). Others have noted that the evidence for comorbidity might be due to patterns in the development of psychopathology in which some disorders naturally precede and "phase into" (and thus "overlap") others in childhood and adolescence. It is possible that more discrete ways to describe adolescent disorders could be found, but that our search has been obscured by the tendency to try to describe them with concepts developed in clinical studies of adults.

Discovering rates and patterns of comorbidity is further complicated by the fact that they are likely to be different depending on the settings and populations in which studies are performed. For example, youths with more severe disturbance more often have comorbid disorders, and they are more often clinically referred or arrested. Therefore, clinically referred or arrested samples of youths are likely to manifest greater comorbidity than would be found in random samples of youths with a particular disorder. Such conditions would produce inaccurate rates of comorbidity. But, of course, it would not change the fact that the published rates are applicable *within* the clinical and juvenile justice settings from which the results were obtained, and with which we are most concerned.

Comorbidity will play an important role in our analysis of the juvenile justice system's obligations to respond to mental disorders of adolescents. Identifying a diagnosis does not necessarily provide a meaningful guide to a youth's mental health needs, if youths receiving that diagnosis tend to manifest any of a variety of other disorders. Moreover, as we shall see later, the considerable overlap of disorders among youths challenges our ability to define discretely different treatment or rehabilitation responses for those with particular diagnoses.

## Race and Gender

The nature of psychopathology in adolescents is likely to be different for boys and girls, and for youths of different racial and ethnic backgrounds. The emergence of mental health problems and the form they take may be influenced by social context interacting with developmental processes (Mash & Dozois, 1996). Boys and girls develop in different social contexts that might contribute to gender-based differences in prevalence or types of disorders. Similarly, during normal development, youths of different ethnicities may develop somewhat different personality characteristics because of the social contexts in which they grow up, leading to different mental disorders or to differences in the way disorders are manifested (Murray, Smith, & West, 1989).

Gender differences in psychiatric diagnoses of adolescents are fairly well documented. Conduct Disorder and ADHD, for example, are less prevalent among girls than boys (e.g., Szatmari, Boyle, & Offord, 1989), rates of depression are higher among girls (e.g., Offord et al., 1987), and girls are more likely to develop comorbid disorders (Loeber & Keenan, 1994). Until recently, very little was known about the relative prevalence of mental disorders among girls in the juvenile justice system, in part because their smaller numbers failed to attract research interest. More recent studies in juvenile detention centers, however, consistently find higher rates of almost all types of mental disorders and mental health problems (including anger and aggression) among girls than among boys (e.g., Cocozza & Skowyra, in press; Grisso et al., 2001; Teplin et al., 2002).

While ethnic differences in rates of mental disorder have been documented for adults (e.g., Warner et al., 1995), there have been few epidemiological surveys of the mental health problems of African American, Latino, or Asian adolescents in the general population (Isaacs, 1992; Cauffman & Grisso, in press). A recent exception is a study of diagnoses (using the Child and Adolescent Psychiatric Assessment, an interview structured to provide DSM-IV diagnoses) among a random sample of over 1,000 youths in rural North Carolina (Angold et al., 2002). About 20 percent of both non-Hispanic white and African American youths met criteria for one or more disorder. There were no ethnic differences for ADHD, Conduct Disorder, Substance Abuse Disorder, or Anxiety Disorders. But non-Hispanic white youths had higher rates of "any depressive disorder," Oppositional Defiant Disorder, and "any affective or anxiety disorder" than did African American youths.

For juvenile justice samples, very few studies of mental disorders have reported their data in ways that allow one to examine racial or ethnic differences. The Cook County Detention Center study by Teplin et al. (2002) is an exception. Higher rates were reported among non-Hispanic white males than among African American males for most disorders and Latino males for some disorders. Non-Hispanic white males were more likely than African American males to present with substance abuse and anger symptoms, whereas Latino males were more likely to exhibit signs of depressed-anxious mood as compared to African American males. Among girls, non-Latino white females presented with more substance abuse and trauma when compared to African American females, whereas Latino females were more likely to endorse somatic complaints and suicidal ideation when compared to African American females.

More research in a greater range of juvenile justice settings eventually may give us greater confidence when applying Teplin's findings beyond Cook County. But if they do, how are they to be explained? Are the differences due to actual tendencies for certain disorders to be more or less prevalent for certain ethnic groups? Or are they the result of differences in arrest patterns—for example, that mental disorder greatly increases the likelihood of arrests for non-Hispanic white youths but that a greater range of African American youths are arrested? Most important, is it possible that our DSM-IV system for classifying mental disorders does not work the same when applied to youths of different ethnic backgrounds? (For a review of concerns about application of the DSM system with African American youths, see Johnson, 1993). Just as certain behaviors and emotional conditions may be normal at one age and not another, they may also be differentially normal or abnormal for boys and girls, or for youths of different ethnic backgrounds, at different ages and stages of development. But our present research base does not allow us to address such possibilities.

## Alternatives to Diagnostic Categories

Thus far, we have encountered evidence that the predominant system for identifying and classifying mental disorders—the DSM-IV—has serious limitations for describing disorders of adolescence because it is rooted in adult psychopathology. It is less useful for adolescents than for adults in describing the cause and course of mental disorders, and it manifests substantial comorbidity of disorders when applied to adolescents, creating diagnostic groups with considerable heterogeneity. Finally, we have found that strict reliance on the DSM-IV diagnostic scheme may not take into account the contextual differences in the development of psychopathology among girls and boys, and among youths of different ethnicities. Therefore, in this search for responses to the mental health needs of adolescents in the juvenile justice system, we begin our journey on very unsteady ground. The field's predominant classification system has been the basis for the prevalence estimates of mental disorder among juvenile justice youths. While it might be trusted to provide gross estimates of the extent of the need, it is less clear that we can rely on it to describe the specific nature of those needs. In this light, it makes sense to consider alternatives to the DSM-IV classification system for identifying youths' psychopathology. Developmental psychopathology offers two general approaches that do not use diagnostic classification.

The first alternative describes youths according to *conceptual dimensions of psychopathology* that are expressed on scales, rather than placing them into diagnostic groups. The prototype for this approach in child and adolescent psychopathology is a system developed by Achenbach (1993; Achenbach & Edelbrock, 1984), which comprises a family of measures called the Child Behavior Checklist (Achenbach, 1991a, 1991b, 1991c; see chapter 3 for further discussion of the CBCL). The system uses a number of dimensions (e.g., "anxious-depressed," "attention problems") that were determined by statistical methods for grouping together symptoms and behaviors in ways that best fit their appearance across large samples of youths. The eight dimensions in Achenbach's system can be further grouped into more global syndromes representing "externalizing" problems (undercontrolled, outward expression) and "internalizing" problems (overcontrolled, inner-directed). Adolescents are not classified into categories in this system. Instead their psychopathology is identified according to the elevation or depression of their scores on the various dimensions or the two syndromes. Their scores may even by high on both the externalizing and internalizing syndromes. Dimensional systems like Achenbach's identify degrees and types of disturbance, as well as patterns of their manifestation, without the use of discrete categories and without presumptions regarding an underlying disease process.

The second alternative is a *problem-oriented approach* that identifies how well or poorly youths have adapted within various personal and social contexts (e.g., Rahdert, 1991; others are described in chapter 3). Frequently these contexts correspond to the everyday social milieus of family relations, peer relations, school functioning, work, leisure activities, and so forth. Whatever the methods used to identify strengths and weaknesses in these areas, they are typically expressed on scales that indicate degree of maladjustment or dysfunction relative to one's age peers.

Both of these alternatives have advantages and disadvantages compared to DSM-IV classification, and we will explore those differences later. But it is not necessary that we choose among them—they all have something important to contribute—although we may have to decide which ways of describing youths' psychopathology are best suited for various contexts and purposes that arise in juvenile justice custody. One strength of these two alternatives, however, is their dimensional quality, which can be very useful for describing degrees of psychopathology (and can even be converted to classify youths into groups by identifying "cut-off scores" on their dimensions). The importance of this is explained later.

## The Clinical Significance of Mental Disorders

Recall from chapter 1 the very high prevalence rates of mental disorders among juvenile justice youths, as well as our conclusion that even these high estimates might be conservative. If meeting criteria for a mental disorder was the deciding factor for requiring some special clinical response to youths in the juvenile justice system, then almost all those entering the system would need clinical attention. In chapter 1, we anticipated that accepting "clinical treatment for all youthful offenders" as the juvenile justice system's mandate required scrutiny and probable refinement of such a mandate.

Discriminating between various types of disorder will provide part of this analysis. In addition, we can seek to identify the relative seriousness of cases involving mental disorders, as well as their potential consequences, for purposes of determining their clinical significance. Not all mental disorders, and not all cases that meet criteria for a particular disorder, necessarily present the same degree of suffering, disability, dysfunction, or short-term and long-term consequences. Therefore, it is important to consider ways to conceptualize *degrees of impairment,* as these might supplement and refine our use of data to classify youths according to specific disorders. What can guide us in conceptualizing seriousness of symptoms, and their functional consequences, when determining the need for a clinical response by the juvenile justice system?

## Classifying "Clinically Significant" Severity of Symptoms

Chapter 3 examines various measures of child and adolescent psychopathology that express *symptom severity* on a continuum, when symptoms are measured according to the dimensional perspective discussed in the previous section. Classification of symptom severity requires some definition of "high" scores warranting special attention. There are three ways to conceptualize a "clinically significant" level of symptom severity.

THE PEER-NORM APPROACH. We may identify high symptom severity according to statistical deviation from the norm of one's peers (as employed, for instance, in the CBCL: Achenbach, 1991b). This requires the collection of symptom severity data from large general samples of children or adolescents, establishing the distribution of scores on a scale, and finding the score that exceeds a particular standard deviation or *t*-score above the mean, or that identifies a particular percentage of youths (e.g., top one-third, one-quarter, or one-tenth). This approach clearly assists in identifying groups of youths (or cases) in which symptom severity can be considered "high" relative to one's peers. The difficulty here is in determining where to place the cut-off. It can be done arbitrarily, as when a test developer decides to call scores "significant" when they are above +2 standard deviations from the mean, or above a *t*-score of 70. No one would doubt that this is high, but it is possible that what we call "high" might vary for different purposes. This can be remedied by research that demonstrates the value of the cut-off for specific purposes (which is the starting point for another approach described below). But without that refinement, there is no particular reason to believe that scoring high relative to one's peers necessarily signifies the need for treatment.

THE CLINICAL CRITERION GROUP APPROACH. A second approach compares an adolescent to groups of youths who have required clinical care. This requires empirical identification of the level of symptom severity manifested by those who have met eligibility criteria for treatment. Typically the criterion sample includes youths currently receiving inpatient or outpatient mental health services, and who therefore have been judged by clinicians (in the course of routine intake activities) to need psychiatric care. A "clinically significant" level of symptom severity, then, is defined as any score that is well within the range of the symptom severity scores of the clinical criterion group. This is the approach taken by Millon, Millon, and Davis (1993) in development of the "clinically significant" cut-off scores for the Millon Adolescent Clinical Inventory.

This empirical approach to conceptualizing severity of symptoms has considerable value, but in practice it requires careful scrutiny. For example, in specific studies using this approach, the level of symptom severity that it identifies as "clinically significant" is heavily dependent on intake or eligibility criteria for the particular mental health programs in which the criterion data were collected. The level of severity of symptoms required in order to obtain treatment in a particular community may vary, for example, as a function of the resources of mental health programs in that community. If resources are very limited in the criterion sample location, so that only youths with extremely severe symptoms receive treatment, research in that setting might lead to higher cut-off scores (a more restrictive definition of "clinical significance") than would be found in other communities. Application of the results to later cases, therefore, would tend to exclude from "clinical significance" some youths who would indeed be considered eligible for mental health services in their own communities. For this reason, the approach is of value only if the cut-off score has been based on data collection in a diverse set of clinical treatment programs, or in a treatment setting that closely matches the one in which we want to apply it.

THE EMPIRICAL CONSEQUENCE APPROACH. A third approach is to set cut-off scores on the basis of empirical evidence of the relation between scores and actual functional consequences of concern. For example, the development of a scale with items that are designed to identify suicidal behavior might include collecting research evidence on whether youths subsequently did or did not attempt suicide. Then statistical procedures can be used to find the right cut-off score, defined as the score that optimally divides youths so that as many as possible who attempted suicide scored above the cut-off score (the method's "sensitivity") and as many as possible who did not attempt suicide scored below the cut-off score ("specificity").

## Chronicity or Multiplicity of Symptoms or Disorders

All three of the approaches just described focus on *intensity* of symptoms in identifying "clinically significant" psychopathology. But this may not be sufficient to identify the seriousness of disorder for purposes of making some decisions about youths' mental health treatment. Two additional considerations are often helpful.

CHRONICITY. We may distinguish between acute and chronic conditions. Some youths may manifest acute symptoms that are not part of a chronic or persistent disorder, but that suggest the need for some type of clinical intervention in order to avoid relatively imminent consequences (such as prevention of suicidal behavior). Others may have chronic and persistent disorders yet manifest a relatively lower intensity of symptoms at a given point in time. This is especially true for some mental disorders that are episodic, waxing and waning in intensity of symptoms across time, so that high symptom levels sometimes are not presented at the particular time of assessment. Moreover, adolescents are more prone to lability and instability in presentation than are adults, especially for mood disorders and anxiety disorders. The fact that their immediate presentation is not acute does not necessarily mean that they are not in need of a clinical response, especially if their disorder may have important longer-term negative consequences.

As we will see in later chapters, the importance of chronicity in understanding the relevance of mental disorder for youths' delinquent behaviors cannot be overstated. For example, one of the best-documented indicators of whether delinquent behaviors will persist through adolescence and into adulthood is whether the behaviors had an onset in the primary school years (Moffitt, 1993). Similarly, in general, the likelihood that adolescents will persist in manifesting mental disturbances of some kind is increased if they manifested mental disorders before the adolescent years (for a review, see Connor, 2002).

MULTIPLICITY. Earlier we noted that many youths in juvenile justice settings meet criteria for two, three, and even four mental disorders. It is commonly observed that adolescents who require the greatest extent of mental health services across the longest period also manifest a large number of symptoms and multiple disorders (Davis & Vander Stoep, 1997). Thus there is some overlap between chronicity and multiplicity of symptoms. But it is helpful to retain both of these ways of identifying seriousness of mental health needs, because some youths have chronic disorders that are relatively specific in their symptom presentation rather than involving a wide array of symptoms and multiple diagnoses.

Later we will examine methods for expressing chronicity and multiplicity of symptoms and disorders among adolescents. The important point for now is that we must consider both of these indexes, as well as symptom severity, when making policy and clinical decisions about our response to youths' mental health needs.

## Conceptualizing Functional Consequences of Mental Disorders

Instead of focusing on symptom severity or chronicity and multiplicity of symptoms, one can identify the clinical significance of youths' psychopathology by examining the *nature and degree of an individual's functional impairment*. This approach measures clinical significance by evidence of the *effects* of disorder and symptoms on the individual's functioning in everyday matters of life, such as social relations with family and peers or meeting obligations regarding school or work. Impaired functioning is expressed in degrees, depending on the extent to which the individual's behavior—as a consequence of mental disorder—departs from developmental and culturally normal behaviors of age peers within one's everyday social setting.

Chapter 3 describes a number of ways to assess functional impairment, some for use specifically with children and adolescents. The "problem-oriented" methods mentioned earlier for describing youths' maladaptive behaviors are primarily focused on functional impairment in various social spheres, using this alone as a measure of psychopathology and need for treatment.

Several developments have promoted increased attention to the concept and use of functional impairment in describing youths' disorders. It is consistent with modern definitions of disorder in developmental psychopathology, which focus less on classification of disorders and more on identifying psychopathology as maladaptative behaviors, deviating from age-peer norms, that represent failures in negotiating developmental tasks in social contexts (Cicchetti & Cohen, 1995; Mash, 1989; Sroufe & Rutter, 1984; Wakefield, 1992). In addition, as discussed later, federal and state agencies have adopted functional impairment as a way to measure eligibility for various public mental health services.

The potential importance of identifying clinically significant disorder according to functional criteria cannot be overstated for purposes of our analysis of the juvenile justice system's treatment obligations. The reason is that many studies find that DSM-IV diagnostic disorder maps imperfectly onto functional impairment. In some cases, youths who meet criteria for *no* mental disorders appear to be at considerable risk of ( Jensen & Watanabe, 1999) or actually manifest (Angold et al., 1999) functional impairment requiring treatment. Conversely, many studies (reviewed by

Canino, Costello, & Angold, 1999) have found that "a substantial proportion of children and adolescents who meet criteria for a diagnosis according to the DSM are functioning within the normal range" (p. 95).
For example, in one study of a Puerto Rican community, while almost
half the children and adolescents met criteria for some DSM disorder, only
17 percent of the sample (about one-third of youths with DSM disorders)
manifested moderate or severe impairment on a measure of the effects of
the disorder in impairing their everyday functioning (Bird et al., 1988).
Similarly, in a juvenile justice sample (Virginia Policy Design Team,
1994), researchers found that about 80 percent of youths in Virginia secure
detention facilities met diagnostic criteria, but only 9 percent were considered to be in *immediate* need (would deteriorate while in detention if not
served), and another 40 percent might need mental health services at some
time in the future.

## A Note on DSM-IV and Clinically Significant Disorder

Before leaving this discussion of definitions of clinically significant mental
disorder, it is worth noting that all three of the approaches that I have
described—severity of symptoms, their chronicity, and level of maladaptive functioning—are employed in the DSM-IV system for describing
mental disorders. That system, however, includes them in ways that have
important limitations.

Specifically, the criteria for some DSM disorders allow for "specifiers"
that require the clinician to classify the patient's current condition as
"mild, moderate, or severe." This judgment is based on the clinician's
assessment of the level of the patient's distress as well as the patient's
degree of functional impairment. Criteria for these specifications, however, are not standardized and therefore allow for differences in judgment
among clinicians. For example, there are no guides for defining what
might be considered mild, moderate, or severe "distress."

Concerning functional impairment, the DSM multi-axial system includes an Axis V designation of "Global Assessment of Functioning" (GAF:
see pp. 30–32 of DSM-IV), using a rating scale that requires the clinician
to focus on the effects of a disorder on the patient's psychological, social,
and occupational functioning. The system has anchors for a 0–100 rating,
providing brief phrases to assist the clinician in deciding how to express
the extent of the patient's functional impairment (e.g., in DSM-IV, p. 32,
scores of 61–70: "Some mild symptoms . . . some difficulty in social, occupational or school functioning . . . but generally functioning pretty well").

The same GAF anchoring phrases are used for adults, adolescents, and children alike. (Not part of the DSM system, the Children's Global Assessment Scale has been developed for use with children and adolescents: Schaffer et al., 1983). The GAF may have value as a repeated measure by a single clinician with a particular patient, thus documenting relative improvements in functioning as a course of treatment. Its value as a tool for identifying clinical significance of disorder and treatment needs, however, has not been substantiated, especially for children and adolescents.

Concerning chronicity, the DSM calls for many diagnoses to be accompanied by a specifier to indicate whether the condition is "chronic," although it provides only vague instructions for how this is applied to children and adolescents. Some disorders, most notably Conduct Disorder, may be specified as "Childhood-Onset Type" or "Adolescent-Onset Type." But these do not necessarily signify chronicity; for example, one does not know the chronicity of childhood-onset Conduct Disorder at the time that it is diagnosed in a ten-year-old.

## Summary

What we call "mental disorder" for purposes of responding to youths' mental health needs is determined not only by the type of disorder, but also by the level of its clinical significance. This can be expressed as severity of symptoms, their persistence (chronicity) or number (multiplicity), and the degree to which the youth's condition results in functional impairment. We will employ all of these definitions at various times in the later analyses of our juvenile justice system's obligations. But we must now consider one more way to define mental disorder for these purposes.

## Defining Mental Disorder within Sociolegal Contexts

The fact that disorder can be clinically classified, and that a person's condition is considered clinically significant, does not necessarily define the condition or its severity as a mental disorder for the three sociolegal contexts. This is because *the context itself* may prescribe or limit what will "qualify" as a mental disorder for purposes of fulfilling society's objectives associated with that context.

For example, there are many areas of criminal and civil law in which certain forms of psychopathology, regardless of their severity in specific cases, are not deemed "mental disabilities" for purposes of the legal obligations or protections that apply in that legal context (see generally

Gutheil & Appelbaum, 2000; Melton et al., 1997). One legal definition of mental disability may be used for purposes of regulating the involuntary psychiatric hospitalization of individuals, while another may be used for defining employment disability, and yet another for questions of insanity in criminal cases. Differences in what is considered a "qualifying" mental disorder in these disparate areas of law reflect society's underlying purposes for the functions of civil, employment disability, and criminal law. Similarly, many sociological perspectives have conceptualized mental disorder not as a medical or psychological "given," but as a culturally shared inferential conclusion (varying from one culture to another) about the nature of individuals' socially deviant behavior (e.g., Mechanic, 1973; Scheff, 1973). Cultures call certain behaviors deviant—and define them as illness, evil, or harmless—in order to justify a particular social response that is believed to be in the individual's interests and/or the interests of society.

Applying this perspective to our present analysis, we must anticipate that different disorders might be relevant for different sociolegal contexts, even though all of them exist within the broader context of juvenile law and policy. This is because the purposes of these contexts—beneficent treatment, due process, and public safety—are themselves quite different. In the final chapters of this book, I seek to define which mental disorders are relevant for the social purposes about which the question of mental disorder is being raised in each of these three sociolegal contexts. In preparation, let us consider briefly the elements of each context that will structure that inquiry.

## Custodial Obligations regarding Treatment

LEGAL DEFINITIONS. All state statutes provide definitions of mental illness, but typically their terms refer to broad conditions of thought, mood, and behavior (not specific diagnoses) that create some level of impairment (e.g., "grossly impairs functioning"). Specific disorders are sometimes noted with regard to Substance Abuse and Mental Retardation, excluding them from the definition of mental disorder (Woolard et al., 1996). The main reason for this is to define conditions under which persons may be committed involuntarily to state mental hospitals, and most states have separate provisions for care and treatment of persons with substance disorders or mental retardation.

Other laws provide definitions of persons who are eligible for mental health services for purposes other than civil commitment. An examination of these, however, shows that they will not take us far in our analysis. For example, Public Law No. 102-321 (establishing the Substance Abuse and Mental Health Services Administration) mandated block grants to fund mental health services for patients who met criteria for "serious mental illness" (SMI), which it defined as any DSM disorder, substance use disorder, or developmental disorder leading to substantial interference with one or more major life activities. According to PL 102-321, "life activities" include "basic daily living skills such as eating and bathing, instrumental living skills (e.g., managing money . . .), and functioning in social, family, and vocational/education contexts."

Concerning children and adolescents, various federal entities (e.g., the U.S. Department of Education and the U.S. Administration on Developmental Disabilities) employ a category of "serious emotional disturbance" (SED) to identify adolescents and young adults whose disorders are sufficiently chronic and severe to identify them as a special, core target population and establish their service eligibility (Bazelon Center for Mental Health Law, 1993). Yet these agencies use different definitions, refer to "significant functional impairment" without operationalizing the term, and specify no particular psychiatric diagnoses (Davis & Vander Stoep, 1997).

Thus, legal concepts such as state definitions of mental illness and federal definitions of SMI and SED provide only vague guidance in determining the responsibilities of the juvenile justice system for responding to youths with mental disorders. Their inclusion of all (or undefined) DSM disorders does little to differentiate among adolescent offenders, most of whom can be classified according to some DSM disorder.

Legal definitions, however, do allow us to make two important points for our future analysis. First, once a youth meets criteria for some DSM disorder, whether it is called a "mental disorder" for purposes of state definitions or federal obligations to provide treatment depends on the *degree of functional impairment* manifested in the youth's behavior. This also means that clinical diagnosis itself is at best a threshold issue for defining the scope of the juvenile justice system's treatment mandate.

Second, the definitions do not disqualify some disorders that one might otherwise assume would be outside the scope of psychiatric treatment for mental health needs. For example, in discussions of treatment for mental health needs in juvenile justice settings, typically little attention is given to functional deficits associated with developmental disabilities, such as mental retardation and the learning and communication disorders. Moreover, both the juvenile justice system and the child mental health system have long seen Conduct Disorder as a target for correctional rehabilitation rather than clinical treatment provided by mental health professionals. Conduct Disorder is diagnosed not with reference to symptoms of an emotional or mental nature, but on the basis of a "repetitive and persistent pattern of behavior in which the basic rights of others . . . are violated" (American Psychiatric Association, 1994, p. 85). Yet the standards noted earlier do not exclude any of these disorders from treatment eligibility, as long as they create significant functional impairment.

The question of the inclusion or exclusion of these disorders, however, is largely moot in light of our earlier discussion of comorbidity. The great majority of youths in the juvenile justice system with Conduct Disorder or Mental Retardation are comorbid for other psychiatric disorders as well (Teplin et al., in press). Thus, even if these disorders *were* excluded from eligibility, this would alter the reason but not the case-by-case obligation for treatment of adolescent offenders.

THE CONTEXTS WITHIN THE CONTEXT. Within the sociolegal context of custodial care, definitions of disorder and impairment for purposes of defining our treatment obligations may not be the same throughout a youth's custody. They may differ during various stages of juvenile justice processing. By "stages," I mean steps in the process, beginning with arrest, referral to the juvenile court, intake processing, secure detention if it is warranted, diversion or full adjudicative processing, waiver (transfer) to criminal court, decisions about disposition for adjudicated youths, and implementation of dispositional options ranging from community-based interventions to secure correctional facilities. For general discussion, these stages can be divided into pretrial and posttrial contexts.

Analysis of the custodial obligations of the system must take into account that the relation between the state and the youth is not the same across pretrial and posttrial legal contexts. Inherent in this relation are two primary factors: (a) the state's obligation to meet adolescents' developmental and psychological needs, and (b) the state's obligation to avoid intrusions that may jeopardize the constitutional rights of persons who are (or may be) deprived of liberty. A youth in pretrial detention is both a temporary ward of the state and a defendant in a legal proceeding that challenges that custodial arrangement. The duality of this relationship places pretrial limits on the juvenile justice system's responses to the youthful defendant's mental health needs, to the extent that unbridled assessment and treatment might jeopardize the youth's legal defense regarding the alleged delinquency. Once the delinquency is proven (adjudicated), the posttrial balance shifts to favor the state's custodial obligation.

I suggest that what is called a "mental disorder" or "functional impairment" that triggers the system's custodial obligation to provide treatment may be different in these two "contexts within the context." After adjudication, the system's custodial obligation might be triggered by any disorder or degree of functional impairment that would apply (according to public mental health regulations) in considering eligibility for services in the public health system generally. At the pre-adjudication stage, however, the types of mental disorder and the degrees of functional impairment that require a treatment response is not solely a clinical matter. They must be weighed against the system's competing obligation to respect the constitutional rights of autonomy and protection against state powers that are afforded defendants not yet adjudicated. This assertion takes into account the fact that assessment and treatment may produce self-incriminating information that would jeopardize the youth's defense, and it can involve increased restrictions on liberty and procedural delays in adjudication.

In later chapters I examine how this principle should be applied for various disorders, levels of symptom severity, and degrees of functional impairment. By way of example, however, this might mean that the state is justified—indeed, might be obligated—to seek pretrial treatment in an inpatient psychiatric facility for a youth in pretrial detention who is experiencing an acute psychotic episode. But in the same pretrial context, the system might be obligated *to refrain* from comprehensive assessment and treatment of a youth's dysthymic (depressed) condition, even if it is producing important emotional distress and impairment of certain everyday functions. In contrast, the same dysthymic condition might trigger an obligation to treat the youth after adjudication and placement in custody of the state's juvenile corrections authority.

The consequences of this principle will be greatest, therefore, at the pretrial stage. Policy regarding how the competing interests should be weighed can be guided by at least two dimensions: (a) the severity of disorder or functional impairment (representing the degree of necessity for immediate treatment), and (b) the seriousness of the alleged offense (representing the degree of liberty that might be lost by inadequate protection of the defendant's rights). We will return to these dimensions in chapter 5.

## Due Process Obligation

Chapter 1 introduced the justice system's obligation to identify and respond to youths' mental disorders to the extent that those disorders might jeopardize their defense. I described three areas of law relevant for this obligation: waiver of *Miranda* rights to avoid self-incrimination and advice of counsel, competence to stand trial, and questions of culpability such as the insanity defense.

Determining the relevance of various mental disorders for each of these purposes must begin with modern law's functional approach in all three of these areas (Grisso, 2003). It is not the mere presence of mental disorder that creates conditions of invalid waiver of rights, incompetence to stand trial, or insanity, but rather sufficient evidence that an individual's mental disorder actually impairs functioning in a way that is legally relevant. For example, pertaining to the validity of youths' waiver of *Miranda* rights, the U.S. Supreme Court in *Fare v. Michael C.,* 442 U.S. 707 (1979), affirmed that no single factor (such as age, intelligence, or mental disorder) was ever dispositive of the question, but that each case must be weighed in light of the "totality of the circumstances" that might be relevant for judging whether the waiver was made "voluntarily, knowingly and intelligently."

Case law on the relevance of mental disorders for adolescents' competence to stand trial and criminal responsibility is virtually nonexistent. Statutes in many states, however, have recently been modified to apply these concepts in juvenile court as they are defined for adults in criminal court (Redding & Frost, 2002), so our analysis can begin there.

With regard to competence to stand trial, statutes and case decisions in criminal law make it abundantly clear that while mental illness or mental retardation are predicates to incompetence in most states, neither their presence in general, nor any specific disorder, is dispositive of the question of competence (Grisso, 2003; Melton et al., 1997). The question focuses on whether the functional consequences of the disorder for this defendant are such that his or her degree of deficit in ability to understand the nature of the proceedings or to participate with counsel in the defense (*Dusky v. United States,* 362 U.S. 402 [1960]) creates a substantial risk of an unfair trial.

With regard to criminal responsibility (the insanity defense), the question before the court is whether, due to "mental disease or defect" at the time of the alleged offense, the defendant could not appreciate (or know) the wrongfulness (or illegality) of the act or could not conform his or her conduct to the requirements of law. (The precise wording varies from state to state, but most approximate the formulation above. For variations, see Borum, 2003b; Melton et al., 1997). Thus mental disorder or mental retardation are predicates, but they are not determinative of the legal question. Many states, however, exclude disorders "manifested only by repeated criminal or otherwise antisocial conduct" (American Bar Association, 1989), thus avoiding the risk of excusing the illegal behaviors of persons whose "inability to appreciate" the wrongfulness of their acts may be related merely to antisocial character. This has generally been interpreted as excluding Antisocial Personality Disorder as defined in DSM-IV as a predicate for insanity (Melton et al., 1997).

Chapter 4 considers which mental disorders might make a difference in youths' capacities in ways that are relevant for analyzing the juvenile justice system's obligations regarding due process for mentally disordered adolescents. Two concerns will guide that analysis.

First, we must look for disorders that are most likely to produce the functional deficits about which the law is concerned in each of the three legal questions involving due process protections. The only disorders excluded *per se* in law are in the area of insanity, where diagnoses based simply on repetitive antisocial behavior do not qualify. When applied to youths, this could lead us to conclude that Conduct Disorder would not apply, because that diagnosis is based largely on repetitive illegal behaviors. However, as we have noted frequently already, this would exclude only a small percentage of youths in the juvenile justice system, because most youths with Conduct Disorder also manifest other mental disorders.

Second, the functional deficits that need attention are narrower than in a custodial treatment context, which is concerned with general functional impairment in everyday life. All three due process areas are concerned primarily with cognitive or motivational deficits, as well as their influence on performance within relatively narrow contexts. Thus we seek mental disorders that are more likely to impair attention, comprehension, and appreciation of matters with legal relevance for avoiding self-incrimination (waiver of interrogation rights), participating in a defense (competence), and knowing and appreciating the consequences of what one is about to do (criminal responsibility).

The law's focus on functional deficits means that one is not limited to the use of disorders in adult criminal cases as a guide for identifying disorders relevant to the due process obligation in juvenile cases. This is important, because such limitations would be prejudicial, in light of the substantial differences between psychopathology of adults and adolescents. For example, Schizophrenia—the most frequent diagnosis among adults found incompetent to stand trial—typically does not develop until young adulthood (American Psychiatric Association, 1994).

But possibly of greater importance, the consequences of mental disorders with regard to cognitive capacities relevant in these areas of law may be different for youths than for adults. The capacities to which these three areas of law refer generally can be translated into functions that behavioral and neuropsychological researchers call by such names as "attention," "comprehension," "reasoning," "problem-solving," "deciding," and "planning." Collectively these are often called "executive functions," and, as discussed in chapter 4, there is ample evidence that they are still developing during adolescence, not having reached average, adult levels of maturity. Maturation of these capacities in part requires experience in exercising them in increasingly adult-like contexts of responsibility. But maturation of executive functions is also limited by the pace of normal neurological development. Thus normally developing adolescents are at some greater risk of deficits (compared to average adults) in the types of capacities that are involved in these areas of due process.

To the extent that many mental disorders may delay normal development, it is likely that a wider range of mental disorders among youths than among adults may have an impact on their cognitive capacities associated with these due process areas of concern. The task of identifying which disorders among youths are most salient with regard to the cognitive capacities in question is undertaken in chapters 4 and 6. The point here is that the developmental context in which adolescents' mental disorders are manifested may lead to different conclusions about their relevance for due process obligations than we would reach in similar analyses for adult defendants.

## Public Safety Obligations

As described in chapter 1, the public safety obligation has two primary objectives: (a) to assess risk of violence in order to provide adequate security, and (b) to provide rehabilitation and treatment in order to reduce dangerous recidivism. How should mental disorders be defined for these purposes?

If there are particular mental disorders of adolescence that are empirically associated with a substantially higher degree of risk of harm to others, then those disorders will determine the focus of the system's assessment and treatment efforts in fulfilling the public safety obligation. In chapter 4 we will examine whether such a set of disorders can be found, but we should not expect a highly satisfying conclusion. For example, some disorders may be related to aggression in adolescent *clinical* populations, but they might "wash out" when one is working with a *juvenile justice* population. The fact that some majority of juvenile justice youths have been referred because of their impulsive, angry, and aggressive behaviors could reduce the likelihood that differences between diagnostic groups will emerge.

We will almost certainly find no differences in aggressive potential between youths with or without mental disorders (or between disorders) if we frame the question in terms of "whether youths will engage in aggressive or assaultive behaviors." Much research tells us that most boys engage in assaults (that is, get into physical fights) that are serious enough to do harm at some time during their adolescent years (e.g., Elliott, Huizinga, & Morse, 1986). However, differences between diagnostic groups in juvenile justice populations still might arise if we frame the question another way: "Do some mental disorders increase the risk of specific *types* of aggression, more *frequent or repetitive* aggression, and long-range *persistence* of aggressive behavior?" It is here that we might look with guarded optimism.

Framed in that way, the question is most appropriate for pursuing the system's objective to identify youths who require special security for public protection. As described in chapter 1, there are many points in juvenile justice processing that require assessments of risk of harm to others, and the nature of the risk that needs to be predicted is not the same at all of these points. Pretrial detention questions focus on the likelihood of harm to others in the next few days if the youth is not detained; at the other extreme, hearings regarding potential waiver of a juvenile offender for trial in criminal court ask whether the youth is likely to continue to be a danger as an adult. Thus knowledge of how particular mental disorders or dimensions of psychopathology might increase or decrease immediate risks, long-range risks, and types of harmful behavior will be more relevant than global relationships between psychopathology and aggression.

Concerning the system's obligation to treat mental disorders in order to reduce recidivism, we must both broaden and narrow our search for relevant mental disorders in an important way. Specifically, we need to recognize that *we are looking for (a) disorders with (b) symptoms that are (c) associated with future aggression and (d) are within the domain of clinical intervention.* Factors (a) and (b) in this formula broaden our perspective, recognizing that the relation between mental disorder and aggression, when it exists, may be due to symptoms (e.g., depressed mood, anger, impulsivity) that are characteristic of many mental disorders of adolescence. Factors (c) and (d) narrow our perspective. Recall the distinction in chapter 1 between "rehabilitation" and "clinical treatment." The juvenile justice system has an obligation to provide *rehabilitative services* to all youths in their care, whatever their psychological conditions, in order to reduce recidivism. It has a public safety mandate to provide *clinical treatment* for mental health needs, however, only to the extent that specialized clinical services are also necessary in order to reduce dangerous recidivism.

Thus, the mere fact that an adolescent has a DSM diagnostic condition and is assaultive does not create a public safety obligation to provide clinical treatment. There must be a connection between the symptoms of the condition and the youth's aggression. Moreover, there must be a reason to believe that clinical treatment can alter the relevant symptoms. A clinical intervention cannot be "necessary" if it does not have a history of altering—at least sometimes—the symptom condition that is related to aggression.

Therefore, for purposes of the mandate to provide treatment in the interest of public safety, this formula further limits our search to those disorders and symptoms associated with aggression that one can reasonably expect to modify with clinical care. As we will see in chapters 4 and 7, this may place some mental disorders outside the treatment-for-safety obligation, even though they may be related to future aggression.

## Postscript: Is Conduct Disorder a "Disorder"?

Before concluding this chapter, it is important to consider a significant question that earlier discussions have skipped: Should Conduct Disorder be considered a mental disorder? The question arises in part because Conduct Disorder (CD) is diagnosed solely on the basis of a youth's persistent and repetitive manifestation of any three of fifteen behaviors involving aggression, destruction of property, theft, or "serious violation of rules." The "symptoms" of this "disorder," therefore, are solely behaviors punishable by authority, rather than the types of phenomena—cognitive, affective, and other psychological conditions—that are part of the criteria for most other DSM disorders.

One purpose of a classification system for disorders is to assist in the construction and discovery of underlying causal processes associated with a disorder. Richters (1996), for one, has argued that no such underlying process has ever been found for CD. It is true that research has found relations between CD and many factors that can increase aggression, such as impulsivity, poor learning and problem-solving skills, and biochemical and neurobiological deficits associated with disinhibition and harmfully maladaptive outcomes. But a correlation does not indicate cause; often it is not clear whether studies of these factors among CD youths are identifying causes, spurious correlates, or perhaps even consequences of aggression (Richters, 1996).

Lambert et al. (2001) explained this in a different way in an article titled "Looking for the Disorder in Conduct Disorder." They found that youths diagnosed with CD showed a very wide range of pervasive impairments. They attributed this in part to the fact that the CD criteria (doing any three of fifteen bad or antisocial things persistently) are so varied that a wide variety of youths are drawn into the diagnosis. Imagine, Lambert et al. proposed, that one flipped through the DSM-IV manual picking symptoms at random, then called this meaningless collection of symptoms a "disorder." The internal logic and psychometric value of employing those symptoms to identify youths who manifest "random symptom disorder" would not be too different, they suggest, from the internal logic of using DSM-IV criteria for CD to identify youths as having a "conduct disorder."

Finally, there is little reason to believe that engaging in repetitive and persistent illegal and disobedient behavior is the consequence of a particular underlying causal condition. As we will see in chapter 4, persistent delinquency is associated with *many* disorders of adolescence (e.g., ADHD, depressive disorders, learning disorders, and anxiety disorders, especially Posttraumatic Stress Disorder). Moreover, in contrast to CD, research on these other disorders has revealed a number of plausible underlying causal processes. Since the majority of youths with CD have one or more of those diagnoses as well, is it not possible that a CD diagnosis—like a juvenile detention center—simply acts as a collection point for a lot of adolescents who engage in aggressive and illegal behaviors for reasons best explained by a range of other disorders?

Nevertheless, it would be premature to completely reject CD as a potentially useful category. Its status as a mental disorder needs to be questioned, but it may yet have a limited role to play in research and clinical considerations.

## Conclusion

This chapter has taken stock of ways to define mental disorders as a first step on our path toward an analysis of the juvenile justice system's obligations to respond to mental disorders among young offenders. The chapter described classifications of disorders, their clinical significance, and their relevance for various contexts. This has raised many warnings about difficulties that we will confront in later chapters when we apply these concepts in the process of defining the obligations. Many of these difficulties are related to the fact that psychopathology in adolescence cannot be understood outside of the context of adolescent development. This makes the terrain entirely different and more complex than the territory of adult psychopathology and its relation to legal questions. Moreover, the chapter has pointed out that diagnoses alone do not define the juvenile justice system's obligation to meet adolescents' needs for mental health services. We must also take into account the severity, chronicity, multiplicity, and functional significance of youths' disorders, as well as the fact that what qualifies as a mental disorder requiring treatment may vary across sociolegal contexts.

The focus has been on conceptual definitions of mental disorders. But to arrive at a complete picture of the juvenile justice system's obligations, we must now explore two further issues. First, any prospect for meeting the obligations we have discussed here will require that the system identify mental disorders in youths reliably and efficiently. Chapter 3 examines that proposition. Second, the final section of this chapter identified the need to know the relation between various mental disorders of adolescence and the functional abilities, impairments, and characteristics that are relevant for our three sociolegal contexts. Chapter 4 takes stock of those characteristics.

## Chapter 3

# Assessing Mental Disorders in Adolescents

The juvenile justice system's ability to respond to young offenders with mental disorders depends substantially on its ability to identify them. This chapter examines the potentials and challenges facing the system when identifying youths with disorders relevant for the three sociolegal contexts of custodial treatment, adjudication, and public safety. This requires attention to three broad assessment issues: (a) *availability* (what methods are available, and what do they claim to do?); (b) *reliability* (to what extent can we depend on their results?); and (c) *applicability* (what are the practical implications of their use in the three sociolegal contexts?).

The discussion bypasses the question of clinicians' abilities to make diagnoses based on unstructured interviews and clinical intuition. The days when society depends on the diagnostic judgment of clinicians are rapidly drawing to a close. Reliance on their art has been replaced by demands for "evidence-based methods" (objective, data-based accountability) in a world in which managed care and state budget regulatory offices control the availability of treatment resources and require more proof of need for care than a clinician's general impression. Moreover, we know little about the abilities of clinicians—unaided by assessment tools—to make reliable diagnoses with children and adolescents. Structured tools and instruments are the focus of this chapter.

The range of options for assessing youths' mental disorders is extensive, and it is not possible here to provide detailed guidance to clinicians regarding the values and limits of all of these methods. A number of sources can be consulted to obtain reviews of (and references to) the wider range of interview methods, screening tools, rating scales, and psychological tests that are available for use with adolescents in the juvenile justice system (e.g., Hoge & Andrews, 1996; Grisso & Underwood, in press).

## What Methods Are Available?

A method is "available," for present purposes, if it (a) assesses characteristics of youths related to mental disorders, (b) has been developed for, or has a history of use with, boys and girls in the juvenile justice system, ages twelve to seventeen, and (c) is published in English and Spanish. Here I discuss four categories of measures that meet these requirements and briefly describe some representatives of those categories. This provides a general notion of the available options, which will aid later discussion of issues in identifying adolescents' disorders.

### DSM Diagnostic Interviews

A number of well-researched tools use structured or semistructured interviews employing standardized questions to determine whether youths meet criteria for various diagnostic categories of the *Diagnostic and Statistical Manual of Mental Disorders* (DSM-IV) (American Psychiatric Association, 1994). There are, for example, the Diagnostic Interview for Children and Adolescents (Herjanic & Reich, 1983) and the Schedule for Affective Disorders and Schizophrenia for school-aged children, also known as the Kiddie-SADS (Puig-Antich & Chambers, 1978). But the Diagnostic Interview Schedule for Children (DISC) is the most comprehensively developed tool and serves as a prototype for this class of instrument. The DISC grew out of research conducted under the aegis of the National Institute of Mental Health and benefits from a history of various versions dating back to 1979. The most recent is the DISC-IV (Shaffer et al., 2000), which uses diagnostic criteria consistent with the current DSM-IV. The version it replaced, the DISC-2.3 (Shaffer et al., 1996), corresponded to criteria in an earlier version of the DSM (DSM-III-R). As noted in chapter 1, both of these versions have been used in important research on the prevalence of mental disorders among adolescent offenders.

The procedure for the DISC-IV involves asking questions of respondents, exactly as they are written and in a specific sequence, with branching sequences depending on the respondent's answers. Examiners have the choice of asking questions that will provide a current (past four weeks) diagnosis, diagnoses for status during the past twelve months, and diagnoses during the youth's lifetime. Examiners also may ask questions related only to select diagnoses. The DISC-IV includes an assessment of significance of impairment (consistent with DSM-IV levels of mild, moderate, and severe) for diagnoses made for a given individual.

Shaffer et al. (2000) report a DISC-IV administration time with youths of one to two hours, and they recommend about three to six days of training for DISC-IV administration. Processing the answers to achieve diagnoses typically must be accomplished with a computerized algorithm. The DISC-IV usually is administered in a face-to-face interview format, but it is available on CD, including a version that verbally asks the youths questions that they answer at a computer keyboard. Wasserman et al. (2002) have tested this computer-assisted "Voice DISC-IV" in juvenile correctional facilities.

## *Personality and Behavioral/Emotional Problems Inventories*

Several important paper-and-pencil inventories for clinical use with adolescents measure their characteristics on certain personality dimensions or on constructs that identify behavioral and emotional problems. Three of these instruments, developed in the early 1990s, have been used with some frequency in juvenile justice settings. They are the Minnesota Multiphasic Personality Inventory-Adolescent (MMPI-A: Butcher et al., 1992), the Millon Adolescent Clinical Inventory (MACI: Millon, Millon, & Davis, 1993), and a "family" of instruments under the name Child Behavior Checklist (CBCL: there are several manuals and guides for these various instruments—for a description of all of them, see Achenbach & McConaughy, 1997). There have been recent, comprehensive reviews of each of these three instruments (MMPI-A: Archer, 1999; Forbey & Ben-Porath, 2001; MACI: McCann, 1999; CBCL: Achenbach, 1999).

The MMPI-A uses dimensions that were derived from the adult MMPI, in use since the 1950s (and used with adolescents as well as adults until the development of the MMPI-A in 1992). It consists of 474 true–false items (reading level approximately sixth grade) that can be administered in paper form or with computer or audiotape. These items contribute scores to ten clinical scales (e.g., "Depression," "Paranoia") that represent personality and behavioral tendencies, not DSM diagnostic conditions. Other scales on the instrument assist in detecting problematic response styles, such as overreporting or underreporting of clinical abnormalities. A youth's scores are compared to norms based on results of administration of the instrument to a large number of adolescents, allowing one to identify the age-relative degree of pathology on each of the scales. The MACI is much the same type of instrument, but its 331 items contribute to seven "Clinical Syndromes" (e.g., Anxious Feelings, Impulsive Propensity), several personality characteristics (e.g., Inhibited, Conforming), several "Expressed Problems" scales (e.g., Identity Diffusion, Family Discord), and several scales examining response styles. Both instruments require from one to two hours to administer.

The CBCL comes in Parent, Teacher, and Youth Self-Report forms. Shorter (112 items) than the other two inventories, it focuses on eight behavioral and problem dimensions (e.g., Withdrawn, Anxious/Depressed, Aggressive Behavior) that can be grouped into two broader types or styles of pathology, called "externalizing" (outward expression) and "internalizing" (inward feelings and thoughts). The CBCL also has a "competencies" section that is intended to identify specific social capacities and problems in everyday life. Youths are compared to age-peer norms. Administration requires about thirty to forty-five minutes. There is an enormous research literature on the reliability and validity of the CBCL, less with the MMPI-A, and least for the MACI.

### Symptom Inventories

A number of instruments assess specific symptoms without providing diagnostic classifications (see Grisso & Underwood, in press, for a comprehensive list). Two that have gained substantial use in juvenile justice settings are the Brief Symptom Inventory (BSI: Derogatis, 1993; Derogatis & Melisaratos, 1983) and the Massachusetts Youth Screening Instrument-Second Version (MAYSI-2: Grisso & Barnum, 2003; Grisso et al., 2001). These instruments are designed to obtain information about symptom conditions or mental/emotional distress—nine for the BSI (e.g., Paranoid Ideation, Psychoticism) and six for the MAYSI-2 (e.g., Angry/Irritable, Depressed/Anxious, Suicide Ideation). Both are designed for quick administration and scoring (BSI: fifty-three items, ten minutes; MAYSI-2: fifty-two items, ten minutes). The BSI was originally developed for adults but has been used with adolescents. The MAYSI-2 was developed and normed specifically for adolescents in the juvenile justice system.

### Measures of Functional Impairment

Functional impairment instruments seek to measure the degree to which psychopathology is actually interfering with a youth's everyday functioning. They therefore typically focus on evidence of the individual's current performance, behavior, and interpersonal relations at home, at school, and with peers. (For a review of many measures of this type, as well as their purposes, see Canino, Costello, & Angold, 1999).

The Children's Global Assessment Scale (CGAS: Shaffer et al., 1983) is patterned after the DSM-IV Global Assessment of Functioning in that it uses a 0–100 rating scale with verbal case anchors, but the CGAS provides anchors that are more appropriate for children and adolescents than in the DSM-IV's method. Two others, though, are more often seen in juvenile justice settings. The Child and Adolescent Functional Assessment Scale (CAFAS: Hodges & Wong, 1996; Hodges, 1997; for recent reviews, see Bates, 2001; Hodges, 1999) is a quick method for clinicians to rate youths (based on whatever case information is available) on adequacy and deficits in functioning within various life domains (e.g., home, school) and with regard to various potential problem areas (substance use or self-harmful behavior, for instance). It was developed specifically to assist in identifying those with "serious emotional disturbances" (SED) for purposes of determining services eligibility and assessing performance outcome (e.g., identifying functioning before and after services are provided). It is said to be used statewide in child mental health systems in about one-half of the states (Hodges, 1999), many of them by legislative authority in order to document eligibility for services. The extent of its use specifically in juvenile justice facilities in those states, however, has not been reported. The Problem-Oriented Screening Instrument for Teenagers (POSIT: Rahdert, 1991; McLaney, Del Boca, & Babor, 1994; Dembo et al., 1996), a 139-item questionnaire, was developed by the National Institute on Drug Abuse as a quick method for identifying youths whose level of impairment in ten areas might require further evaluation and services. The POSIT is used extensively in juvenile justice intake assessment programs in a number of states (e.g., Dembo et al., 1998).

Another class of problem-oriented instruments developed specifically for use with adolescents identifies the potential for suicidal or self-injurious behavior, or the history, frequency, and consequences of substance use. Scales to assess suicide potential, of which there a considerable number, typically are brief and rely on self-report. (For reviews, see American Academy of Child and Adolescent Psychiatry, 2001; Grisso & Underwood, in press). Some of them have undergone research to establish their ability to identify suicidal youths. A very large number of instruments are available for use specifically with adolescents to assess extent of alcohol and drug involvement and psychosocial factors associated with substance use. (For surveys of these instruments, see Center for Substance Abuse Treatment,

1999; Winters, 2001). Some of them are embedded in other problem-oriented instruments (such as the POSIT), but most are free standing, and many of them have been adequately researched and found to have acceptable psychometric qualities.

## About the Instruments

As mentioned earlier, the methods noted here are only representatives of a much larger field of instruments—certainly at least several hundred—that have been developed for assessing youths' clinical conditions. However, most of this larger field of tools has been used only in research or only occasionally in applied clinical settings. As one explores the adolescent mental health and juvenile justice programs across the country, the dozen instruments identified here are the ones that repeatedly arise in actual practice.

The BSI is the only instrument among them that was originally developed for adults and has been pressed into service with youths without modification. What limited data are available suggest caution in its use with age groups (children or adolescents) for which it was not designed (e.g., Broday & Mason, 1991; Piersma, Boes, & Reaume, 1994).

The other instruments developed specifically for use with adolescents have appeared mostly within the past ten years; a few were based on earlier prototypes, but most are first-generation instruments. Their recent evolution is probably related to several factors. Many advances in the field of developmental psychopathology during the 1980s stimulated interest in developing instruments in this area, prompting at the same time an increase in the conceptual capacity necessary for carrying out this work. In addition, a sea change in the economics of mental health care during the 1980s and 1990s, involving managed care and cost containment (Young, 1998), created the need for assessment tools to meet the accountability requirements for evidenced-based practice (hard data on case-by-case mental health needs and treatment outcome). This produced a market incentive for the development of child mental health assessment tools. The market is substantial, because the states' juvenile justice systems recently have begun adopting assessment practices that screen every youth entering their systems for mental health needs.

Two implications of the recent history of these instruments are relevant. First, they have not had much time to establish their research or applied track record. Most of them can provide some evidence for their reliability and validity, but often the evidence is based on the initial studies performed by the test authors themselves during the tests' development with initial samples of youths. Moreover, often the research has examined an instrument's utility and meaning only in the context of clinics or in-patient psychiatric programs. For example, no studies have reported the reliability and validity of the BSI, MMPI-A, and MACI specifically with youths in juvenile justice custody. Initial assessments of a method's reliability and validity may or may not hold up when later compared with results obtained from testing adolescents in different clinical and delinquent settings, geographic areas, or ethnic groups.

Second, these instruments are in active competition for the child mental health and juvenile justice assessment market. Buyers must beware, because sellers (and consumers, too) might be tempted to implement the instruments for purposes that exceed their design. As seen in their description, these instruments are not generally interchangeable. One should not use a symptom screening device to make diagnoses, and a comprehensive diagnostic tool like the DISC-IV does not produce a picture of specific areas of functional impairment in everyday life. The choice of an instrument for a juvenile justice program must be informed by the program's specific purposes in wanting a tool. We will return to this issue later when examining the assessment objectives associated with each of our three sociolegal contexts.

## How Reliable Are the Methods?

"Reliability" has a variety of technical meanings in the field of psychometrics, some of which we will encounter in a moment. For this discussion, however, I use the term in the broader sense, asking to what extent we can depend on instruments of the type described earlier to inform us with some degree of accuracy about the mental disorders and mental health needs of youths in the juvenile justice system. The discussion focuses especially on the way that the developmental status and circumstances of youths raise extraordinary challenges for these instruments.

### Measuring Imperfect Concepts Well

Chapter 2 described the difficulties encountered by developmental psychopathologists in defining discrete mental disorders and their symptoms. Their frustration is most evident in the problem of comorbidity of disorders, as well as the degree to which various symptoms of disorder in adolescence (e.g., depression, anxiety, anger) are shared across current diagnostic categories. In terms that were quoted earlier, there do not seem to be any natural "joints" at which to carve the beast. Yet that is precisely where the test developer must start—first with the process of determining which diagnostic concepts and symptoms to measure, and then with the task of turning them into items and scales.

Sometimes the test developer's process can contribute to the refinement of the original concepts. For example, efforts like Achenbach's statistical procedures for developing the CBCL sometimes introduce a degree of order into chaos, showing us more coherent arrangements of symptoms into categories and clusters than were evident in clinical practice. (Achenbach's work has provided support for the notion of grouping youths' problems within "externalizing" and "internalizing" concepts, which have gained wide acceptance in child psychopathology.)

Typically, though, tests developed on the basis of current diagnostic structures will reflect the comorbidity and symptom nonspecificity of the structures that they operationalize. In other words, the scales that the tests measure will have considerable overlap. Youths scoring high on Conduct Disorder are likely to score high on various other diagnostic categories, and youths who report depressed mood often will also report being troubled by other negative emotions such as anger and anxiety. This is seen empirically when one examines the correlations between scales within any personality instrument (e.g., the MMPI-A or MACI), behavioral/emotional problem tool (e.g., the CBCL), or symptom inventory (e.g., MAYSI-2), many of which have average interscale correlations of about .35 to .50. (These figures are considered rather higher than one would wish, and higher than is generally found in adult measures of psychopathology.)

In other words, our instruments tend not to divide youths "cleanly" into those who are conduct disordered on the one hand and dysthymic on the other, or depressed youths here and angry youths there. Instead, they reflect accurately what we know about adolescents' disorders from developmental theory and clinical experience. As chapter 2 explained, distinct types of disorders are more a feature of adult psychopathology than childhood or adolescent psychopathology, which have more comorbid variations. Ironically, then, if a tool for assessing youths' mental disorders is well developed, it will have limited ability to identify one disorder from another (or will show considerable overlap among disorders), because that appears to be the way that psychopathology really is in adolescence.

## Dealing with Moving Targets

There are several things about adolescent development that make youths "moving targets" when it comes to identifying their mental disorders and their implications. Some of these we discussed in chapter 2, especially the matter of discontinuity of disorders in adolescence. This means that there is some chance—greater in adolescents than in adults—that the disorder one discovers today when testing a youth will not be the youth's disorder for the longer-range future (even if it goes untreated), and may indeed be a precursor for some other disturbance at a later time.

In addition, the normal course of change during adolescent years creates the possibility that some youths may manifest disorders at one point in their adolescence that simply do not persist. For example, their disorder as it appeared at a particular time arose in response to their difficulty in mastering a particular developmental task (like managing increasing independence in early adolescence) for which they finally find a solution. Or their behavior regressed to an earlier form of adaptation (temper tantrums that are no longer appropriate at their age) in reaction to a difficult change in their life (their parents' divorce, for example), but regained a normal developmental course when they subsequently received adequate parental support. Finally, basic studies of adolescents' emotional lives indicate that their thoughts and feelings tend to be more labile than those of adults (Steinberg & Cauffman, 1996). From day to day, youths are more susceptible to brief but dramatic changes in mood, so that they might honestly report some current thoughts or feelings that we would not consider typical for them if we were able to assess them repeatedly at random intervals.

Thus, when a clinician sees, or a youth reports, substantial evidence for "anger," it could represent (a) an uncharacteristic reaction to a current circumstance or situation in the youth's life, (b) a currently characteristic response of the youth that may endure through a developmental phase but not longer, or (c) a characteristic that will transcend his developmental phases, perhaps even continuing into adulthood. This has significant consequences for the identification of disorders in adolescence with data obtained at a given point in time, and for grasping their longer-range significance. First, some of the data that one might be seeing at any given point are "states" rather than "traits," related to momentary emotions or temporary developmental phases, rather than enduring characteristics. They should not be ignored; indeed, they might have great significance in signaling the need for immediate clinical attention. For example, serious depressed mood and suicidal thoughts are not insignificant simply because they are momentary. But the data are less dependable for making longer-term predictions or extended treatment plans. Second, even if what one sees is not temporary, the overall results still are likely to have a shorter "shelf life" than for adults. With adolescents, one should not presume the current validity of a diagnosis made more than a few months earlier, or that last year's diagnosis necessarily explains a youth's current clinical episode.

Some sense of the magnitude of this "moving-target problem" is provided by the results of a major, longitudinal study of 4,000 inner-city youths in Pittsburgh, Denver, and Rochester, in which youths' serious delinquency, drug use, and mental health problems (externalizing and internalizing indexes on the CBCL) were assessed annually for three years (Huizinga et al., 2000). Among all youths who were identified as "having mental health problems" at the start (that is, were in the top 10 percent of the sample on the CBCL), about 75–80 percent did *not* meet those criteria when retested after one year, and only 5–10 percent of them continued to score high on the measure after two years. Interestingly, delinquency followed the same pattern; among youths meeting criteria for a serious delinquent behavior in the starting year, only about 20–25 percent "persisted"—continued to engage in serious delinquency yearly—over a two-year period.

It is not surprising, therefore, that when test developers examine the relation between diagnoses or symptom scores for the same youths at two different points in time, their "test–retest reliability" (the correspondence of the two scores) is only modestly good for most disorders and quite inadequate for others. Test–retest research procedures typically minimize the time between testing, usually two to three weeks, because the objective is to examine the stability of the test, not to document changes in youths' conditions that might normally occur over longer periods of time. Even so, the average test–retest reliability correlations are in the area of .65 to .85 for various scales in instruments like the MMPI-A, the MACI, the MAYSI-2, and the DISC-IV, and they are in the range of .35 to .60 for at least some scales in each of these instruments. Test–retest correlations in the former range are acceptable but do not bring a gleam of satisfaction to the psychometrist's eye, and those in the latter range are considered troubling.

The relevance of these observations depends on what a test intends to measure. Test–retest reliability is more important for tests that claim to measure characteristics that should endure more than a few weeks (most diagnostic conditions) and less important if they claim to measure thoughts and emotions that might be expected to change over that amount of time among many youths.

## Relying on Youth and Parent Reports

Most of the instruments described earlier rely either on youths' reports of their thoughts, feelings, and behaviors in response to standardized questions, or on the reports of others—usually parents—who have observed the youth over time. Thus, the reliability of the data on which standardized diagnoses and symptom descriptions are based depends on the abilities and inclinations of informants to provide accurate and relevant information. This is a matter that requires some caution and must be taken into account when reviewing the options for assessing mental disorders in juvenile justice contexts.

YOUTH OR PARENT? One might expect that it would be better to ask parents about their children rather than to expect youths to be able or will ing to provide reliable information in the context of their arrests and adjudications. But this expectation has its limits. Every experienced examiner in a juvenile court clinic has observed the fear, embarrassment, or barely contained rage on the part of parents as they react to the recent arrests of their children. It should not be surprising that their observations are often quite different than those offered by parents who are seeking help for their children at mental health clinics.

In addition, parents sometimes cannot report things that youths can report about themselves. Child diagnosticians used to rely primarily on parents' reports of their children's conditions, believing that children and adolescents were incapable of providing reliable information. Several important studies (e.g., Lapouse & Monk, 1958; Rutter & Graham, 1968), however, altered this view. The weight of the evidence suggested that mothers reported the *observable behaviors* of their children somewhat more reliably, but that children reported more *"internalized" difficulties* (fears, disturbed thoughts and emotions), and they reported them more reliably (test–retest) than did their mothers. Over the years, therefore, practice has evolved to virtually require youth-reported information in clinical assessments, as well as caretaker information whenever the matter being assessed goes beyond the youth's thoughts and feelings. (Grills and Ollendick [2002] provide a very readable, complete review of the research on this issue.)

Several instruments—the DISC-IV, the CBCL, and the CAFAS (in its use of records that often contain others' reports of children's behaviors)—employ both adolescent- and parent-reported data. What is one to do with discrepant data obtained from these two sources? There are methods for integrating discrepant information (Grills & Ollendick, 2002). But typically one either believes one informant more than the other or one relies on both informants for different types of information, depending on which type (behaviors or internal states) they are more likely to report reliably.

Sometimes, though, one has no choice but to rely on youths themselves as the only source of information. Parents usually are not available, for example, when youths are first detained after arrest, a point at which assessment to determine emergency or immediate treatment needs may be critical. The information instruments can provide at that point is almost entirely based on the reliability of the youth's own self-report.

YOUTHS' RESPONSE BIASES. Youths (and adults) do not always report their thoughts, feelings, and behaviors as they actually are. This may result from the emotional circumstances in which juvenile justice assessments sometimes occur, as well as from youths' awareness of the implications of admitting to various thoughts, feelings, and behaviors in the context of custody.

As an illustration, imagine a youth who has been arrested by police officers in his home in the middle of the night, taken from his own bed to the police station, booked, threatened explicitly or implicitly with being removed from friends and family for a period of anywhere from a week to several years, and taken in shackles to a detention center, strip-searched, and led to a small room with a cot and locked door and told that he would have to stay there "for a while." The next morning, after being roused at 6:00 A.M. and fed along with fifty other youths whom he does not know, he is led to a room where a staff member proceeds to ask him questions to identify where he lives and attends school, then gives him a test booklet to complete that asks, among other things, the following questions:

- Have you been feeling lonely much of the time?
- Have you felt angry a lot?
- Have you been bothered by worried and nervous feelings?

Other questions ask:

- Have you thought a lot about getting back at someone you have been angry at?
- Have you used alcohol and drugs at the same time?

How a person answers such questions so soon after being admitted to detention may well be quite different than one's answers given under different circumstances. For the first three questions, the youth might endorse these "feelings" because of the painful experience of the past forty-eight hours, reflecting his transient rather than typical characteristics.

As for the last two questions, one would not be surprised to find that a youth was disinclined to admit to aggressive and illegal acts when faced with an authority figure representing the legal system that will decide his fate. In fact, the last time the youth was arrested, his attorney might have cautioned against responding too openly to questions that might get one in trouble. There is some comfort in the very consistent report of clinicians in the juvenile justice system that youths more often than not will report negative information about themselves more readily than one might expect. But Wasserman et al. (2002) observed that in their study in juvenile justice settings, as in other studies (e.g., Atkins, Pumariega, & Rogers, 1999; Randall et al., 1999; Teplin et al., 2002), the rate of identified Attention-Deficit/Hyperactivity Disorder cases has been so low that it is likely that youths in juvenile justice custody are underreporting the aggressive and impulsive symptoms that are often associated with that disorder.

When instruments have been developed specifically with youths in juvenile justice circumstances, it is possible for the test's norms to compensate somewhat for these sources of situational bias in responding. But most of the instruments we considered earlier were developed in community mental health and inpatient psychiatric settings for clinical populations of adolescents and their parents. In these settings, children and parents are there to be helped, and their relation to doctors is typically collaborative and hopeful when doctors ask them questions about their thoughts and feelings. Unlike youths in pretrial detention, typically they are going home at the end of the day and have been promised confidentiality when they were given assessment instruments.

Youths' possible inclination to conceal their thoughts or feelings is not always the problem. Clinicians frequently report that girls in the juvenile justice system often tend to *overreport* their negative emotions and thoughts, either because of social role differences that make the expression of feelings more acceptable to girls than to boys, or because they have learned that doing so may elicit greater attention and support. There is little research to substantiate these observations. As chapter 1 explained, girls in the juvenile justice system do have higher average scores than boys on almost every measure of mental or emotional disturbances. But it is not clear whether this reflects overreporting or simply greater psychopathology among girls than boys in juvenile justice settings. Some studies, though, have found poorer agreement for girls than for boys when their self-reports are compared to information obtained from parents (e.g., Angold et al., 1987; Rapee et al., 1994).

Virtually absent from the research on this issue are data regarding the reporting of symptoms by youths of varying ethnic and cultural backgrounds. There are intuitive reasons to suspect that ethnicity, and differences in ethnicity between youth and examiner, may make a difference in the reporting of symptoms and problems. Some of the instruments described earlier have examined ethnic group differences in scores (which we will consider later), but those data do not address reliability of reporting.

Most tools for assessing mental disorders and problems of youths are vulnerable to these reporting biases of adolescents. The MACI and MMPI-A have indicators built into their instruments meant to detect under- or overreporting of symptoms and problems. But this does not resolve the issue, because they were not developed with populations of youths in juvenile justice custody at the time of testing.

Despite these cautions, there is no reason to believe that the problem is so great that it invalidates the use of youth self-reports (or parent reports) in adolescent assessment. But it is a source of error that must be weighed in practice, and it must be given greater attention in many situations in the juvenile justice process, depending on the likelihood that the results of the assessment may be interpreted by youths or parents as representing substantial gains or losses.

### Validity

The "validity" of an instrument is the degree to which it measures what it purports to measure—in this case, whether it identifies the mental disorders, symptoms, or impairments that it is intended to identify. There is no single way to establish an instrument's validity, and no single study can do so. Indeed, there is no rule regarding the number and kinds of studies it takes to conclude that a test is "valid." Moreover, a test may be valid for some purposes (e.g., identifying depressive disorders) and invalid for others (e.g., identifying which youths with depressive disorders are in need of treatment).

There are many methods for testing an instrument's validity, and they go by many names—face, internal, concurrent, construct, predictive, and so forth (see, e.g., Anastazi, 1988). But they can all be categorized as representing one of two broad approaches: *theoretical* and *concurrent.*

Theoretical approaches examine whether the instrument has a record of finding results that are consistent with our theoretical notions of mental disorders. By analogy, imagine we came across historical records that we had good reason to believe accurately pointed to the location of a buried treasure. We use a device at that location that is said to detect precious metals. If it registers, we have indirect evidence that the device does what it is supposed to do, even if we are not immediately able to dig up the treasure. Similarly, if theory tells us that youths with Major Depression are more likely than other youths to have parents who manifested Major Depression, and if the measure we use to form our depressed and nondepressed groups helps us to substantiate that prediction, the measure moves up a notch in our belief in its validity for identifying Major Depression. If a disorder is expected to produce a high suicide risk, and if our measure of suicide potential achieves higher scores with the group diagnosed with that disorder than with youths in general, our confidence that the measure assesses what it is supposed to assess increases.

Concurrent approaches to validity examine the degree to which the instrument produces scores or diagnostic groups that comport with results obtained with other methods for determining those groups. For example, if a measure of Major Depression usually identifies the same youths that are identified by a panel of highly expert clinicians, the measure gains a degree of recognition regarding its validity for measuring the disorder.

When examining an instrument's validity, a difficulty inherent in both of these approaches is that the instrument is always being compared to something else (theoretical expectancy, or some other definition of the "right" answer). Therefore, whether the results are positive or negative, one's conclusions about validity can only be as good as the validity of that to which the instrument is being compared. Typically, the validity of the thing to which it is being compared is either unknown, or what is known about it is based on past studies that compared *that* thing to something else (which, of course, is of unknown validity or is considered valid because *it* was once compared to something else).

The logic seems circular, yet a substantially reliable field of clinical assessment has been built under these conditions. But it is important to understand that to declare an instrument "valid" establishes no firm anchor and, indeed, has meaning only in a particular psychometric sense. Moreover, tests too often are declared to be "valid" without specifying that they are valid only for some specific purpose. For example, we might prove that a test identifies 90 percent of youths who later manifest suicide attempts and, in doing so, falsely identifies as suicidal only 30 percent of youths who do not attempt suicide. In general, this might be considered a highly valid test; it certainly establishes a strong relationship between the test and the thing it intends to measure. Now imagine that you operate a detention center where, out of every 1,000 youths admitted, 100 have actual suicide tendencies and 900 do not. The test will identify 360 of these 1,000 youths as potentially suicidal: that is, 90 percent of 100 youths who actually are (90), and 30 percent of 900 youths who are not (270). Therefore, if you provide suicide precautions or hospitalization to all those scoring positive, you will be doing so for almost all youths who need it, but 75 percent of those to whom you provide it (270 out of the 360) do not need it. Would you still consider the test "valid?" Or is it valid for some purposes, but not for yours?

*Norms*

The manuals of most instruments provide norms with which one can compare a youth's scores. Norms are developed by administering the instrument to large samples of adolescents (often including clinical and non-clinical samples) in order to determine the range of scores and consequently what is considered high and low relative to one's peers, and to provide ways to identify where a particular youth falls in that range.

It is important for norms to be age-appropriate for the youths one is assessing, and many instruments do provide separate norms for younger and older adolescents. But one of the nagging problems with many measures of psychopathology reviewed earlier is the questionable use of their norms with various ethnic subgroups in juvenile justice settings.

According to federal statistics (Snyder & Sickmund, 1995), the ethnic proportions of those in juvenile pretrial detention centers nationally are as follows: 43 percent African American, 35 percent White (non-Hispanic), 19 percent Hispanic, and 3 percent other ethnicities (e.g., Asian, Native American). In contrast, the norming samples for the MACI, MMPI-A, CBCL, BSI, and DISC-IV range from 58 to 89 percent White (non-Hispanic), with African American youths comprising less than 15 percent of the samples for the MACI, the CBCL, and the MMPI-A. Figures are not available for the proportion of Hispanic youths in some test norms, but they were less than 12 percent for the MMPI-A and 6 percent for the MACI. Moreover, none of these instruments' manuals contain separate tables showing the average scores of youths by ethnicity on the instrument's various scales. None publish statistics (such as scale alpha coefficients) to show whether the scales as constructed have adequate internal consistency for each ethnic group, and none have employed special statistical methods that determine whether individual items in the instruments are consistently interpreted the same or differently by various ethnic groups taking the test. This is important because, without that information, one does not know whether youths of different ethnic backgrounds approach the test questions differently, thus perhaps nullifying the intended meaning of the scale for certain ethnic groups.

Similarly, when researchers have compared an instrument's scores to some other criterion to test the validity of the instrument, almost never (with the exception of the CBCL) have those comparisons been made separately for youths of different ethnicities. Thus one does not know whether the evidence for the validity of the instrument applies equally well to African American, Hispanic, and Asian youths as to White (non-Hispanic) youths.

Why such limitations of these instruments have not been resolved is not clear. Correcting them would not be impossible. For example, almost all of the types of information noted above have been provided for the MAYSI-2 (Cauffman & McIntosh, in press; Grisso et al., 2001). The difference might be in their starting points. The MAYSI-2 was developed and normed in juvenile justice settings, with minority ethnic youths comprising 56 percent and 85 percent of its Massachusetts and California samples, respectively. Similarly, the use of the DISC-2.3 by Teplin et al. (2002) and the DISC-IV by Wasserman et al. (2002) in juvenile justice samples both have ethnic minorities in high proportions, and Teplin et al. (but not Wasserman et al.) reported separate prevalence rates for youths of different ethnicity. In contrast, most developers of measures of adolescent psychopathology have begun with outpatient and/or inpatient clinical samples, drawn from settings where the greatest proportion of youths are non-Hispanic White. This produces fairly small samples of ethnic minority youths, discouraging separate analyses because of the potential instability of the results.

The fact that most child psychopathology instruments have not been studied within juvenile justice settings raises other concerns as well, and we will return to those in the next section.

## Summary

The field offers a reasonable number of adequately developed instruments from which to choose when trying to identify youths with mental health needs. Moreover, there are several instruments to accomplish the several objectives—for example, arriving at diagnoses, estimating degree of functional impairment—that will arise in various contexts within the juvenile justice system.

But the degree to which they provide reliable case-by-case information about youths is limited in several ways, including inherent difficulties in classifying youths' disorders, error associated with the temporal meaning of child clinical data obtained at any given point in a youth's life, and error associated with reliance on youths' and parents' reports of youths' behaviors and feelings. In addition to these sources of error associated with the developmental status of adolescents, we are currently faced with inadequate information about the reliability or meaning of performance on these instruments specifically in juvenile justice settings, and especially with the multi-ethnic population of adolescents whose mental disorders and impairments we are attempting to assess.

This does not mean that the juvenile justice system cannot use the instruments described earlier. But there is a need for caution, as well as for substantial future research to identify the meaning of scores on these instruments for youths of various ethnic backgrounds.

## Applicability: Instruments in Context

Ultimately, one's choice of methods to assess disorders among adolescents will depend also on their compatibility with the demands of the juvenile justice context in which they are used. This requires four types of considerations:

- *Justice Processing:* Where and when is information needed in the processing of delinquency cases?
- *Feasibility:* Do instruments meet the practical demands of the system?
- *Relevance:* Do instruments tell us what the system needs to know, given its purposes for wanting to know?
- *Resilience:* Can instruments endure the conditions under which they will be used?

### Justice Processing: Where and When Mental Health Information Is Needed

INTAKE. Soon after arrest, juvenile justice personnel must make decisions about which youths will be referred to outpatient or inpatient mental health services in the community. Often these decisions are made by intake probation staff or intake assessment centers. Screening procedures may help to identify those who are most likely to need more careful evaluation for making these decisions (Cocozza & Skowyra, in press; Grisso & Underwood, in press).

PRETRIAL DETENTION. Some youths are placed in secure pretrial detention centers soon after their arrest. Typically decisions must be made within a few days regarding the need for continued detention, requiring some information about their mental status to the extent that it is relevant for the question of risk of harm to self or others (one of the criteria justifying continued detention). In addition, staff of detention centers frequently are expected to make decisions about youths' immediate needs, especially as they relate to potential suicide risk, risk of harm to other youths in the facility, and possible acute mental disorder that would require professional consultation or a petition for immediate inpatient commitment.

PRE-ADJUDICATIVE LEGAL QUESTIONS. Questions are raised in some cases that require information about adolescents' clinical status as it pertains to specific legal decisions prior to trial (see generally Grisso, 1998). Among these are questions concerning a youth's potential transfer to criminal court for trial, which require making a judgment about likelihood of rehabilitation and degree of danger posed if the youth were retained in the juvenile justice system. Any evidence of mental disorders might be relevant for this decision. In addition, questions of a youth's competence to stand trial and of criminal responsibility (related to the insanity defense) often hinge specifically on the presence and effect of mental disorders.

DISPOSITION AFTER ADJUDICATION. If youths are found guilty (delinquent), courts frequently require information about their needs when deciding on their placement, in light of the need for services or the danger posed to the community. Typically this information is collected prior to trial to provide its timely use if the youth is adjudicated delinquent. Courts' disposition options fall generally into various types of community programs with probation contact or referral to the state's juvenile corrections authority that also has various placement options (although typically focused on more secure placements). Community options include the possibility of court-ordered clinical services, and juvenile authority secure placements may include options for clinical treatment.

CORRECTIONS. When someone is referred by the court for placement with state correctional programs for youth, the corrections authority of many states provides for an intake assessment to determine, among other things, whether the youth has special mental health needs that require services while in the custody of the youth authority or that suggest the need for more or less secure placement. These results are used for rehabilitation, treatment, and placement planning. Some progressive youth authorities also provide for mental health assessments near the time of program completion, especially when the youth has been in secure facilities and is being considered for return to the community where services might be provided through community agencies during continued custody under the youth authority.

### Feasibility: The Practical Demands on Mental Health Assessment Methods

Recommendations for the use of particular types of assessment methods must take into account the costs of their use, as well as the need for special expertise in administering the methods. Cost is a multifaceted factor. Specific costs include testing materials, the expense of training and maintaining expertise of personnel, the personnel time required for administration of the instrument, costs involved in processing the assessment information and documenting results, and financial compensation associated with the time and level of professional expertise involved. Secondary financial considerations include the possibility of delays in case processing (e.g., reduction in cases-per-day due to longer processing time, longer bed-days in detention or assessment centers), as well as expenses of increased consultations, comprehensive evaluations, and referrals that might be generated by the results of screening procedures.

The instruments described earlier vary widely in these costs for relatively obvious reasons. Some test developers require a per-case fee for administering certain psychological tests, while other tests may be used without cost for materials. Various instruments require more or less time per case and may or may not require administration and interpretation by more costly doctoral-level examiners.

The level of expertise required for various assessment methods must be weighed against the availability of specialized examiners at various points in juvenile justice processing, as well as the volume of cases at those points. At the intake stage, general observation suggests that intake probation information is collected by social work probation officers, and detention intake assessments are performed by nonprofessional detention staff at the time of the youth's admission, with doctoral-level professionals performing more in-depth evaluations in a minority of cases. The number of intake evaluations in a given year is enormous. In 1996, about 1.75 million youths were processed through the juvenile justice system in the

United States on delinquency charges, and about 320,000 youths were admitted to pretrial detention centers (Snyder & Sickmund, 1999). For jurisdictions that have routine screening (every-admission) evaluations at their intake probation and detention intake levels, this represents a very large number of youths annually in most metropolitan areas, even with the increased availability of technology in recent years for processing intake information. For example, Miami/Dade County intake assessment centers (which screen all youths soon after arrest) performed over 120,000 screening evaluations during a recent eighteen-month period.

Mental health professionals (psychiatrists and psychologists) are more likely to be involved in evaluating adolescents' mental health needs related to pre-adjudicative legal questions like competence to stand trial. The number of youths evaluated for questions of competence or criminal responsibility is not known, although some states (Florida and Virginia, for instance) perform several hundred competence-to-stand-trial evaluations annually for children and adolescents.

Typically court probation officers are required to provide some type of disposition-related behavioral and mental health information to judges in virtually every case that is adjudicated. In only a minority of these cases will psychologists and psychiatrists perform comprehensive evaluations. Similarly, evaluations of youths entering juvenile correctional programs after adjudication will be performed by specialized social workers, with occasional assistance from psychologists and psychiatrists in special cases.

Fiscal responsibility and management of scarce resources requires that cost and required level of expertise must be taken into account when deciding what assessment methods should be used. Indeed, very high assessment costs may actually subtract from available resources for providing treatment to youths who are identified as having mental health needs. On the other hand, costs must not be reduced at the expense of selecting methods that provide reliable information that we need in order to meet our obligations. Brief screening devices for identifying symptoms should not be used throughout the juvenile justice process merely because they are cheaper. Cost must be weighed against a method's ability to tell us what we need to know at a particular point in the process.

## Relevance: Telling Us What We Need to Know When We Need to Know It

Our consideration of what methods to use in order to identify youths' mental health needs must take stock of what juvenile justice personnel need to know about youths' mental disorders, at various stages in the adjudicative process and for various purposes related to our three socio-legal contexts. I do not attempt that here, except to describe a general template for the later analyses of this issue (chapters 5–7).

The type and depth of mental health information that the system needs varies considerably from one step in the adjudication process to another. For example, we must ask whether probation intake staff really need to know specific diagnoses for every youth who comes through the door. Alternatively, might a brief screening instrument that provides a rough index of symptoms such as depressed mood and anger be sufficient? Do detention staff need to know an adolescent's diagnosis, or is it sufficient for them to learn that the youth is or is not a suicide or assaultive risk? Is it sufficient for staff who are preparing to make disposition recommendations to only know about symptoms provided by a brief screening instrument, or is something more needed?

The point of these questions, although prosaic, must be kept clearly in mind. *No instrument will serve all purposes for mental health evaluation at all points in the juvenile justice process.* Earlier I noted that the instruments we reviewed were in competition for the juvenile justice market. They should not be, because most of them are not interchangeable in light of the differences across juvenile justice contexts in what the system needs to know. A final analysis of the system's obligations to identify youths' mental health needs will suggest different types of instruments for different points in juvenile justice case processing, tailored to the type of information relevant for objectives at each of those points.

### Resilience: Meeting Challenges to Validity and Ethical Use

Like all products of science and industry, assessment tools are at the mercy of their users. They may be deployed with care and sensitivity or with ignorance, and occasionally their misuse suggests less than appropriate motives of the users. Some instruments may be more resilient than others when used roughly, but none are immune from being misused. Wonderful plans for screening and assessing youths' mental disorders in the juvenile justice system can easily go awry in practice.

UNSTANDARDIZED ADMINISTRATION. Students of psychological assessment are accustomed to hearing their professors intone the oft-repeated adage, "A test is no more valid than its administration." Standardized tools are immediately unstandardized if they are introduced and administered to youth in a different manner than was intended, and having been unstandardized, the results the test produces are invalid, even when the instrument itself enjoys impressive evidence for its validity.

The point here is not about professional expertise. Many of the instruments described earlier have been developed to allow non-Ph.D. and non-M.D. juvenile justice personnel—with various degrees of inservice training—to administer the instruments competently, score them, and translate the scores into diagnostic categories, levels of distress, or degrees of impairment. But the care with which they will do this cannot be guaranteed by the instrument. Often the degree to which instruments will be administered as intended depends on staff motivation. My own team of trainers (for the MAYSI-2) has conducted staff trainings of juvenile justice personnel who quickly embraced the instrument with enthusiasm, an attitude that is often seen among public sector workers who are committed to the youths in their charge. We have also conducted staff trainings of juvenile justice personnel who stubbornly resisted anything having to do with the instrument, fully intending to subvert its use with half-hearted implementation, an attitude that is often seen among public sector workers who are committed to minimizing changes in their established routine.

MISUSE OF THE RESULTS. Tests may be misused in many ways, but in the present context it is especially important to attend to misuses that are related to the two-sided relationship between youths and their juvenile justice custodians. The system is obligated to provide for youths' needs in a manner that is humane and beneficent, which in some states is still interpreted as requiring a rehabilitative and therapeutic objective. But the system has many other objectives, including "moving cases along," maximizing adjudications, and getting kids off the streets. Ironically, increased assessment of youths' mental disorders offers opportunities to further these latter, less-beneficent objectives.

For example, one way to reduce crowding in a juvenile justice system's pretrial detention center is to set the cut-off scores on mental health screens low enough to increase the number of cases that "need" to be transferred to inpatient psychiatric beds, thus freeing more beds in detention. Youths who admit to drug use or angry feelings in pretrial mental health screens may find that their answers get into the hands of prosecutors, thus influencing court decisions about their guilt (or more likely, strengthening the prosecutor's hand in a plea bargain).

There is not much that test developers can do about such misuses. But knowing that they can happen suggests the need for two precautions. First, we should recognize that more assessment is not necessarily better assessment. In fact, one should probably err on the conservative side, concluding that *the state should do no more by way of assessment than that which is essential to meet its treatment, due process, and public safety obligation.* Nonessential assessment increases the risk of unjustified intrusion on privacy, multiplies the opportunities for information to be misused, wastes public funds that could be allocated to other purposes (e.g., treatment of youths' mental disorders), and sets up youths and parents to expect benefits that too often are unfulfilled. Second, recommendations for particular assessment methods or tools should be accompanied by requirements for the conditions in which they should be used. This means attending to the assessment process, not merely the tool, and providing assurances that the results will be used in ways that are appropriate from both clinical and legal perspectives.

## Conclusion

Many good tools have been designed to provide the types of information that the juvenile justice system needs in order to identify youths with mental disorders and functional impairments. Their capacity to assist the system, however, is limited for a number of reasons. Some of these reasons are inherent in psychopathology in the context of child and adolescent development, which produces conceptual and measurement issues of great complexity. Other are related to the development of the tools in clinical and general community samples, raising questions about the meaning of their scores when we rely on youths' and parents' reports in a very different juvenile justice context. And one must be concerned about the utility of norms that often do not reflect the ethnic composition of youths in juvenile justice settings.

Ultimately the value of assessment tools for meeting the system's objectives will depend also on their ability to fit within the juvenile justice system's financial constraints and need for efficiency. In addition, tools must be chosen with regard to specific decision objectives at various stages in case processing, because classes of tools will vary in their value for different purposes. Finally, the potential for misuse of assessment data requires that the practice of identifying youths' mental disorders and impairments should be targeted, efficient, and bounded by requirements that limit the uses of data obtained from assessments of youths' mental health needs.

*Chapter 4*

# The Consequences of Mental Disorders in Adolescence

The mere fact that youths have been identified as having mental disorders and functional impairments is not enough to determine how we should respond to their disorders. We also need to know the relation of those disorders to the objectives of our three sociolegal contexts.

- What does the treatment literature tell us about the *prospects for treating youths' mental disorders* and mental health problems?
- What mental disorders of youths are *relevant for protection of the due process rights* of youths during their adjudication?
- What do we know about the *relation between mental disorders and aggression* for purposes of attending to public safety?

These questions form the three sections of this chapter. Our later analyses of how the juvenile justice system should be responding to young offenders' mental disorders depend substantially on our answers to these questions.

## The Treatment Context: What Are the Prospects for Treatment?

An extensive body of scientific literature describes research on treatments for child and adolescent psychopathology, and makes recommendations for clinical application of treatment methods. It focuses on treatments for specific DSM diagnostic disorders (e.g., Attention-Deficit/Hyperactivity Disorder [ADHD], anxiety disorders), for general symptom conditions (for instance, depressed mood, anger and aggression), and for specific disorder-related outcomes (e.g., suicide). It addresses preventive interventions, emergency interventions, and long-term management of chronic conditions. It describes inpatient and community-based interventions. It identifies the value of psychopharmacological treatment, forms of individual psychotherapy, group therapies, and psychosocial approaches involving systematic interventions in the lives of youths, their parents, and other relevant people in their social networks. It analyses systems of mental health service delivery, including referral processes, networks of service provision, and economic schemes for managing the costs of mental health care for children and adolescents.

This literature is vast and complex. Yet, until the past decade, most treatment of youths' mental disorders was guided by theory and clinical art. Only recently has the field of child and adolescent psychopathology begun to *demonstrate* the value of clinical treatments for youths' mental disorders. This new era has been stimulated in part by advances in scientific methods for examining treatment effects, and in part by a managed care health system in which reimbursement for care requires a demonstration that the treatment to be provided has some value (Weisz & Jensen, 1999).

The lexical icon for this movement, found in the introduction of virtually every recent review of treatment methods, is "evidence-based practice." Treatment is no longer defined simply as anything that a mental health professional provides. Especially if it is to be reimbursed by insurers, *"treatment" is an intervention for which there is research evidence of an effect that is appreciably more beneficial than no intervention.*

This section takes stock of what is known about evidence-based benefits of treatments for young offenders with mental disorders. It addresses three questions:

- *Dimensions of Treatment:* How can we organize the topic of "treatment" so that it helps us to think through the system's obligations?
- *Values of Treatment:* What does research say about the benefits of various treatments for mental disorders, so that we can begin to identify what the system should be required to provide, and what it should *not* be required to provide because of lack of value?
- *Systems for Treatment Delivery:* Treatment is not simply something one goes out and orders; it requires a plan for its administration. What do we know from mental health services research regarding the juvenile justice system's options for managing the delivery of necessary treatment services to youths?

## Dimensions of Treatment in a Juvenile Justice System Context

The term "treatment" is often used in a monolithic way in juvenile justice rhetoric to refer to anything that is intended to modify youths' behavior. Chapter 1 proposed a distinction, however, between juvenile justice systems' "rehabilitative interventions"—the behavior modification, special and occupational education, monitoring, and group counseling activities around which many corrections programs are based—and "treatment" interventions designed to address youths' mental disorders. The meaning of "treatment" in the juvenile justice context can be further refined by considering several concepts related to its implementation: (a) objectives of mental health care, (b) modes of treatment, (c) clinical targets, and (d) definitions of treatment success.

OBJECTIVES OF MENTAL HEALTH CARE. The objectives of clinical treatment vary depending on the course of disorder at the time of clinical intervention. For example, a man develops chest pains and rushes to a hospital's emergency room. Cardiac arrest is diagnosed and treatment is provided with the goal of averting the immediate life-threatening consequences. When the crisis is over, the man is moved to the hospital's recovery area for several days to receive treatment with a different objective — namely, monitoring and stabilization to ensure that the underlying disease process is in remission. For some diseases, this period of treatment may continue for weeks or months, even after the patient has returned home. Once in remission, a third type of treatment frequently occurs, focused on health maintenance to avoid relapse in a patient who is now known to be at risk of the disease that has been successfully treated at the crisis and stabilization levels.

Similarly, treatment may mean all of these things when applied to potential obligations of the juvenile justice system with reference to youths' mental health needs. I refer to these three objectives of treatment as *crisis-related* or *emergency treatment, stabilization,* and *maintenance.*

*Crisis-related treatment* may be required for some youths on admission to detention facilities or sometime during pretrial detention, community probation, or a stay in a correctional facility. This emergency intervention often is in response to behaviors—such as suicide threats, "out-of-control" aggressive behaviors, psychotic-like episodes, or drug withdrawal reactions—that require rapid response with the sole objective of reducing the immediate harm associated with the behavior. Effective crisis-related treatment depends on a system's ability to identify an impending crisis, to obtain clinical assistance quickly, and to have in place procedures for transporting a youth to facilities with specialized treatment resources for dealing with the crisis.

Mental health service directed toward *stabilizing* a youth's condition is often necessary following a crisis, and focuses on achieving a condition that allows the youth to function with less distress and greater effectiveness when returned to the routine of the detention center, correctional facility, or community-based program. This level of care is also needed, however, in many cases that do not involve a preceding crisis. For example, a youth may manifest significant anxiety causing considerable distress and greatly reducing the ability to function in rehabilitation programs or in the community, but without that anxiety involving a highly disruptive episode that would be labeled a "crisis." Treatment for stabilization typically requires the availability of treatment services within juvenile justice facilities or, if the youth is not in a secure setting, in community justice or mental health programs.

Finally, treatment for juvenile justice youths might involve *maintenance* services that ensure continuity of care after maximal functioning had been achieved, to prevent relapses and perpetuate the benefits of stabilization treatment. This level of care might arise during the "rehabilitation" phase of juvenile justice custody, but most importantly after custody has been relinquished.

I use this three-part treatment scheme in chapter 5, when considering the system's custodial treatment obligations. It is also useful in gauging the relevance of our review of treatment effects later in this section.

MODES OF INTERVENTION. There are at least three fundamental modes of treatment that are available to mental health and juvenile justice systems. They are (a) *psychopharmacological* agents, (b) *psychotherapies,* and (c) *psychosocial* interventions. In theory, all three may be applied in any of the health service contexts dedicated to one of the treatment goals just described.

Psychopharmacological treatment of mental disorders involves administration of medications that chemically alter mood, cognition, or behavior, their effect typically being achieved by altering the process of brain neurotransmission. (These are reviewed in more detail later.) The distinction between psychotherapies and psychosocial interventions is not a bright line; indeed, one can view them as ranging across a spectrum. At one end of this spectrum is any mode of treatment primarily involving a therapist and patient in conversation, for any theoretical or practical reason, focused on changing the patient's behavior, thinking, or emotional condition. At the other end is an intervention that seeks these changes by altering the environmental circumstances in which the patient is expected to function in everyday life. Midway along this spectrum are a variety of methods that involve direct work with the patient in the context of people and social systems that are important in the patient's life.

Examples of interventions that may be arrayed along such a spectrum are listed below. (The methods described here are not necessarily "preferred" methods—a notion dealt with later—but are used simply to exemplify what the spectrum may include.) Thus, moving along the spectrum from one pole to the other, one might encounter the following methodologies:

- Youth-focused—Kendall's (1994) individual cognitive-behavioral therapy for youths with anxiety disorders, as well as Assertiveness Training (Huey & Rank, 1994) and Problem-Solving Skills Training (Kazdin, 1996), together with various psychodynamic approaches to assist youths in developing insight into their behavior, typically through the patient-therapist relationship carried out in individual therapy sessions
- Youth in Group—Cognitive-behavioral group treatment for adolescents with depression (Clarke et al., 1999), as well as a variety of peer group methods for treating drug abuse and dependency (Jarvis, Tebbutt, & Mattick, 1995)
- Youth and Family—Functional Family Therapy (Alexander et al., 1988) that focuses on reducing youths' clinical problems by improving interpersonal functioning and communication within the family, with all members participating in the therapy
- Youth and Systems—Multisystemic Therapy (Henggeler et al., 1986; Borduin et al., 1995), in which the therapist works on a daily basis with the youth by intervening directly in the youth's social systems (e.g., family, school, work place) while the youth is involved in them
- Systems—Therapies that train parents (e.g., the Oregon Social Learning Center program: Patterson, 1975, and McMahon & Wells, 1998; also Barkley, 1997), teachers (e.g., Gittelman et al., 1980), or others in the youth's social spheres of interaction to alter the behaviors of youths with disruptive behavior disorders or ADHD by altering their own behaviors in response to the youth (typically without the youth's involvement in the treatment)

All of these approaches may be called "psychotherapy." But it is of value to distinguish them as increasingly "psychosocial" in nature as they move further along the spectrum away from the traditional mode of individual therapy involving the youth alone.

The degree to which one can proceed toward the psychosocial end of the spectrum typically is inversely related to the degree of security surrounding a youth's incarceration. Treatments in secure detention and correctional facilities are confined almost entirely to methods in the less psychosocial part of the spectrum, because the people and social situations that would be needed to employ more psychosocial modes of treatment typically are not available in those settings. Psychopharmacological interventions also involve special requirements that need to be considered when implementing treatment. For example, prescribing must be done by child psychiatrists, who typically are not full-time employees of juvenile justice facilities and sometimes are not even to be found in the communities in which juvenile justice facilities are located. Other implications of various treatments will become clearer when we review the research on the effectiveness of psychopharmacology and psychosocial interventions with adolescents.

CLINICAL TARGETS. All forms of treatment seek to reduce symptoms and problem behaviors associated with some disorder. Some treatments, however, seek to do this by targeting the *disorder,* while other treatments aim at *specific symptoms.* (See Connor, 2002, for a discussion regarding these two strategies in adolescent psychopharmacology.) For example, for a youth who is both seriously depressed and prone to aggressive outbursts, some medications for the treatment of depression will reduce depressed affect as well as the aggression associated with the youth's condition. In addition, though, some medications (e.g., risperidone, an atypical antipsychotic drug: e.g., Simeon et al., 1995) appear to be effective in reducing aggression among youths regardless of their psychiatric diagnosis, so that the medication may be used to target aggression apart from the underlying disorder. Similarly, a psychotherapy for depression may reduce the youth's aggression if it successfully treats the depression (and if the aggression is related to the disorder). But treatment for a similar youth might target a reduction in aggression by assignment to a group anger-management therapy that is not designed to treat depression.

Whether one treats the disorder or the symptom is, of course, a clinical question that has no single answer for all cases. What one must consider, however, is that clinical questions in correctional settings may not always be the same as clinical questions in clinical settings. Imagine a medication targeted for reducing aggression that works more quickly, efficiently, or cheaply than one that treats the disorder. Treating the disorder, however, may offer a more fundamental and lasting change in the conditions giving rise to the youth's aggression. Whichever of these approaches is chosen may be influenced by the way one balances objectives. The first is more aligned with immediate public safety obligations and the second with general treatment obligations and longer-range concerns. There need not be a conflict between these two approaches, but the potential for conflict is present if either obligation is one-sidedly paramount over the other.

DEFINING TREATMENTS OF VALUE. Researchers who study the potential benefits of methods of treatment examine their value in terms of "efficacy" and "effectiveness" (e.g., Hoagwood et al., 1995). To examine a method's *efficacy,* therapy researchers employ the treatment mode under highly controlled conditions. As an analogy, imagine the test of a new pesticide in which it is applied in exactly the same carefully measured and uniform amount per square foot of lawn as is a pesticide already in use. A significant advantage in weed control for the new pesticide demonstrates its efficacy. For tests of therapies, study patients must be selected according to rigorous specifications to ensure that they have the disorder for which the method is intended to be of benefit. The method itself is carefully designed and systematically documented, and the "research doctors" who will be providing the treatment undergo special training in the method to ensure that they will always follow its procedures in a standardized way. The group to which the study patients are compared—the control group—is also carefully chosen to ensure its members have the same diagnosis as the study group, but they receive some other (or no) intervention. Efficacy is expressed as the proportion of patients in the experimental group, compared to the proportion in the control group, who demonstrate a specific beneficial outcome (as measured with standardized instruments).

In contrast, a method's *effectiveness* refers to its value in the real world where researchers cannot control the quality of its application. Using the same analogy as above, we may test the new pesticide's effectiveness by giving it to a number of homeowners, along with instructions for its use, but with no further intervention by the researchers other than their measurement of weed control in the homeowners' yards as the summer proceeds. Similarly, the effectiveness of a method of therapy refers to its value when ordinary clinicians in actual clinical settings provide it to whatever patients obtain their services. Presuming that the method has been shown to be efficacious, will it be of benefit where it really counts—in the real world, complete with its time pressures, individual differences between doctors, and patterns of referral determined simply by whoever (with a specific type of disorder) comes through the clinic door? And if it is of benefit, what real-world circumstances make a difference in increasing or decreasing the likelihood of that benefit?

I later use the distinction between efficacy and effectiveness when examining research on the beneficial effects of various treatments. But two caveats should be noted in the context of that distinction's more general use. First, it does no good to simply require that the juvenile justice system provide "treatment" unless the *efficacy* of that treatment is "evidence-based." Second, the mere fact that the juvenile justice system employs an efficacious treatment does not mean that it will be effective. *Wherever we require treatment, we must also require that the system provide the means— the personnel, training, and quality-control monitoring—that will allow the efficacy of the treatment to be translated into effective practice.* Treatment without efficacy *and* effectiveness is at risk of offering little benefit, at the possible cost of resources that could meet other important objectives of the juvenile justice system.

## What Treatments Have Value?

During the 1970s and 1980s, "Nothing Works" was the bumper-sticker message from those who summarized what we knew about interventions in juvenile justice (e.g., Martinson, 1974). Today we know that some interventions with juvenile justice youths are of value (Greenwood, 1996; Lipsey, 1992). But those findings must be distinguished from our present concern. The Martinson and Lipsey reviews focused on "what works" to reduce recidivism among delinquent youths in general, not "what works" in the treatment of delinquent youths with mental disorders. In fact, the message regarding the value of clinical treatment of delinquent youths typically has been, "We don't know whether anything does or doesn't work." Very recently, however, we have begun to get some answers, and the news is both good and bad.

Kazdin (1988) claimed that he found over 200 types of child and adolescent psychotherapy in the literature, most of which have never been examined in controlled research. Reviews of research on child and adolescent treatment methods, however, have included well over 300 outcome studies (Weisz & Jensen, 1999). There have been many excellent, comprehensive reviews of research on the efficacy and effectiveness of psychopharmacological, psychotherapy, and psychosocial interventions for adolescents' mental disorders. The discussion here is based on general conclusions that can be drawn from commonalities across the results of those reviews.

Some of the best recent reviews covering a broad range of disorders and treatments include Burns, Hoagwood, and Mrazek (1999), Hughes, La Greca, and Conoley (2001), Mash and Barkley (1998), Weisz and Jensen (1999), Weisz et al. (1987), and Weisz et al., (1995). Especially important is a series of reviews initiated by the National Institute of Mental Health assessing the research on the beneficial effects of psychotropic medications (antipsychotic agents: Campbell, Rapoport, & Simpson, 1999; selective serotonin reuptake inhibitors: Emslie et al., 1999; tricyclic antidepressants: Geller et al., 1999; psychostimulants: Greenhill, Halperin, & Abikoff, 1999; mood stabilizers: Ryan, Bhatara, & Perel, 1999), as well as a recent review by Connor (2002) focused on psychopharmacological treatments for aggression in adolescents. (See also Connor et al., 2002, for a meta-analytic study of the value of stimulants in the treatment of aggression in youths with ADHD.) Other reviews that cover research on a specific type of treatment, or for treatments of a single disorder, are cited later.

PSYCHOPHARMACOLOGICAL TREATMENT. One cannot expect a single, bottom-line answer to the question whether psychopharmacological agents "work." The results of research on this question will vary when one examines efficacy or effectiveness with various types of medication, some of them disorder-targeted and some symptom-targeted (e.g., to reduce aggression), and employed across a number of different diagnostic groups. But some generalizations within these subdivisions are now possible.

Looking first at *efficacy* (well-controlled research studies in the "lab"), more psychopharmacological research has focused on *ADHD* than on any other childhood/adolescent disorder. There is considerable, reliable evidence for the efficacy of stimulants such as methylphenidate (Ritalin) in reducing aggression in ADHD youths (review by Connor et al., 2002), as well as general improvement in the condition as manifested in better school achievement and problem-solving (review by Weisz & Jensen, 1999). This does not necessarily mean that ADHD youths on Ritalin become like youths who have never had ADHD (Elia et al., 1991), and the effects generally have been studied only over periods of a few months rather than involving long-term follow-ups. But symptom reduction across studies has been relatively consistent, especially when used in conjunction with behavioral interventions.

Studies of the psychopharmacological treatment of *depression* in youths (Geller et al., 1999) have focused on tricyclic antidepressants, with little evidence of benefit for youths past puberty. More recently, selective serotonin reuptake inhibitors (SSRIs, newer antidepressants with safer side effects than tricyclics) have received "tentative support" (Weisz & Jensen, 1999) for the treatment of Major Depression. Interestingly, the value of antidepressants (even the older tricyclics) has been more clearly demonstrated for the reduction of aggressive behaviors in youths with disruptive behavior disorders (e.g., Conduct Disorder), especially in the context of ADHD (Connor, 2002).

Mood stabilizers (e.g., lithium) have been used increasingly in the treatment of adolescents with *Bipolar Disorder,* which often is manifested in manic-like symptoms involving extreme emotionality and impulsiveness. The results have been mixed, both for reduction in general symptoms of Bipolar Disorder (Ryan, Bhatara, & Perel, 1999) and with regard to reduction in aggression specifically (Connor, 2002). Concerning youths with *Schizophrenia,* several studies have demonstrated the relative efficacy of antipsychotic medications for reducing thought disturbance, although with mixed results with regard to degree of improvement, as well as serious cautions regarding the side effects of available medications (Campbell, Rapoport, & Simpson, 1999). Interestingly, few studies have examined the effects of psychopharmacological treatments for *anxiety disorders.* Those that have been conducted offer "no convincing evidence of benefit from any agents for childhood anxiety disorders" (Weisz & Jensen, 1999, p. 143), except for the well-studied efficacy of SSRIs for youths with Obsessive Compulsive Disorder.

It is worth noting that the use of even efficacious psychopharmacological agents with youths has its risks in the form of side effects, which range from minor discomforts (e.g., dry mouth) that are experienced in many cases to serious and even irreversible conditions in a smaller percentage of cases. Often these more serious side effects, such as tardive dyskinesia (uncontrollable twitching of hands or facial muscles), are associated with prolonged use.

Turning to the *effectiveness* of these psychopharmacological agents (when applied in actual practice in the real world of clinical care), Weisz and Jensen (1999) concluded that such studies "are noticeably absent from the research literature" (p. 145). This is especially important because some medications are not used in the disorder-targeted fashion when applied in actual clinical programs for youths. For example, in clinical settings treating youths with episodic acute aggressive behaviors, it is quite common for medications to be used for sedation—simply to stop the current aggressive outburst—by administering them on a p.r.n. basis (*pro re nata,* or "as needed") (Vitiello, Ricciuti, & Behar, 1987). There has been almost no research "to support the use of p.r.n. medications for acute aggression in psychiatrically-referred youth" (Connor, 2002).

The mere fact that psychiatrists may report, or experience, that such practices are of value is not evidence for the effectiveness of sedatives. For example, Vitiello et al. (1991) examined the effects of a sedative medication, compared to a placebo, on acute disruptive behaviors in children and younger adolescents. Further, some youths received the sedative or placebo in oral doses and some in intramuscular injections. Aggressive behavior was more greatly reduced by intramuscular than by oral administration, regardless of whether youths received the sedative or the placebo, while the mere fact of sedative or placebo condition had no different effect. In other words, the results suggested that decreases in youths' aggression were explained better by their desire to avoid the needle than by whatever the needle was delivering.

PSYCHOTHERAPY AND PSYCHOSOCIAL INTERVENTIONS. There has been far more research on the beneficial effects of psychotherapy and psychosocial interventions than on psychopharmacological interventions. Primary reviews of the general child and adolescent clinical literature in this area were noted earlier, to which may be added reviews of treatment effects specific to youths with aggressive behaviors that resulted in their adjudication (e.g., Frick, 1998; Greenwood, 1996; Schoenwald, Scherer, & Brondino, 1997; see also reviews of treatment programs for adolescents produced by a project called Blueprints for Violence Prevention at the Center for the Study and Prevention of Violence, 2002). Generally, both the efficacy and the effectiveness of such interventions increase as one moves from the youth-focused forms of intervention to the psychosocial forms.

Least beneficial are various modes of *individual psychotherapy* focused on developing the client's "insight" through the therapist–patient relationship; on average they have resulted in no significant benefit compared to nontreatment controls (Weiss et al., 1999). In his meta-analysis of treatments for juvenile justice youths, Lipsey (1992) found that individual counseling provided outside the juvenile justice system—for example, by community providers during probation—actually had a negative effect (that is, was worse than nothing, with recidivism as the outcome variable). (See also Kazdin, 2000b, reviewing traditional individual psychotherapy with conduct-disordered youths.) This is not to say that delinquent youths never benefit from individual psychotherapy or counseling based on a one-to-one therapist–client relationship, and it is possible that counselors who work within the juvenile justice system may be more capable of adapting psychotherapeutic methods to the capacities of delinquent youths. But such therapies typically depend on verbal abilities and conceptual processing of problems (e.g., thinking about things in the abstract), both of which are strengths for only a minority of delinquent youths.

Appreciably better results have been demonstrated for interventions that use a *cognitive-behavioral approach.* These therapies typically focus on cognitive restructuring—changing one's awareness of social cues and interpretation of what one encounters, and promoting strategies for delay, reflection, problem-solving, and responding. Thus the focus is on increasing one's interpersonal skills, self-control, and problem-solving in social contexts. Efficacy studies leave no doubt about the value of cognitive-behavioral therapies, either in individual or group therapy, in treating youths with conduct problems (e.g., Kazdin, 1996, 1997; Kendall et al., 1990; Lochman et al., 1987; Lochman & Wells, 1996) as well as depression (as reviewed by Kaslow & Thompson, 1998) and anxiety disorders (e.g., Kendall, 1994).

Connor (2002), however, has described three factors that may lower the degree of benefit of these therapies in actual practice. First, cognitive-behavioral therapies tend to have less beneficial outcomes when conducted by less experienced clinicians (Kazdin, 2000b). This is significant for our purposes, since the structured nature of these therapies, together with the limited financial resources available to the juvenile justice system for hiring staff, may encourage the system to use clinicians who are less trained than those who conducted therapies in the studies demonstrating the efficacy of the methods. Second, these therapies are likely to be somewhat less effective for youths who are significantly delayed in their cognitive development (Durlak, Fuhrman, & Lampman, 1991), as are many youths in the juvenile justice system, and who therefore might not bring as much cognitive capacity to the therapy process. Third, the benefit is reduced for youths who are facing severe family dysfunction, which often may undo whatever the therapy has achieved (Kazdin, 1997).

Recognition of the latter point—that youths are significantly influenced by dysfunction within their families—has resulted in considerable development of treatment methods that include the *family in therapy with adolescents.* These approaches, many of which have demonstrated efficacy with a broad range of diagnoses among adolescents, conceptualize adolescents' disorders as representative of maladaptive interactions within the family and therefore take the family, not the individual youth, as the identified unit for treatment. In their various forms, they focus on teaching parents to manage their children's behavior (e.g., Barkley, 1997;

McMahon & Wells, 1998) and on reconstructing expectations and inter-personal interactions of family members (e.g., Functional Family Therapy: Alexander et al., 1988).

Reaching the very psychosocial end of the psychotherapy spectrum, *Multisystemic Therapy* (MST) (Borduin et al., 1995; Henggeler, Melton, & Smith, 1992; Schoenwald, 1998) has set the standard for efficacy among treatments targeted for delinquent adolescents. The therapy is nonspecific regarding types of youth disorders. It involves a "therapist" who is actually a social engineer, virtually living alongside the youth and family as they carry out their daily activities, negotiating events that arise between the youth and anyone in any "systems" within which the youth functions—family, school, work, and peer groups. The method has been clearly dem-onstrated to be cost effective and to achieve its objectives of improved functioning, increased family cohesion, and reduced recidivism with last-ing effects (e.g., Henggeler, Melton, & Smith, 1992; Henggeler et al., 1993). For our purposes, it is most relevant for treating Conduct Disorder, and it is significant that the treatment outcome studies have involved youths with significant impairments and serious prior offenses.

Until recently there has been little quality research on the value of treatment of adolescents for substance use disorders (Kaminer, 2001). That picture is changing, with several new reports of successful interventions with substance-abusing and substance-dependent adolescents using MST (Hengeller, Pickrel, & Brondino, 2000), Functional Family Therapy (Waldron, Brody, & Slesnick, 2001), the Twelve-Step Approach (Winters, Stinchfield, & Opland, 2000), and cognitive-behavioral therapy (Kami-ner, Burleson, & Goldberger, 2000). (See generally Monti, Colby, & O'Leary, 2001.)

Most of the studies on psychotherapy and psychosocial interventions for adolescents with mental and substance use disorders have been con-trolled efficacy studies. But what about the effectiveness of these methods in the real world? Unfortunately, effectiveness studies have been rare, and the few that have been done show little evidence for positive effects com-pared to control groups (Weisz et al., 1995). In what has perhaps been the largest test of the value of real-world mental health treatment services for children, the Fort Bragg Project (Bickman, 1996) involved an invest-ment of $80 million for a well-designed study of the value of an enriched, state-of-the-art system of mental health care and treatment for all children in a catchment area in North Carolina during a period of several years. Compared to another "services as usual" site, the Fort Bragg Program produced far better access to treatment and greater user satisfaction, but no better clinical or functional outcomes. Bickman's own conclusion was consistent with the title of his 1996 article, "A Continuum of Care: More Is Not Always Better." He concluded, in part, that merely providing a lot of treatment is not the answer; we must look for ways to teach clinicians how to provide efficacious treatments well.

REDEFINING THE "EVIDENCE-BASED PRACTICE" REQUIREMENT. In summary, *efficacy* studies provide substantial evidence that various psychopharmacological and psychotherapeutic interventions have beneficial effects for youths' mental disorders and aggressive behaviors. This is very good news. After several decades of knowing little about the value of treatment for adolescent offenders, we now know that some treatments can make a positive difference—not just for youths with mental disorders, but for youths with mental disorders *and* consequent delinquent behaviors. These treatments can reduce symptoms as well as delinquency recidivism. And studies have even begun to show us what kinds of treatment are more or less likely to be beneficial with what kinds of youths.

The bad news is that we have little evidence that these treatments are *effective,* that is, that they achieve their capacity (as demonstrated in controlled efficacy studies) when they are put in place in everyday practice. Therefore, few treatments are "evidence-based" as we defined that term at the outset of this section on the treatment context; many pass the efficacy test, but for most their effectiveness is not known. And what evidence does exist suggests that treatments that are promising in the lab are much less satisfying in the chaotic real world of clinical care.

This presents a dilemma. If we insist that treatments be evidence-based before the system is allowed or obligated to provide them, no treatment will be forthcoming if this guideline requires demonstrations of both efficacy and effectiveness. Clearly we must lighten our requirement, allowing treatments to be applied on the basis of efficacy demonstrations even when we are not sure that they will work (be effective) when put into everyday clinical practice. After all, we cannot obtain evidence for effectiveness until we do provide (and study) efficacious treatments in the real world.

What also emerges from this review, however, is that merely "trying out" efficacious treatments in real-world clinical circumstances is not likely to result in effective treatment. Something must be done in practice to maximize fidelity to the concepts and methods that contributed to their success in controlled efficacy studies. Asking how that might be achieved brings us to our final consideration—the systemic context in which treatments are provided.

## Systems of Service Delivery

Whether efficacious treatments will work in practice depends significantly on conditions that are outside the theory and formal procedures of the treatments themselves. There are at least four perspectives to consider in this regard, all of them related to the context in which treatment services might be delivered to youths in the juvenile justice system: (a) quality control, (b) professional availability, (c) consumer issues, and (d) systemic contexts for service delivery.

QUALITY CONTROL. As we decide on the system's treatment obligations, we must recognize the need for quality control that will ensure that a treatment with known efficacy is implemented in a manner that maximizes its effectiveness in practice. Among other things, this requires adequate staff and professional training, as well as periodic monitoring to ensure that the procedure is implemented according to the manual.

In addition, the effectiveness of a treatment may depend on other procedural and administrative details that are not in the treatment manual. Determining whether a treatment with known efficacy will be effective, desirable, or even possible in juvenile justice practice typically requires a more detailed look at the actual procedures involved in its implementation. Cost-benefit and quality-control analysts, for example, are not content with defining a treatment merely by repeating its description given in the treatment manual. They typically need to examine the microlevel clinical procedures that are actually required to implement and complete the treatment with a given patient (Yates, 1996). Often these are not manualized.

For example, the obligation to provide psychopharmacological services to detention center youths with mental disorders is not as simple as asking the on-call psychiatrist to drive to the detention center, interview the youth, make a diagnosis, and prescribe an efficacious medication. The psychiatrist first is faced with the fact that many youths will present with more than one diagnosis, requiring a decision to focus on one of them or to focus instead on a particular symptom (e.g., aggression). In any of those cases, several medications may be considered for use, although the range may be restricted by the institution's formulary (availability and restrictions for specific types of medications). Sound judgment is involved in making that decision, sometimes requiring information about the family (e.g., the family's history of psychopathology). It is potentially dangerous to begin medicating without knowing whether the youth has already been taking prescribed (or illegal) drugs, the youth's reactions to past attempts at medication, and a general medical history (e.g., allergies, past medical and psychiatric diagnoses). Such information typically must be obtained from some reliable source before venturing too far.

Considerations also must be given to the length of time before one can expect to see the effects of the medication, especially when the behaviors associated with the disorder are dangerous and in need of a rapid response. Dosage should start at a level that is low enough to be safe yet potentially effective. A reliable mechanism for administering the medication across the next few days or weeks (e.g., trained and reliable front-line staff or nursing) will be necessary, and the actions of that person or those persons must be included in the procedural analysis. Once the medication procedure begins, the youth's condition must be monitored daily for the possible need to increase dosage in order to obtain the desirable effect or decrease it to reduce undesirable side effects—a process called "titration"—or to abandon the first choice and try another medication altogether. Once a desired effect has been obtained, decisions must be made about maintenance medication as well as the possibility of additional medication to reduce side effects.

This example allows us to make two points based on clinical considerations for any treatment that is contemplated when making recommendations for the care of adolescents in the juvenile justice system. First, an analysis of the actual microlevel procedures required to implement a treatment is crucial in order to know specifically what is being required when we obligate the juvenile justice system to be responsible for various treatments. Moreover, understanding procedures at this level of detail may be important for maintaining quality control. It is at this level of procedural detail that the difference between adequate efficacy and poor effectiveness may occur. Unstandardized implementation at the microlevel of clinical practice may be the source of reduced effectiveness when a treatment with known efficacy is put into practice. *Thus, to do it right, we must ensure that practitioners are not only "providing the service," but that they are abiding by the macrolevel procedures of the manual and effectively managing the microlevel clinical and administrative procedures embedded in the service.*

Second, if we do *not* require that treatment must be done right, no amount of good intentions will absolve us of the harm that results. Without the precautions described in the preceding description, prescribing medications for youths would be so dangerous as to justify the conclusion that it would be better for them to receive no treatment at all—and the same may be said for virtually all forms of psychotherapy and psychosocial interventions. Administered outside of protocol, treatments are likely to be ineffective, wasteful of precious resources, and open to abuses and perversions that can make them destructive of the welfare of youths. *Treatment without attention to clinical quality is not treatment and is likely to have worse consequences than if no intervention at all were provided.* Obligating the system to provide a treatment also obligates the system to ensure that it is competently provided.

PROFESSIONAL AVAILABILITY. Treatment requires qualified people to administer it. Depending on the type of treatment, this will mean people with a medical degree, a Ph.D. in psychology, a master's degree in psychology, or specialized training in psychiatric nursing or psychiatric social work. Having the degree, however, is not enough; most persons in those professions will not be qualified for our purposes, because only a minority of them have training in services for adolescents. Moreover, among those who are trained to work with adolescents and families, only some will be trained specifically to provide the treatments reviewed earlier.

Contrast this requirement with the fact that many areas of the United States have no psychiatrist—much less a child psychiatrist—within several hours drive of the local detention center. When we require that properly licensed social workers must provide particular psychosocial interventions, we must recognize that in many communities, clinical social workers leave detention centers for more fulfilling and financially rewarding positions the day that they obtain their licenses. Paying psychiatrists and psychologists one-quarter to one-third of their standard hourly fee for providing services to juvenile justice agencies—as is the case in some jurisdictions—tends to attract the very best (who accept the loss of income because they genuinely care about kids) and the less competent (who for various reasons cannot obtain better employment elsewhere).

As one formulates obligations for the juvenile justice system to provide treatment, one must recognize that how these obligations are fulfilled will require attention to the availability of professionals to administer them, as well as mechanisms to train them and monitor their performance.

CONSUMER ISSUES. Although youths are the "patients" in clinical relationships, parents typically are the "clients" or consumers of mental health services for children. In general child clinical practice, youths do not present themselves for treatment; they are brought by their parents or schools. Youths cannot independently consent to most treatments without their parents' consent, and in some jurisdictions the juvenile justice system may not medicate a youth without the parent's consent. In aftercare planning, the system often must depend on parents to ensure that their children continue to go to their psychotherapy appointments or maintain their medication schedules. And, as noted earlier, parents themselves often are the "patients" in some of the more efficacious psychosocial interventions. The roles of parents in youths' treatment are pervasive and important.

This is not to say that parents should always be involved in their children's treatment. Juvenile justice personnel are well aware of cases in which a parent's abusive or neglectful behaviors so endanger the child that direct parental involvement in the child's treatment is not desirable. But short of these circumstances, parental involvement should be the norm.

The juvenile justice system faces various obstacles in its enlistment of parents to facilitate treatment for youths' mental health needs. The parents of some delinquent youths are caring and concerned, but many struggle with their own personal and financial difficulties or mental illnesses. Early in the adjudicative process, a parent is often angry at their child because of his or her behavior that precipitated arrest; they might not always have their child's best interest at heart when making decisions or abiding by commitments regarding their youth's treatment. Youths sometimes are housed in pretrial detention or correction facilities that are several hours from their homes, and many parents of delinquent youths have no personal means of transportation to maintain therapeutic contact with the child or treatment staff. Obligations to provide treatment to youths in the juvenile justice system require meeting all of these challenges, because the most efficacious treatments for adolescents are predicated on some type of parental involvement.

SYSTEMIC CONTEXTS FOR SERVICE DELIVERY. Discussing treatment without considering systems of service delivery is like building a ship in the desert; it won't get far without the right medium to convey it. Efficacious treatments without a mechanism for their delivery are—like the ship without water—pretty, but useless.

During the 1990s, as evidence mounted regarding the efficacy of some treatments for adolescents' disorders, applied researchers turned their attention to the development of better models and practices for systems to deliver those mental health services to children, adolescents, and families (see, e.g., Bickman & Rog, 1995; Burns, 1999; Burns & Hoagwood, 2002; Nixon & Northrup, 1997; Stroul, 1996). "Better" generally means decreasing the use of inpatient care, increasing community-based service, improving coordination between services in the community, creating continuity of services across the child and adolescent years into young adulthood, promoting involvement of families and schools, and maximizing limited resources in a world of health care in which the true driving forces are managed care, Medicaid, and privatization of services with public funds (together with expenses associated with malpractice and civil rights litigation). Some models for service delivery, such as the "wraparound approach" (Burchard, Bruns, & Burchard, 2002), have achieved a level of articulation and acceptance that qualifies them as interventions themselves rather than simply ways to deliver services.

Most of this research has not yet focused on models of the delivery of treatment service within the juvenile justice system. It has, however, documented the nature and scope of the population of youths whose lives are spent in and out of both the state's mental health and juvenile justice systems. Youths who have juvenile justice referrals in a given year are several times more likely than their neighborhood peers to have come to the attention of the community mental health and social service agencies (Rosenblatt, Rosenblatt, & Biggs, 2000; Stiffman et al., 1997; Vander Stoep, Evans, & Taub, 1997; Westendorp et al., 1986). Moreover, among clients of child mental health services with "serious emotional disturbances"—the 10 percent who use a vastly greater proportion of child mental health services—well over one-half of males and only a somewhat lower proportion of females have juvenile justice or, in adulthood, criminal justice records (Davis & Vander Stoep, 1997).

Traditionally this overlap population of seriously delinquent and seriously mentally ill youths is labeled "not ours" by whichever system they happen to be in at a given moment. In recent years, however, some jurisdictions have witnessed collaborative efforts between juvenile justice and mental health systems to provide mental health services to those youths for whom they "share" responsibilities. At least some states have found ways to pool mental health and juvenile justice funds to create consultation and referral services for young offenders in juvenile justice custody who need mental health services (e.g., McMackin & Fulwiler, 2001). Medicaid will not pay for the treatment of those in secure juvenile justice institutions after having been found delinquent. In some jurisdictions, however, Medicaid is available for services provided to youths in pretrial detention, offering the potential for juvenile justice programs to develop arrangements with private providers who can bill Medicaid for services rendered to mentally disordered youths in detention centers.

As we think about the juvenile justice system's obligation to provide treatment to those with mental disorders, we must consider the fact that it cannot afford to become a mental health system for delinquent youths.

Certainly there are some types of treatment services that it must take the responsibility to provide. There are other treatments that it could not provide without duplicating the functions of a community's public mental health system, but which it might obtain through collaboration and coordination with mental health agencies. These systemic issues of service delivery will play a significant role in our later analysis of the juvenile justice system's implementation of its treatment obligations.

*Summary*

The various ways to describe treatments provide different dimensions for analyzing the juvenile justice system's obligations, including objectives and modes of treatment, disorder- and symptom-targeted treatment, and the value of treatment as judged by studies of efficacy and effectiveness. While research has demonstrated the efficacy (value in controlled laboratory studies) of many types of treatment—psychopharmacological, psychotherapeutic, and psychosocial—with many types of adolescent disorders, far fewer studies have demonstrated the effectiveness of those treatments in real-world clinical circumstances. The juvenile justice system may be able to go forward in the implementation of apparently efficacious modes of treatment despite a lack of evidence of their effectiveness in application. But in doing so, it must implement those treatments with fidelity, because it is likely that merely providing efficacious treatments, without attention to quality, will be no better (and perhaps worse) than providing no treatment at all. Finally, the success or failure of even the best treatments will depend on a variety of clinical, professional, and consumer issues in service delivery, as well as the development of model systems for funding and delivering mental health services.

## The Adjudicative Context: How Are Mental Disorders Related to Legally Relevant Capacities?

James, fourteen years old, has been charged with assault with a deadly weapon and attempted murder. He was running from the scene—a street corner—with three older youths. The evidence against him gives the prosecutor some chance to make the charges stick. It's not at all certain, however, because the other youths are not providing evidence about each other, there was only one shooter, and there isn't substantial evidence to identify conclusively who among them it was.

James's three friends are one year short of being adults under criminal law. The prosecutor has filed for transfer hearings on all four cases, asking the judge to allow the state to prosecute the youths in criminal court as adults. James's transfer hearing is today. He and his attorney are sitting in the holding cell when the prosecutor calls the attorney out to talk. The attorney returns to the cell to find James's mother there, sitting on a bench in the corner, sobbing uncontrollably. James, as usual, looks blank. It's the look that his mother has gotten used to seeing since about a year ago when he suddenly became depressed and moody and would sometimes hit the wall with his fist. He'll talk to you, look at you, but it's almost like he isn't there—the psychologist said he was trying to control some terrible feelings inside him by distancing himself from everything around him, more or less denying the importance of whatever is going on.

"Look, I've got to talk to both of you right now," the attorney says to James and his mother. "The prosecutor just offered us a deal. He'll call off the transfer hearing this afternoon, James, if you'll admit you were there—not that you were the shooter, just that you went there with them. And you need to tell him who held the gun and pulled the trigger. Now you've got to think carefully about this. If you get transferred—which is likely—and you are found guilty even of just being an accomplice—which is a 50-50 thing—you can get anywhere from ten to twenty-five years, at least some of it in prison. But if you take this deal, there's no transfer—you stay a juvenile, maybe two or three years in DYS custody, probably at juvenile secure over in Plymouth. After a year or two I might be able to get you out, and back home. Now I know you're going to be worried about the other guys' friends on the street—that they might try to get you. But who knows, maybe they won't even be friends anymore— or maybe you could leave your mom, go stay with your aunt in Virginia. . . . Hey, buddy, pay attention here! You listening to me? This is your life, man. What you and your Mom decide in the next couple of minutes is going to make all the difference in what kind of life you are going to have from now until you're forty years old."

James's case is fictional, but most juvenile defense attorneys can recount several stories with the same dilemma. It might be a youth's decision to waive the right to silence and confess (sometimes to things the youth didn't do) at a police interrogation, or to be of no help to the attorney in reconstructing the crime event when preparing a defense, or to decide against accepting a plea bargain that any lawyer would consider an excellent deal. Sometimes it's the attorney's feeling that the youth's "mental problems" didn't even allow him to really grasp what was going on at the time of the crime.

In all of these cases, though, the critical issue is the youth's ability to make decisions. From the time of police interrogation through the trial, law requires that the defendant must be the sole decisionmaker in matters that pertain to waiver or assertion of important constitutional rights. Parents can help their children at these times, of course, as can attorneys. But they cannot "stand in" for the youth to offer the court decisions on his or her behalf. Moreover, as in James's case, parents frequently are in no condition even to offer advice, and attorneys can only advise, not make the decision on behalf of their client. Thus youthful defendants—whom, as adolescents, society considers too young to be making decisions about smoking, drinking, driving, contracting for major financial commitments, voting, or marrying—are the only people authorized to make trial-related decisions that can seal their fate for the rest of their lives.

Are youths as capable as adults of making these decisions? The question especially raises doubts in cases like James's that involve a double jeopardy, with the effects of mental disorder potentially compounding the effects of immaturity on one's decisions as a defendant. What does knowledge of youths' mental disorders tell us, if anything, about potential deficits in their abilities to do things that are important for protection of their rights during adjudication? As a first step in addressing this question, one must (a) *identify abilities that are legally relevant,* especially for waiving rights in interrogation, participating in one's trial (competence to stand trial), and judging defendants' culpability within the framework of the insanity defense. The second step is to (b) *examine what is known about the development of those abilities in youths in general.* This will provide a developmental background against which to (c) *determine whether and how research on mental disorders of adolescence provides us any more specific guidance.*

## What Abilities Are Relevant?

The abilities associated legally and psychologically with decisionmaking about the exercise of constitutional rights have been categorized and described in considerable detail (e.g., Appelbaum & Grisso, 1988, 1995), especially in the context of waiver of *Miranda* rights (Grisso, 1981, 2003), defendants' participation in their defense (competence to stand trial, including pleading decisions: e.g., Bonnie, 1992; Grisso, 2000, 2003; Hoge et al., 1992; Melton et al., 1997), and concepts associated with criminal responsibility and the insanity defense (Melton et al., 1997). At the broadest level, most of these analyses focus on sets of abilities that have been labeled "understanding," "reasoning," and "appreciating the significance of information." To these have been added "judgment" in decisionmaking, although it stands somewhat outside the mainstream with regard to analyses of abilities associated with legal competence to make decisions.

At the most basic level are defendants' abilities to *understand* information that is critically relevant for their decision. If offered the right to consult an attorney, do defendants grasp what an attorney is and what protections an attorney is supposed to provide? When pleading guilty, do they know what the consequences might be? When they engaged in the act for which they are charged, did they know that it was illegal?

*Reasoning* refers to the process of working with information that is understood in order to reach a decision. When defendants weigh their choices in a plea bargain, for example, are they at least capable of focusing on, imagining, thinking about, and comparing the positive and negative consequences of the options they are provided?

The concept of *appreciation* arises especially in some cases involving persons with mental disorders. It recognizes that some defendants may be able to tell you the facts (they understand) and may have the ability to compare and weigh their options (they can reason), but nevertheless have a distorted view—as a consequence of their mental disorder—regarding how the facts apply to them. For example, imagine that a defendant understands that a defense attorney is supposed to try to prove the defendant's innocence, but that her paranoid delusion about her own attorney causes her to believe that he is collaborating with the prosecutor. She may understand what an attorney is for, and may be able to reason about her options. But her decision to reject everything that her attorney tells her will be based on a false belief created by her mental disorder. Thus we might have such serious doubts concerning the "validity" of her decisionmaking that we instead find her legally incompetent to decide. Similarly, her paranoid disorder might also have influenced her beliefs about the victim at the time of her offense, rendering it questionable that she should be held responsible for the crime.

Finally, recent theories have been advanced regarding "immaturity of judgment" as a factor to be considered when weighing the legal capacities of children and adolescents (e.g., Scott, 1992; Scott, Reppucci, & Woolard, 1995; Steinberg & Cauffman, 1996; Woolard, Fried, & Reppucci, 2001). Currently there are few legal references that formally recognize the concept when considering youths' capacities to make decisions as defendants, but the concept is compelling and seems implicit in the legal reasoning of some courts. Below some age, the perspective of young people on the meaning of time (future orientation), their susceptibility to influence by peers (autonomy of choice), and their perceptions of the likelihood of risky outcomes (risk perception) are still developing and are not like those of the average adult. In this sense, they are not the decisionmakers that they will be when they attain whatever level of perspective they will have during their own adult years. While these matters might be true in general for children and younger adolescents, they might be true for at least some older adolescents as well who are slower to develop than their peers.

These developing perspectives are important in decisionmaking because they influence how one perceives the consequences of one's decisions. Time perspective is a good example. How heavily would you weigh the potential consequences of a two-year period of confinement? You have a grasp of what two years feels like and what it is worth. Now consider the eight-year-old who was asked (in a competence-to-stand-trial evaluation) to explain what he meant when he said he understood that he could be "put in juvenile jail for a long, long time." He likened it to "a *really* long time, like when my Mom sends me to my room for the whole weekend." Or the explanation of a twelve-year-old who, when offered a hypothetical plea agreement in a research situation, accepted it when he learned that to do otherwise would risk a six-year sentence; as he explained it, "That's half my life!"

Neither of these is a wrong answer. The youths' understanding and reasoning abilities might be fine, and neither had a mental disorder. In fact, many adults might choose the same option as these youths. But adolescents are probably not making such choices based on the same reasons—nor are their time-related perspectives about these decisions the same—as they would be if they were asked the question after they were eighteen or twenty-five. We are not confident that the weight they will give to the factors in their options—their "judgment" involved in the decision—is "mature." We doubt that the bright fifteen-year-old girl who pleads guilty to a crime that could get her twenty years in prison is exercising the same judgment as she would if she were older, when she tells us that she is doing it so that "when my boyfriend [already sentenced for the same crime] gets out, he'll know that I loved him enough to do the same time."

## *Where Do Youths Stand on These Legally Relevant Abilities?*

Let us set aside for a moment questions about mental disorder, delinquency, and even individual differences in development among same-age youths. What do we know about youths of various ages, on average, regarding the abilities we are discussing? There are two broad kinds of scientific information to consider.

DEVELOPMENT OF COGNITIVE ABILITIES. For over 100 years, when measuring absolute levels of performance of intellectual functions associated with the global concept of "intelligence," developmental psychologists have found age curves that continue to rise through adolescence. These abilities include what youths know about the world, their reasoning abilities, and their capacities to think abstractly ("What if . . . ?" and "How are these things alike?"), all of which increase year by year until they begin to reach an "adult-like" level around age sixteen or seventeen. Experimental studies of specific abilities within this domain find somewhat different rates or patterns of development, depending on exactly which ability is being examined. But their sum supports two general conclusions. First, on average, youths tend not to have adult-like *capacities* for understanding and reasoning until sometime in early to mid adolescence. Second, achieving those capacities does not mean that adolescents can necessarily *employ* them with the efficiency or dependability that one associates with adult performance. In other words, on average, youths of fourteen years of age might have some of the tools, but they need a few more years to make them work sufficiently well to match average adult performance.

Explaining why and how adolescents' cognitive abilities require some time to mature to a level that approximates adult performance is a bit more complex than saying that they simply need experience and practice. Recent studies that point to other factors range from research on brain development to evidence of noncognitive, social-psychological aspects of development. For example, recent advances in magnetic resonance imaging of the brain have allowed neuroscientists to study changes in brain activity while youths or adults are viewing objects or performing cognitive tasks. This allows one to locate specific areas of the brain that appear to manage certain cognitive and emotional functions. Moreover, by performing these examinations repeatedly over time as youths develop, or by comparing youths and adults of different ages, neuroscientists are plotting the course of development of those brain areas and functions across childhood and adolescence.

Studies using these methods are discovering that much is taking place in normal brain development in the early to middle adolescent years. For example, the growth of myelin—sheaths on neurons that improve their conductive efficiency—continues through childhood and is not completed for certain areas of the brain until well into adolescence (Giedd et al., 1999). Whereas early childhood is characterized by rapid growth in the number of synaptic connections available in the brain, late childhood and early adolescence involves a "pruning" process (e.g., Huttenlocher, 1990) in which neural connections are gradually reduced so that transmissions become more efficient and less random. (Picture a city developing across centuries, its chaos of early footpaths gradually evolving into a more orderly and efficient set of streets and highways.)

One of the areas of the brain in which this activity is particularly apparent in early and middle adolescence is the prefrontal cortex. This area is especially important for "executive cognitive functions," a term that neuroscientists give to a set of functions that are critical for abstract reasoning, planning, and organizing information so that individuals can respond in an adaptive, goal-directed way to whatever they encounter in their environment (Foster, Eskes, & Stuss, 1994). An important related function of this area is "affect regulation"—the capacity to inhibit or delay one's impulsive and emotional reactions to incoming stimuli so that more effective responses have time to take shape through prefrontal activity (Giancola et al., 1996; Price et al., 1990). A number of studies have demonstrated that development of the prefrontal cortex and its connections with emotion centers in the brain continue well into adolescence (e.g., Casey et al., 1997; Giedd et al., 1999; Luna et al., 2001; Paus et al., 1999).

The significance of the relatively late completion of neural development related to executive cognitive functions is relevant for our discussion because these functions—for example, delaying one's response in order to consider and plan, and integrating information to foresee the consequences of one's possible choice—are all involved in adolescents' decisionmaking about the legal options with which we are concerned. They suggest that youths who are making choices with far-reaching consequences (e.g., about plea bargains, or about how to react to a threatening event on the street) may not be functioning with the same neurological capacities that they will have when they reach adulthood.

Additional evidence that adolescents' problem-solving and decisional abilities have not reached adult levels comes from other studies far removed from neuroscience. For example, on average, adolescents perceive everyday risks somewhat differently than do adults (Benthin, Slovik, & Severson, 1993; Furby & Beyth-Marom, 1990) and have a shorter future time orientation (Greene, 1986; Nurmi, 1991). Maturation of these social and psychological functions as they apply to everyday problems of life continues through adolescence (Cauffman & Steinberg, 2000), a scientific finding that almost no parent would be surprised to hear. What the neurological studies tell us is that this is not merely a matter of youthful in-experience, but rather a more complex mix of neurological and social maturation.

DEVELOPMENT OF PERFORMANCE IN LEGALLY RELEVANT CONTEXTS. A second significant body of research has examined youths' performance in tasks that involve the capacities of understanding, reasoning, and appreciation when they are faced with decisions as defendants. In general, the results are much as one would expect from the prior review of basic scientific studies of adolescents'· cognitive development (for reviews, see Grisso, 1997, 2000b). These studies have examined youths' abilities to understand and reason about *Miranda* warnings and the options to talk or remain silent (e.g., Abramovitch, Peterson-Badali, & Rohan, 1995; Grisso, 1981), as well as their abilities to grasp and process information (e.g., about the trial process, attorneys, and making plea agreements) that is considered important for competence to stand trial (e.g., Peterson-Badali & Abramovitch, 1993; Peterson-Badali, Abramovitch, & Duda, 1997).

The findings of these studies are generally consistent with those of the recent MacArthur Juvenile Adjudicative Competence Study, currently the most comprehensive investigation of youths' capacities as trial defendants (Grisso et al., 2003). The study used objective measures of how well juvenile offenders grasped trial-relevant matters, and involved over 900 youths and 450 adults, some in juvenile or criminal custody and some with little court involvement. The results indicated that those fifteen years old and younger were three times more likely than young adults to have serious deficiencies in their understanding or reasoning about trial processes and defendant decisions. The risk of incompetence to stand trial was greatest for youths younger than fourteen and for adolescents with IQ scores below 80. The effects were similar across genders and ethnic groups. On additional methods requiring hypothetical decisions about waiving rights and dealing with plea bargains, adolescents' choices and their manner of arriving at them also manifested differences from adults, tending to be less focused on essentials and more strongly influenced by concerns about compliance with authority.

## Does Mental Disorder Make a Difference?

A significant body of research has confirmed the effects of mental disorders on adult defendants' legally relevant capacities. The most common disorder found in cases of incompetent adult defendants is Schizophrenia, followed by other psychotic disorders and Mental Retardation (Nicholson & Kugler, 1991). Similarly, acquittal due to insanity among adults typically involves disorders in the psychotic spectrum, although defendants in only a minority of cases involving psychotic disorders are acquitted due to insanity (Cirincione, Steadman, & McGreevy, 1995). In contrast, there have been no studies that examine whether youths with specific mental disorders perform more poorly than other adolescents (or adults) in tasks of understanding, reasoning, or appreciation in legal contexts, and no studies of the mental condition of youths found not guilty by reason of insanity.

In a study of the capacities of delinquent youths to understand and appreciate *Miranda* rights as given by police officers, Grisso (1981) found that these abilities were significantly poorer for younger adolescents than for older adolescents and adults, as well as for youths with general deficits in intelligence (especially youths with IQ scores in the mental retardation range). But the study did not examine the relation of *Miranda* comprehension to youths' mental disorders.

A few studies have examined relations between youths' capacities associated with competence to stand trial and their mental disabilities. Cowden and McKee (1995) found that clinicians judged youths to be incompetent to stand trial significantly more frequently when they had serious psychiatric diagnoses or remedial educational histories. The types of disorders, however, were not specified. McGaha et al. (2001) reported that among youths in Florida who were found incompetent to stand trial and were remanded to programs to "restore" their competence, functional deficits related to their incompetence were due to mental retardation in about one-half of the cases, with serious emotional disturbance as the cause in most of the remaining cases.

Grisso et al. (2003) found that youths with levels of intelligence associated with mental retardation clearly performed more poorly than youths with average intelligence on abilities related to competence to stand trial. But the study did not include identification of youths' mental disorders, and no significant differences were found between those who reported more symptoms of mental or emotional distress and those who reported fewer.

In fact, virtually no published studies have examined the relation between adolescents' mental disorders and their decisionmaking abilities in *any* realm of practical, everyday life. The closest approximation, perhaps, is a study (Cauffman, 2002) in which youths with significant mental disorders obtained lower scores on measures of psychosocial maturity than did youths without diagnostic disorders, and they made less mature decisions about avoiding dangerous risk than did nondisordered same-age peers or adults.

While we do not know the specific effects of symptoms of mental disorders on youths' actual decisionmaking, we do know that they influence cognitive abilities that are important for basic understanding and reasoning functions on which decisionmaking depends. Kazdin (2000a) has reviewed cognitive deficits associated with various mental disorders of adolescence that can influence decisionmaking. For example, the symptoms of psychotic disorders often include gross disorganization of thought, sometimes involving delusions that distort reality during problem-solving. Anxiety disorders and ADHD are likely to impair attention and focus in decisionmaking situations, as well as increase the risk of impulsive decisions. Depression is associated with distortions in information processing, as well as reduced motivation to take hold of a problem sufficiently to fully consider its implications (Kazdin, 2000a).

One of the most important policy questions raised by these observations is whether the nature of disorders that create antecedent conditions relevant for due process concerns is, or should be, different for youths than for adults. As noted earlier, incompetence to stand trial in adults typically has been found in cases involving Schizophrenia. Rarely will an adult be found incompetent as a consequence of mood or anxiety disorders or the adult variant of ADHD. Yet due to developmental differences between adolescents and adults, the latter disorders may have an effect on youths' decisionmaking capacities that is no less detrimental than that of more serious psychotic disorders for adults. This is an important possibility that plays a significant role in the analysis in chapter 6 of the juvenile justice system's obligation to ensure due process for adolescent defendants with mental disorders.

In summary, there is substantial evidence that youths in general are still developing capacities that are relevant for making decisions as defendants and for our considerations regarding their responsibility for their illegal behaviors. Youths with mental disorders, therefore, may begin with a lower baseline of ability than adults, and any effects of mental disorders simply compound the risks of immature decisionmaking. Moreover, a greater range of disorders, not only serious psychotic disorders, may be relevant in juvenile than in adult cases. But the specific nature of the effects of various mental disorders on legally relevant abilities is not yet known empirically, in the absence of decisionmaking research with delinquent or nondelinquent samples of youths with mental disorders. This will necessarily limit how definitive we can be in our recommendations in chapter 6, where the focus is on identifying youths with mental disorders that could influence their decisionmaking as defendants or their criminal responsibility.

## The Public Safety Context: How Are Mental Disorders Related to Aggression?

Imagine that you are a legislator sitting in a hearing to gather information that will help you decide a matter of policy regarding youths with mental disorders and their likelihood of doing harm to others. The committee has invited two experts to testify about this matter. The first provides the following information (the expert's supporting research citations have been inserted):

> There is substantial evidence that youths with mental disorders present a greater risk to public safety than do youths without mental disorders. About seven in ten youthful offenders in the juvenile justice system have at least one mental disorder (Teplin et al., 2002), compared to only two in ten in the general population of adolescents (Kazdin, 2000a). Moreover, aggression has been associated with almost all forms of adolescent psychopathology, both clinically and empirically (Connor, 2002), but especially with ADHD—which is one of the better predictors of physical aggression (Loeber et al., 1998)—and Conduct Disorder (numerous studies). Moreover, Conduct Disorder does not go away; 87 percent of youths with this diagnosis in adolescence continue to have it three years later (Lahey et al., 1995), and 67 percent of them go on to have criminal records in adulthood (Kratzer & Hodgins, 1997). About two-thirds of youths with psychotic disorders have been found to have violent histories (Inamdar et al., 1982), and juveniles who commit murder are more likely to show psychotic symptoms than other violent (non-homicidal) youth with conduct disorders (Lewis et al., 1988; Myers et al., 1995).

As you frown and make a note to schedule your teenager for a psychological evaluation, the next expert takes the microphone:

> The evidence that youths with mental disorders are likely to commit acts of violence is weak at best. Little is known about hostile aggres-

sion and youths' depressive or anxiety disorders; one study found that depression slightly raises the risk, but no more so for physical aggression than for nonviolent and minor offenses (Huizinga & Jakob-Chien, 1998). Most youths with ADHD do not commit violent crimes; in fact, ADHD is found in juvenile justice settings no more frequently (2.3 percent: Wasserman et al., 2002) than in the general population (3–6 percent: Barkley, 1996), is related to delinquency mainly when it coexists with Conduct Disorder (Frick, 1998), and usually does not continue into adulthood (10–15 percent: Mannuzza & Klein, 1992). While Conduct Disorder applies for many youths in juvenile justice settings, it is unrelated to recidivism in some studies (Wierson & Forehand, 1995). Moreover, Conduct Disorder symptoms tend to diminish across time in 60–80 percent of cases (Cohen et al., 1993; Huizinga et al., 2000), and fewer than one-third of such youths graduate to adult Antisocial Personality Disorder (Robins, 1966). Youths who commit murder are no more likely to have mental disorders—psychotic or otherwise—than high school students in general or youths with other violent and nonviolent offenses (Benedek & Cornell, 1989; Katz & Marquette, 1996).

The experts, of course, have reported selectively from the literature to support their respective advocacy positions. But they have not reported falsely. The reason why their mutually contradictory testimony—and all of their assertions—can be true is related to the bewildering complexity of differences in what is being studied by each of the authorities that they cite. The differences between studies that create the most chaos in cross-study comparisons are the following:

- *Definitions of the target behavior,* which include, for example, "aggressive behavior," "delinquent behavior," "physically harmful behavior," "serious violent and serious nonviolent behavior," "persistently delinquent behavior," and "arrest for physically harmful behavior." Moreover, each of these terms may be operationalized differently across studies.
- *Definitions of significance of results,* which include tests of differences between mean scores, tests of differences between proportions (percents), bivariate correlations, regression analyses, odds ratios, effect sizes, and receiver operating characteristic analyses (to name a few). All of these statistics are important for certain purposes, but they are instructive for *different* purposes. A given data set can produce a substantially signifi-

cant relation of a disorder to aggressive behaviors with an analysis of variance, but at the same time might show only a modest correlation, a large odds ratio, and inadequate predictive power according to an "area under the curve" analysis.

- *Different population sampling fields,* which include random community samples, public school samples, community mental health clinic samples, inpatient clinical samples, inpatient forensic clinical samples, juvenile justice system samples, juvenile pretrial detention samples, and juvenile corrections samples. For example, any relation between physical violence and depression will be relatively low in a sample of youths drawn from the general population, relatively higher in a juvenile detention sample, and possibly higher still if drawn from an inpatient psychiatric facility (where civil commitment often requires a finding that youths are mentally ill and dangerous).
- *Differences in reference groups,* for example, when discussing the relation between delinquency and ADHD, stating the proportion of delinquent youths who have ADHD will suggest a smaller relation between the two than stating the proportion of ADHD youths who are delinquent.
- *Differences in the time frame,* for example, studies differ in whether they examine the relation of mental disorder to lifetime aggressive tendencies, to aggressive tendencies recently, to a recent aggressive act (e.g., the reason for present arrest), or aggression prospectively—which may be within the next few months, a year, subsequently at any time during the adolescent years, or into adulthood.

It is helpful to begin the review of mental disorders and aggression in this way, because it shows that efforts to force a general conclusion about their relation based on current research will probably produce an oversimplified and distorted message. While looking at this research, one should also keep in mind that the objective is to assist juvenile justice decisionmakers at three points in the juvenile justice process: (a) *the pretrial detention decision* (likelihood of harm to others if not detained), (b) *the disposition decision* (degree of security and nature of treatment that is necessary to protect the public from harm during the youth's rehabilitation), and (c) *the waiver of jurisdiction and extension of jurisdiction decisions* (likelihood of continued harm to others in the future when the youth ages into adulthood).

These decisions are all about future aggression, but they place different demands on decisionmakers. For example, detention decisions are made about a much more varied set of youths than are disposition or waiver decisions, because various types of youths (first-time offenders, minor offenders, very young offenders) are less likely to reach the latter decision points. The three decisions also focus on somewhat different time frames for anticipated aggression, ranging from immediate (within the next few weeks if not detained) to very long range (several years from now in adulthood). In all cases, though, we are interested in whatever research can tell us about *the risk of (a) physical harm to others (b) in the future (c) among youths with mental disorders (d) identified at time of contact with the juvenile justice system.*

In the three subsections that follow, I briefly review some relevant and important "principles" in the development of aggressive behavior in childhood and adolescence, as well as what is known clinically about the relation of aggression to specific psychiatric diagnoses of adolescents. I then reflect on the value of these perspectives for identifying and responding to youths' potential aggressive behaviors related to their mental disorders.

## Aggression from a Developmental Perspective

Aggression is normal as an evolutionary, biologically based response to one's environment. The capacity for hostile and harmful behavior ordinarily is shaped and channeled by society as the person develops, so that it fits society's needs (e.g., for soldiers and police officers) and is exercised in socially appropriate ways (e.g., self-defense, sports). The shaping process involves complex social responses that are intended to teach self-restraint and inhibition. This process is more or less successful partly as a function of variations in psychosocial (e.g., family) and environmental (e.g., neighborhood) factors, and partly as a result of biological and psychological differences among youths. There is substantial evidence, for example, that hormonal, neurological, and psychophysiological differences among children make self-restraint and inhibition more difficult and more resistant to social influences for some youths than for others (e.g., Raine, 1996). Moreover, a child's history of stressful or traumatic experiences can itself influence the development of neurotransmitter systems in the brain or the development of neuroanatomical areas of the brain involved in inhibition or disinhibition of aggression (for a review, see Ferris & Grisso, 1996).

If we think of childhood and adolescence as a journey, there are predictable changes in the terrain on which the path to self-restraint is traveled.

Typically these different terrains are viewed as three broad phases of the journey: infancy, the elementary school years, and the adolescent years. The developing infant is gradually taught not to express internal impulses spontaneously in socially annoying or harmful ways. New demands for self-restraint arise in the preschool and elementary years in the context of developing relations with other children, and again in early adolescence in relation to new capacities brought about by biological changes, increasing opportunity for independent (unsupervised) activities, and peer group demands.

The initiation of each of these phases and its new demands seems to be characterized by a "surge" of aggressive behavior—not for each youth, but as an average for youths at a given phase—that then declines somewhat (on average) across that phase. For example, Tremblay (2002) documented that mothers report a surge of aggressive activity (frustration and rage reactions) in their infants when they are about two to three months of age, with an overall decline during the next few years. Similarly, an increase and decline in seriously harmful behaviors toward others has been well documented during adolescence (e.g., Elliott, 1994).

Beyond that, the nature of the general terrain is not the issue so much as the search for the various pathways taken by youths as they traverse it. Some youths display no aggressive tendencies early in a given phase of the journey. Others do so for a period of time before apparently adjusting successfully (some rapidly, others gradually) to new self-restraint demands of that phase. And, of course, a proportion continue aggressive behaviors throughout that phase (in infancy and toddler years, about 10 percent: Tremblay, 2002; in elementary school years, about 8 percent: Haapasalo & Tremblay, 1994; and in the adolescent years, 10–20 percent: e.g., Elliott, 1994). There is a tendency for youths who have manifested greater hostile aggression throughout one phase of the journey to continue to do so during the subsequent phase as they enter new terrain. But researchers have also found subgroups whose prior-phase behavior does not predict their behavior in the next phase, especially youths who were seen as nonaggressive earlier but for whom aggressive behavior arises "unexpectedly" as they move on.

The search for order in these pathways has encountered increasingly complex patterns during the past fifteen years of criminological and developmental investigation (Loeber & Hay, 1994; Loeber & Stouthamer-Loeber, 1998; Moffitt, 1993; Moffit et al., 1996; Tolan & Gorman-Smith, 1998). But a few general principles have evolved to guide our thinking about aggression and serious harmful behavior in adolescence.

First is the principle of *desistance*. Most youths who engage in or are arrested for physically harmful behaviors do not continue to present a significant risk for those behaviors as they age into late adolescence and early adulthood (e.g., Elliott, 1994; Huizinga, 1995; Loeber & Hay, 1996). For most youths who engage in physical harm to others at some time in adolescence, their behavior is "adolescent-limited" (Moffitt, 1993). Ironically, this does not mean that total arrests for serious violent behaviors are lower for young adults than for adolescents; violent arrest rates per age group peak at about ages eighteen to twenty-three and then decline (Zimring, 1998). This peak appears to be a surge of increasingly serious and repetitive violence among a minority of delinquent youths who do persist in violent behavior past adolescence (Loeber & Stouthamer-Loeber, 1998).

The second principle pertains to *age of onset*. In general, if physically aggressive behavior is apparent in the preschool and early elementary school years and persists well into adolescence, there is an increased likelihood that it will persist into adulthood as well (called "life-course-persistent" aggressors by Moffitt, 1993). This is not always true (Magnusson, Stattin, & Duner, 1983), of course, but the odds are much greater that early-onset aggressors will graduate to adult violent offending.

The third principle is that *the first and second principles do not necessarily hold for women and ethnic minorities*. Several studies and reviews (e.g., Loeber & Stouthamer-Loeber, 1998; Moffitt et al., 2001; Silverthorn & Frick, 1999; Zoccolillo, 1993) find that a "delayed-onset" pathway, in which hostile aggression first becomes evident in adolescence, is more typical than early childhood onset for girls whose aggression in adolescence continues into adulthood. Regarding ethnic minority youths, the applicability of the early-onset pathway to African American and Latino youths, especially those in high-risk inner-city environments, is still being sorted out. Tolan and Gorman-Smith (1998), for example, found the expected relation between early onset of aggression and violent delinquency in adolescence when examining a group of youths who represented ethnic proportions for U.S. adolescents, but not among a sample of African American and Latino youths from poor, high-crime neighborhoods in Chicago. As with many "race" differences in criminological studies, these findings may be related to socioeconomic rather than specific ethnic differences, reflecting special risk factors associated with growing up in harmful surroundings (Hawkins, Laub, & Lauritsen, 1998). Nevertheless, the results do suggest that caution be used in applying the general developmental principles of aggression to low-socioeconomic minority youths.

## Aggression from a Clinical Perspective

When we consider the relation of mental disorder to violent behavior among delinquent youths, we must combine what we know about the development of aggression in general with what we know about the relation of mental disorders in adolescence to anger, impulsivity, and other mental states that promote aggression. There is a good deal of evidence for such connections.

AFFECTIVE DISORDERS. So pervasive is irritability and hostility among youths with Major Depression and Dysthymia that DSM-IV criteria allow "irritable mood" to be substituted for "depressed mood" in identifying depressive disorders among children and adolescents (e.g., pp. 327 and 349, American Psychiatric Association, 1994). The relation between adolescent depressive disorders and anger, irritability, and hostility is thoroughly documented (Biederman & Spencer, 1999; Goodyer & Cooper, 1993; Knox et al., 2000). The significance of anger as a motivator for aggression is well known (Novaco, 1994). The role of depression-related irritability as a forerunner of aggression lies in its implications in social contexts. Youths who clearly manifest a sullen, angry, and belligerent attitude are more likely to get angry responses from other youths (and adults), thus increasing the risk of events that escalate to physical aggression. And an irritable adolescent is more likely to interpret ordinary annoyances by others as direct threats, increasing the risk that the youth will respond with defensive aggression.

ANXIETY DISORDERS. Clinicians (and some clinical researchers: Connor, 2002; Walker et al., 1991) find that most adolescents with anxiety disorders are shy, withdrawn, and tend to avoid fearful situations, resulting in less aggressive behavior than is normal for youths of their age. The exception is Posttraumatic Stress Disorder (PTSD), which involves (a) exposure to a traumatizing event, (b) persistent reexperiencing of distress about the event through recollections or dreams, (c) avoidance or numbing regarding the related emotions, and (d) being "on edge" as manifested in startle responses, outbursts of anger, or hypersensitivity to possible harm (American Psychiatric Association, 1994). The relation between PTSD and youths' aggressive reactions has been well documented (for a review, see Connor, 2002). It appears to be related to the conditioning of neurobiological fear responses that underlie our natural tendencies to react aggressively and self-protectively when events occur that remind us of the original trauma (Charney et al., 1993; Fletcher, 1996). Most youths with PTSD do not engage in serious harmful acts, but their risk for such behaviors is increased. For example, in juvenile justice samples, both boys (Steiner, Garcia, & Matthews, 1997) and girls (Cauffman et al., 1998) with Conduct Disorder and PTSD have been found to be more impulsive and aggressive than youths with Conduct Disorder alone.

PSYCHOTIC DISORDERS. Serious psychotic disorders like Schizophrenia are rare prior to early adulthood. The presence of delusional beliefs among persons with Schizophrenia, often including paranoid notions about harm from others, might suggest an increased risk of aggression. Yet research on adults indicates that they present less risk of violence than persons with other serious mental illnesses (indeed, no greater risk than persons with no mental disorders: Monahan et al., 2001), and the evidence for increased risk among youths with Schizophrenia is weak (Connor, 2002).

DISRUPTIVE BEHAVIOR DISORDERS. Attention-Deficit/Hyperactivity Disorder (ADHD), Oppositional Defiant Disorder (ODD), and Conduct Disorder (CD) form a cluster of disorders the DSM-IV calls "Attention-Deficit and Disruptive Behavior Disorders." They are clustered for good reasons:

- ODD tends to precede CD, with about 80–90 percent of CD youths having been diagnosed ODD at an earlier age; but ODD does not predict CD well, because only about 25 percent of ODD youths are later diagnosed CD.
- About one-half of youths diagnosed with ADHD will eventually be diagnosed CD, and more than two-thirds of CD youths also carry a diagnosis of ADHD.

(For reviews, see Barkley, 1996; Biederman, Newcorn, & Sprich, 1991; Connor, 2002; Frick, 1998; Loeber et al., 1998). Extrapolating from these statistics, if one were to randomly choose from the files of a clinical treatment facility a group of 100 youths with ADHD and/or CD diagnoses, one could expect roughly forty of them to be ADHD only, about twenty CD only, and about forty diagnosed as having both disorders.

Substantially higher rates of physically aggressive behavior are found for youths with ODD, CD, or ADHD disorders than for youths in general or with other mental disorders (Connor, 2002). This is not surprising, of course, since impulsive and/or aggressive behaviors form a substantial part of the criteria for obtaining these diagnoses in the first place. But it is significant because these disorders, especially CD, identify youths who are at greater risk for *continued* illegal and aggressive behaviors in adulthood. For example, about two-thirds of adolescents with CD diagnoses have criminal records as adults (Kratzer & Hodgins, 1997), although only some of these will be arrested in adulthood on offenses involving physical harm to others. While only about 30 percent of youths with CD diagnoses develop Antisocial Personality Disorder in adulthood (among which are our most serious adult offenders) (Robins, 1966), this is a far greater proportion than for youths with other non-comorbid affective, anxiety, or psychotic disorders.

Recently special attention has focused on the long-range consequences among youths who meet criteria for *both* ADHD and CD (especially if they manifested ODD earlier in childhood). Studies have suggested that these youths have a substantially greater rate of delinquency in adolescence, of harmful behavior to others as their adolescence proceeds, and of continued harmful aggression and offending as they enter adulthood (e.g., Barkley, 1996; Biederman et al., 2001; Frick, 1998; Fischer et al., 1993; Loeber, 1990; Mannuzza et al., 1993). This does *not* mean that most or even the majority of youths who are comorbid for these disorders are eventually arrested for violent crimes in adulthood. Moreover, some evidence suggests that other characteristics, especially a callous and unemotional personality style together with substance use, may be better indicators than ADHD when attempting to identify which CD adolescents will continue their aggression into adulthood (Loeber, Burke, & Lahey, 2002).

Youths with CD have also been in the spotlight as a result of a significant movement among clinical delinquency researchers to find the "fledgling psychopath." Psychopathy is a personality type (not currently part of DSM-IV) that, in adults, has been related to repeated, long-term criminal behavior (Hart & Hare, 1997). Measures of psychopathy in adulthood are more powerfully related to future illegal aggression than any other single characteristic investigated by violence-prediction researchers (Quinsey et al., 1998; Monahan et al., 2001). The psychopathic personality is high on antisocial characteristics (e.g., impulsiveness and irresponsibility) found in Antisocial Personality Disorder (APD), but differs from APD in combining these with several characteristics suggesting a selfish, callous, and remorseless life-style. These characteristics are durable (relatively resistant to change) and quite likely to have been developing during childhood and adolescence. So it is not surprising that intense interest has developed in recent years in determining whether psychopathy (or some early form of it) can be identified among youths (e.g., Brandt et al., 1997; Christian et al., 1997; Frick et al., 1994; Lynam, 1998; Rogers et al., 1997). The search has narrowed to the group of youths with hyperactive and early-onset disruptive symptoms, assisted by special tools intended to assess child/adolescent variants of adult characteristics of psychopathy (Forth, Kosson, & Hare, 1997; Frick et al., 1994; Lynam, 1997).

While evidence is mounting that disruptive disorders comorbid with other disorders (e.g., ADHD, depression, or substance use) raise the risk of future violence, currently the research does not allow one to call this group psychopathic or even pre-psychopathic (Edens, Skeem, Cruise & Cauffman, 2001; Hart, Watt, & Vincent, 2002; Salekin, Rogers, & Machin, 2001; Seagrave & Grisso, 2002). As yet there is no evidence that youths with high scores on the junior psychopathy scales during adolescence actually manifest psychopathy in adulthood. Moreover, the mere fact that adolescents manifest characteristics associated with the construct of psychopathy—for example, grandiose, manipulative, irresponsible, impulsive—does not mean that they are psychopathic. Notice that one or more of these characteristics is very likely to be named when one asks almost any parent "Please describe the teenager in your family." As explained in chapter 2, a great many youths manifest these tendencies as transient features of normal developmental tasks (Edens et al., 2001; Seagrave & Grisso, 2002). Thus it is impossible at present to say whether hyperactive/disruptive youths manifesting psychopathic-like characteristics are tomorrow's adults with psychopathy and violent behavior.

SUBSTANCE USE DISORDERS. A significant body of research tells us what is perhaps obvious: there is a strong relation among adolescents' substance use and aggression, seriousness of delinquent behavior (for reviews: Brady, Myrick, & McElroy, 1998; Huizinga & Jakob-Chien, 1998; Loeber & Dishion, 1983), and continuity of aggression among CD youths as they transition to adulthood (Loeber, Burke, & Lahey, 2002). For example, in one general community sample of adolescents, prevalence of problem alcohol use was 15 percent for nondelinquent youths, 38 percent for minor delinquent youths, and over 50 percent for youths with serious violent and nonviolent offenses (Loeber et al., 1991).

Note, however, that while these statistics show that the risk of serious offending is far greater among youths who have problems of alcohol use, about one-half of serious offenders do not. Moreover, the difference in substance use between youths who engage in serious violent versus serious nonviolent behavior is not substantially different, and the rates themselves differ considerably across studies from various sites (Huizinga & Jakob-Chien, 1998). Finally, the relation of Substance Use Disorders to delinquent behaviors appears to vary depending on their presence with comorbid conditions. For example, the seriousness of delinquent behavior is related more strongly to Substance Use Disorder among youths with Conduct Disorders alone than among those with "internalizing" disorders alone (e.g., depressive disorders) (Randall et al., 1999). This is an area, however, in which there are substantial differences among ethnic groups. Prevalence studies (e.g., Teplin et al., 2002) consistently report lower rates of disorders related to substance use among delinquent African American youths than among delinquent non-Hispanic white youths.

## Using the Data in the Public Safety Context

Developmental criminology and developmental psychopathology have made significant progress toward understanding the relations between adolescent mental disorder and aggressive offenses. What guidance can they give us to address policy (see chapter 7) regarding youths' mental disorders and public safety? At least one lesson is that modesty and caution are necessary when translating the results for policy considerations. The following review of some of the pertinent caveats that are required does not criticize the existing scientific research on mental disorders and aggression; indeed, most of it is useful. But we must recognize inherent limits for interpreting and applying their results in order to avoid turning good science into bad practice.

MENTAL DISORDER, DELINQUENCY, AND AGGRESSION. Clearly there is some relation between mental disorder and aggression. But this will not necessarily help juvenile justice personnel to separate delinquent youths into those who are more or less likely to be harmful to others. A good illustration of the reason for this caution is found in Huizinga and Jakob-Chien's (1998) description of a general community sample of youths who self-reported (a) violent, (b) serious nonviolent, or (c) minor illegal behaviors, and youths who reported (d) none of the above behaviors in the past year. When there were differences among these four groups on a measure of mental health problems (e.g., depression, hyperactivity) in the Child Behavior Checklist the differences most often were found between youths who report *none* of these behaviors and the other three groups. Most of the scales showed no significant differences in mental health problems between youths at the various levels of offense—for example, between serious violent offenders (serious physical harm) and serious nonviolent offenders (delinquent but not physically harmful to others).

This is important because all of the youths in the juvenile justice system are in those three groups that show few differences among them in mental disorders. Even if mental disorder is greater among seriously aggressive delinquent youths than among nondelinquent youths, identifying mental disorder *among* a group of delinquent youths might not take us very far in identifying which of them will be more aggressive in the future.

FIGURE AND GROUND REVERSAL. Relations between youths' mental disorders and physically harmful behavior can be expressed two ways: the proportion of violent youths who are mentally disordered, and the proportion of mentally disordered youths who are violent. The proportions are substantially different depending on the reference group. For example, Huizinga et al. (2000) offered a helpful set of analyses pertaining to persistent serious delinquent youths and youths with persistent mental health problems (not including those with drug use problems alone) "Persistent" meant continued evidence for at least two years. *Among all persistent delinquents,* about 13–20 percent (different rates in different cities) had persistent mental health problems. But *among all youths with persistent mental health problems,* about 30–45 percent were persistently delinquent. This is not a problem of science, but it can be a source of confusion when one is *translating* science for policy implications. The relationship between mental disorders and violent behavior "looks" quite different when the figures from either source are quoted simply as a "violence and mental disorder overlap" without specifying the reference group from which the figures are obtained.

COMMUNITY/CLINICAL DATA AND JUVENILE JUSTICE DATA. Our knowledge of the relation of mental disorders to youths' harmful aggression is based substantially on the study of youths selected from the general community or encountered in clinical (psychiatric) settings. Far fewer studies have begun with a group of youths, all of whom were referred to the juvenile justice system where their mental disorders or mental health problems were identified, who were then followed for comparison regarding their future aggression. This is important for at least two reasons.

First, as noted in chapter 3, some error in identification of mental disorders is associated with the context in which assessment is performed. Adolescents assessed at the time of referral to juvenile justice are in circumstances that can increase (for some) or decrease (for others) the appearance of particular symptoms, and measurement at one point may identify some youths whose mental health problems are transitory rather than persistent (Huizinga et al., 2000). As a consequence, we must be careful about how much we say about the relation of mental disorders and aggression for youths encountered in juvenile justice settings, based on data that were collected in very different community or clinical settings.

Second, the aggression outcome measures used in community and clinical studies often do not represent the outcomes with which we are concerned in juvenile justice contexts associated with public safety. No studies, for example, have examined specifically what courts want clinicians to consider for the pretrial detention question—namely, the degree to which mental disorder is related to harmful aggression *during the next few weeks or months* before adjudication. On the other hand, several studies have examined outcomes representing what the courts want to know in longer-term dispositional questions—namely, the degree to which youths with mental disorders are more or less likely to continue to engage in aggressive behaviors during and beyond their adolescent years.

STATISTICAL RELATIONS AND CLINICAL PREDICTIONS. The fact that a relation between two things has been demonstrated—even a strong relation—does not necessarily mean that the relation has practical importance. For example, many researchers state that "mental disorder predicts aggression" when describing these relations. When they say this, they simply mean that mental disorder offers something of value in our attempt to understand or account for aggression. They usually do *not* mean that they would be willing to bet large sums of money on the application of this knowledge in specific clinical cases.

For example, if we were told that 20 percent of youths with a particular disorder engage in future violence, compared to 5 percent of youths without it, we would certainly say that this disorder should be considered when we are trying to grasp the relevance of mental disorder for aggression. After all, the odds for future violence in the group with this disorder are four times greater than in the group without it. Yet if we used these figures in a clinical or legal context to predict that all youths with that disorder would be violent, we would be wrong 80 percent of the time, because only 20 percent of youths with that disorder eventually engage in violent behavior.

The day may come when collecting a combination of personality and historical facts about youths will provide decisionmakers with probability statements about future violence in individual juvenile cases. That day has, in fact, arrived for adults. Clinicians can now collect specific pieces of information about a mentally disordered felon (Quinsey et al., 1998,) or a civilly committed adult with a mental disorder (Monahan et al., 2001) and, with proper algorithms, identify within acceptable limits the percentage probability of risk that the individual will commit a violent act upon release from prison or hospital. But this technology is some way off for adolescents.

When it arrives, it is questionable whether mental disorders as such will even be included among the factors in these predictive equations, even though we trust the research that says there is a "relation" between some mental disorders and violent behavior. DSM-IV diagnoses typically play little or no role in the adult prediction schemes cited above, because the researchers who developed the tools found that they contributed too little to the predictive power of the instruments after other factors were taken into account. Some "risk assessment" tools are now in development for use with adolescents, including the Structured Assessment of Violence Risk in Youth (SAVRY: Borum, Bartel, & Forth, 2002) and the Early Assessment Risk List for Boys (EARL-20B: Augimeri et al., 2001). The developers reviewed the best information available in the field before selecting "risk factors" that would maximize the likelihood of validity (which is still under study). Thus it is interesting that both instruments make very limited use of mental disorders to guide clinical judgments about risks of future violence among youths. Both tools include hyperactivity and attention deficit disorder, and one urges consideration of Conduct Disorder when rating a factor called "antisocial attitudes." Beyond this, experts who develop such tools appear to have concluded that *traits or affective states* associated with some mental disorders—for example, impulsivity, anger, psychopathic characteristics, or substance use difficulties—offer better potential for prediction than specific diagnoses of mental disorders themselves.

In summary, we reach the frustrating conclusion that (a) there is a substantial relation between adolescents' mental disorders and their future aggression, and (b) there are serious limitations in the degree to which this relation can be used to advance the juvenile justice system's obligations regarding public safety. Chapter 7 explores how the relation between mental disorders and the risk of harm to others can be used with less equivocation in forming general *policy* regarding public protection, while the state of our current knowledge will limit more seriously our ability to apply it to *predict* future aggression in individual cases.

*Part II*

# Discovering the Obligations

*Chapter 5*

# Refining the Custodial Obligation to Provide Treatment

Using reliable methods, researchers have established that considerably more than one-half of the youths processed through the juvenile justice system meet criteria for various DSM-IV mental disorders (chapter 1). The juvenile justice system should attend to their needs clinically as a matter of custodial obligation. But what is the nature of that obligation? How can it be translated into objectives that are potentially beneficial to youths, families, and society?

Previous chapters provide a number of insights that can help us refine the mandate to provide treatment to youths with mental disorders, and those are summarized in the first section of this chapter. Then, in the three sections that follow—on crisis-related treatment, stabilization treatment, and maintenance treatment—I sketch the juvenile justice system's obligations with regard to these three treatment contexts. The final two sections examine systemic implications, as well as unanswered research and policy questions, for implementing the mandate.

## Charting a Treatment Mandate

It is rare that any social agency can do everything that it might wish to do, largely because financial resources, time, and energy are not limitless. Formulating the treatment mandate begins by considering a number of ways in which the scope of the mandate might be limited in order to better ensure its feasibility. The first four chapters reached conclusions that we now can use to limit the juvenile justice system's obligation in a rational manner:

- Diagnosis does not define the obligation.
- Not all treatment is worthwhile.
- Clinical care is sometimes harmful.
- Justice systems are not ideal settings for clinical care.

## Diagnosis Does Not Define the Obligation

Assuming that youths' mental disorders can be identified with an acceptable degree of reliability, we learned in chapter 2 that this still does not tell us whom the system should treat. Not all mental disorders require clinical care. The earlier reviews focused on disorders that are more likely to require treatment, but there are hundreds of other disorders in the DSM-IV system. Many of them are minor in their effects on youths' functioning, such that clinical care would not be prescribed even in the context of community mental health programming. Moreover, even for youths with the more troubling mental disorders, not all have equal needs for clinical care or equal urgency regarding its implementation. Cases within any category of mental disorder vary with regard to severity and degree of actual functional impairment (chapter 2). Some cases present a degree of impairment for which clinical care may not be necessary, or that allows one to delay treatment without serious suffering or social consequence.

## Not All Treatment Is Worthwhile

As concluded in chapter 4, whatever treatment is required must have a clear purpose and a reasonable promise. For many mental disorders, treatment may be of benefit with regard to some objectives but not others. For example, for some disorders, there may be ways to reduce acute symptoms that constitute conditions of emergency, but little evidence that clinical intervention will produce remission, improve everyday functioning, or avoid reemergence of the disorder. *Some treatments actually have no known efficacy* (no proven value in controlled research studies), and often it is unclear that those with efficacy can be implemented effectively in ordinary clinical or juvenile justice services. Sometimes this might argue for the necessity to increase the system's capacity to implement efficacious and necessary treatment. But at other times this would be fruitless, as when the relevant conditions for treatment simply cannot be met (e.g., implementing a treatment that requires a long time to show progress in cases in which the system will loose jurisdiction of the youth in the near future).

Providing treatment that does not have a clear purpose and a reasonable promise of benefit is wasteful. All clinical interventions have a financial cost, and the cost of some interventions is considerable, including professional time and infrastructure (e.g., hospital beds, transportation, program staff for special mental health treatment units in juvenile justice facilities). Funds spent on treatments of little value are better spent on meeting other basic health and rehabilitative needs of youths.

I do not provide in this chapter a cost-benefit analysis to determine whether the expenses required to obtain benefits through treatment are greater than the financial costs to society of failing to provide treatment. The point here is more basic. *Providing treatment of mental disorders for juvenile justice youths can only be worthwhile if provided with integrity, and integrity (quality) will have a considerable financial cost.* Our review has shown that clinical treatment of youths, like many good things in life, is of little value unless it is applied selectively and with attention to quality as outlined in efficacy research and standardized practice. Integrity and quality of services cannot be obtained without incurring expenses sufficient to implement a treatment as it was intended when first developed and studied for its efficacy.

## Clinical Care Is Sometimes Harmful

Financial cost is not the only reason that clinical care should be limited to treatment that has a clear purpose and sufficient quality to provide a promise of real benefit. *Every treatment intervention runs the risk of harming youths or society.* Those risks are acceptable only to the extent that they are justified by the purpose and probable benefit of the treatment.

Some risks are obvious. Psychopharmacological interventions involve risks of unpleasant and sometimes dangerous side effects, and medical care provided incompetently or under thoughtless conditions increases the probability of those risks. Some treatments can be antitherapeutic; for example, some group therapies are potentially effective but, if not properly implemented, run the risk of negative peer influences that promote delinquency.

Other negative risks are not so obvious. Cases for which treatment has no effect are not merely failed cases; the record or experience of "no effect" can have important negative consequences. A judge, reviewing the record of a youth who was "in treatment" but has again been arrested, notes that the youth "failed to respond to treatment." It is common for courts to presume that this "failure to respond" reflects the youth's lack of amenability to rehabilitation, without examining whether there is any reason to question the efficacy of the treatment itself. Youths and parents themselves may draw similar conclusions. When an initial treatment effort is unsuccessful because it had no known value, was ill chosen for the case, or was poorly executed, the willingness of youths and their parents to engage in future clinical interventions might be seriously curtailed by their conclusions that "therapy is just a waste of time."

Finally, a potential side effect of clinical interventions is the abuse of state's powers. Assessment and treatment in juvenile and criminal justice settings always require attention to risks associated with loss of privacy, autonomy, and due process protections for youths as defendants in legal proceedings and state custody. The content of screening instruments, psychological tests, and diagnostic interviews typically involve the report of behaviors, thoughts, feelings, and inferred personality characteristics that are "legally sensitive." These data can increase the state's ability to adjudicate youths when used at the pretrial stage of legal proceedings, and to seriously restrict their liberty after adjudication. A variety of protections—discussed later in this chapter—can allow beneficial assessment and treatment to go forward while minimizing these risks, but the risks cannot be eliminated. Once again, the point is that assessment and treatment should not be implemented simply because they sound helpful. *Providing any screening, assessment, or clinical treatment that does not have a clear necessity, purpose, and potential benefit incurs risks of harm without adequate justification.*

## Justice Systems Are Not Ideal Settings for Clinical Care

How the mandate for treatment is constructed must be limited also by certain systemic realities. As others have long observed (e.g., Melton, 1989; Mulvey, 1989), the juvenile justice system is not and cannot be a mental health system, and its mandates sometimes are at cross-purposes.

First, some evidence suggests that treatment performed in milieus involving primarily youths at high risk of aggressive behaviors may actually be antitherapeutic. Especially in group therapies involving antisocial youths, negative peer influences on group members sometimes overcome the potential positive benefits, especially for those with relatively less risk in the first place (e.g., Dishion, McCord, & Poulin, 1999). This produces a disadvantage, in terms of treatment outcome, for treatment programs within parts of the juvenile justice system that collect the more aggressive youths who come before the courts.

Second, treatment within the juvenile justice system must recognize certain limits imposed by the legal relation between the state and persons accused of delinquencies. *The state does not have unlimited authority to intervene clinically in youths' lives, especially at certain stages of juvenile justice processing.* For example, the system typically cannot require youths in pretrial detention centers to participate in a variety of therapeutic or rehabilitative activities. Their immediate needs, especially in crisis, must be met during that process. But they are being held for trial, and there is much that the juvenile justice system cannot require by way of a youth's participation in clinical treatment until its authority to do so is established by a trial that finds that the youth has indeed committed an offense allowing the state to take custody.

Finally, from a practical perspective, some clinical interventions are difficult or impossible to implement at certain stages of juvenile justice processing. Group therapies for youths in pretrial detention, for example, would be largely a waste of time, given that most of them do not remain in detention centers for more than a week or two. Therapies designed to encourage discussions of intimate thoughts and feelings related to psychopathology would make little sense at a pre-adjudicative stage, when the adversarial and accusatory nature of the state's relation to the youth are antithetical to the trusting, nonjudgmental therapeutic relationship that such therapies require.

Fortunately, the mandate to provide clinical care to youths with mental disorders need not mean that the juvenile justice system must administer that care. The system can provide treatment in two broad ways. It can administer treatment (or contract with private providers to do it), or it can obtain treatment from other government agencies (such as public mental health services). Its moral or legal obligation is the same in either case, as long as it fulfills its responsibility to ensure that the mental health needs of eligible youths are met.

These conclusions gleaned from earlier chapters will help to refine and qualify the juvenile justice system's custodial treatment obligation. The discussion in the following three sections structure that obligation with regard to the three general objectives of custodial treatment described in chapter 4: *crisis-related treatment, stabilization treatment,* and *maintenance treatment.* In the course of our discussion, it is convenient from time to time to refer to stages of juvenile justice processing when identifying the system's obligations. The terms used for those stages are "intake" (probation intake, pretrial detention intake), "adjudicative processing" (for cases that proceed beyond intake and are awaiting trial on delinquency charges), and "postadjudicative rehabilitation" (after adjudication and under custody of the youth authority, rehabilitation in the community or in juvenile secure corrections facilities).

## Crisis-Related Treatment

Intervention should be available at all points in the juvenile justice system (intake, adjudicative processing, and postadjudicative rehabilitation) for mental health problems that present an *imminent threat of serious physical or psychological harm to youths*. There are two key terms in this definition. "Imminence" refers to the urgency to provide an immediate response in the face of deteriorating mental conditions that may lead quickly to outcomes of a type that will constitute serious damage and sometimes death. "Threat" refers to the obligation not merely to respond when the "physical or psychological harm" occurs, but to anticipate the emergency in order to prevent its potential outcome. Thus the obligation includes the *detection* of a threatened harm, a response to *prevent* it, and the ability to *respond to the consequences* in cases in which detection and prevention efforts have failed.

To examine the obligation to intervene and provide crisis treatment, we must (a) specify a set of *crisis conditions* that trigger this obligation, (b) specify the *interventions* needed to respond to them, (c) determine ways to *identify* youths who need those interventions on a case-by-case basis, and (d) *divert* some youths from the juvenile justice system when their continued mental health care is justified.

### Crisis Conditions

Several organizations concerned about standards for mental health services during juvenile justice custody have offered definitions of crisis conditions requiring intervention services (e.g., American Correctional Association, 1991; Council of State Governments, 2002; Office of Juvenile Justice and Delinquency Prevention, 1994; American Association for Correctional Psychology, 2000; National Commission on Correctional Health Care, 1999). Their recommendations vary in certain respects, but they are generally consistent in their attention to the following conditions:

- Risk of self-injurious behavior, including risk of suicide
- Risk of substance use consequences
- Acute mental and emotional distress

- Risk of discontinued medication
- Risk of imminent harm to others

The first four of these conditions are explored in the subsections that follow, while chapter 7 provides an examination of obligations regarding the risk of imminent harm to others.

SELF-INJURIOUS BEHAVIOR AND SUICIDE. The annual rate of suicide among adolescents in the general population has been estimated (Centers for Disease Control and Prevention, 1998, 1999) to be:

- 1.6 per 100,000 for ten- to fourteen-year-olds
- 9.5 per 100,000 for fifteen- to nineteen-year-olds
- Four times higher among boys than among girls (although girls are twice as likely to engage in suicide "attempts" that are not successful)
- Higher among Hispanic youths than among other ethnic groups

The rate of suicide among youths in juvenile justice facilities has been reported as less than 1 in 100,000 admissions for pretrial detention centers, and about 5 in 100,000 admissions for postadjudication (correctional) facilities (Snyder & Sickmund, 1995). (One cannot compare these rates to those in the general population, of course, because the suicide rates for youths in general are based on whether youths have made attempts during a given year.) Equally important, however, is the rate of suicide attempts, gestures, and self-mutilations that endanger adolescents' lives but do not result in suicide; these occur in about 2,500 cases per 100,000 detention admissions (Snyder & Sickmund, 1995).

Youths engage in self-injurious behaviors (resulting, e.g., in bleeding, poisoning, asphyxiation) for a variety of reasons. Sometimes they intend to kill themselves, but other motives include punishing themselves, expressing anger at others, or gaining attention. Most of them do not die as a result of these behaviors, but death is not the only consequence with which we are concerned. Other damages are considerable, such as the life-long consequences of self-mutilation or brain damage from prolonged oxygen deprivation. This helps focus the objective not only on avoiding suicide (a rare consequence of self-harm), but also on identifying and responding to the imminent risk of serious self-injury for whatever reason and with whatever suicidal or nonsuicidal consequences.

The obligation to identify and respond to the risk of self-injurious behavior is relevant at all points in juvenile justice custody, from intake through postadjudicative rehabilitation. But suicidal thoughts and self-injurious behaviors are often precipitated by moments of high emotional stress and by feelings of loss (Hollinger et al., 1994). This suggests two points of contact during which the system's concern should be especially great: at intake and at the time of the postadjudication dispositional decision.

Concerning juvenile justice intake, because periods of high stress often are precipitants for delinquent acts, youths at intake are quite likely to experience levels of stress that are higher than their own "baseline" across time. Whether the intake contact is between a probation officer and a youth living at home or between a detention staff member and a youth recently admitted to detention, adolescents at intake are only moments removed from stressful family conflicts and street dangers in the community. Moreover, intake through detention can engender a feeling of loss of family or peer support, and intake involving meetings with a probation officer represents a threat of that loss. The second point of heightened stress is when youths learn the outcomes of their adjudication and the court's dispositional decision. When the disposition decision signals their imminent removal from the community for long periods of time, many youths experience the decision itself as representing a significant loss.

Suicidal and self-injurious behavior is most commonly associated with Major Depression or other mood disorders. But consistent with discussions in chapter 2, the presence of those disorders alone should not define the need for crisis intervention to avoid suicide and self-injury. It is true that many youths who are at high risk for self-injury will meet criteria for some depressive disorder, but only a minor proportion of adolescents with depressive disorders engage in self-injury. Moreover, the comorbidity of mood, anxiety, conduct, and attention disorders is such that cases involving suicidal and other self-injurious behaviors are very heterogeneous; suicidal youths are found in almost every diagnostic category.

RISK OF SUBSTANCE USE CONSEQUENCES. At the crisis intervention level of treatment, substance use is of concern in order to avert the consequences of current high levels of intoxication or the immediate dangers of withdrawal from substance addiction. The danger may arise especially for youths who are residing in their communities (intake probation, postdispositional community placement) or are being admitted to pretrial detention centers "off the street." For example, at detention admission, youths who are currently intoxicated may be at higher risk of harming themselves (or others). Those who have been maintaining habitual and daily use may undergo painful and dangerous withdrawal symptoms when faced with the unavailability of substances.

Crises associated with substance use are most likely to arise in cases in which youths meet criteria for DSM-IV disorders of Substance Abuse and Substance Dependence. Substance Dependence involves prolonged, chronic (often daily) use to the extent that the youth has built up a tolerance and strong need for continued use of the substance. Substance Abuse refers to frequent substance use that is maladaptive (endangers the youth or others in various ways), but falls short of physiological or psychological dependence. Both refer to degrees of substance use that seriously impair the youth's functioning.

Most youths who present substance-related crisis conditions will meet the criteria for one or the other of these diagnostic classifications. But the diagnosis alone does not call for emergency intervention. Many youths diagnosed with Substance Abuse Disorder will not present an immediate danger due to current intoxication, and the majority of those with Substance Dependence Disorder will not manifest acute withdrawal symptoms on admission to detention centers. Moreover, occasionally a young person may enter a detention center in a state of intoxication but without a history that would qualify for Substance Abuse or Dependence.

ACUTE MENTAL OR EMOTIONAL DISTRESS. This condition concerns youths who currently are experiencing intense psychological and emotional distress associated with acute symptoms of mental disorders. In the typical cases, their distress has been "building" in recent hours or days and they are in the midst of an episode or eruption of symptoms. Their state is such that delay in responding to their disorder (e.g., until after adjudication) is likely to have serious psychological consequences. Often their pain represents a process of rapid deterioration that may quickly result in increasingly impaired functioning and maladaptive behavior if something is not done immediately to alter its course by reducing the intensity of the symptoms.

For example, a youth who cannot sleep because he sees human forms coming and going through the walls of his detention room may be in need of intervention to deal with an acute, mounting psychotic episode. An adolescent who, over the course of a few days in detention, becomes increasingly withdrawn, isolative, emotionally distant, and unapproachable may be experiencing such intense anxiety that she is trying to protect herself from being overwhelmed by her emotions. Another youth who does not have these psychological defenses at his disposal manifests frequent outbursts, striking out at staff and youths whom he perceives as threats despite an absence of provocation. The intensity of a youth's mental or emotional distress, and the appearance of a condition that is worsening, obligates the system to respond in order to relieve that distress and reverse a process of escalating symptoms and functional impairment.

Youths for whom these episodic crisis conditions occur may meet criteria for any of a number of disorders, such as Schizophrenia, Bipolar Disorder, Major Depressive Disorder, and certain anxiety disorders. Only a minority of those who meet these criteria, however, will be experiencing acute mental or emotional distress of the type described here as engendering a crisis. Youths in these diagnostic groups present with various degrees of symptom severity, so that only some will manifest a level of severity and escalating pattern that requires immediate crisis-related intervention.

RISK OF DISCONTINUED MEDICATION. Some youths with mental disorders are on psychoactive medications at the time that they enter the juvenile justice system. Sometimes they do not mention this to probation and detention staff, and parents often are not available to inform them. Therefore, there is a risk—especially at detention intake—that youths' medications will be discontinued, resulting in relapse and the potential consequences of escalating symptoms of their disorders. Crisis avoidance requires that staff be aware of cases in which this might occur. A wide range of diagnoses are relevant here, consistent with the use of psychopharmacological treatment for many disorders, although they are probably most likely in cases involving mood disorders, psychotic disorders, and youths with Attention-Deficit/Hyperactivity Disorder (ADHD).

## Intervention for Crisis Conditions

Given these four potential crisis conditions related to mental and emotional disturbances of youths, two general interventions are required of the system: the conditions must be identified, and cases thus identified must be provided access to psychiatric and other medical services. Here we discuss the second obligation—necessary services—followed by a discussion of the obligation to identify youths experiencing crises.

MANAGEMENT OF SUICIDE AND SUBSTANCE USE RISK. When probation or facility staff become aware that a youth is at substantial risk of self-injury, crisis intervention must focus on (a) *providing conditions to increase immediate safety* and (b) *altering the psychological condition that elevates the risk.*

Providing safe conditions typically involves creating the physical and psychological environment in which the youth may be monitored and assisted to avoid self-injury. For those being seen in intake probation or on postdisposition probation, this is likely to mean referral to a mental health facility that can provide this environment. Some juvenile detention and corrections facilities may be able to provide safe conditions within the facility if they can ensure separation of the youth from others in a way that allows for staff "in-sight" monitoring and psychological support. Where this cannot be provided, the alternative is referral to a mental health facility that can ensure such conditions. Cases involving withdrawal related to substance dependence will usually require hospitalization or residence in a specialized facility for substance use crises, due to the medical dangers inherent in the process.

In addition to managing the youth's safety, the juvenile justice system is obligated to take steps to alter the psychological condition that is elevating the risk of self-harm or the crisis substance use condition. Typically the type of care required in these cases cannot be handled solely by intake probation officers, detention or corrections facility front-line staff, social workers operating as mental health counselors, or psychologists. Any of these professionals might provide important case management, one-on-one emotional support for the youth, and monitoring of the youth's condition. But self-harm and substance use crisis conditions are substantially medical in nature, and systems must have a method for obtaining psychiatric consultation services to fulfill additional and essential objectives. The psychiatrist's consultation typically will involve interviewing the youth, discussing the case with staff, and making essential medical decisions about the youth's care. Pharmacological interventions with demonstrated efficacy are available for responding to these crises (chapter 4), and often they will be needed. Other alternatives for professional intervention are brief emergency counseling and/or referral to an inpatient mental health facility for at least brief hospitalization until the crisis subsides.

If medication occurs outside a mental health facility—whether on intake probation status or in a detention or corrections facility—a method must be in place for continuous monitoring of the youth's response to the medication over a period of days. This monitoring is necessary in order to observe the effectiveness of the medication and the possible emergence of unwanted side effects. Lack of effectiveness or the presence of serious side effects may require adjustments of dosage or the trial of a different medication. Mental health counselors may provide some of these day-to-day monitoring functions. But nurse qualifications typically are needed for medication management, with periodic reviews by a consulting psychiatrist.

RESPONDING TO ACUTE MENTAL AND EMOTIONAL DISTRESS. The level of crisis described earlier as "acute mental and emotional distress" will sometimes require brief inpatient psychiatric hospitalization to reduce symptoms below a crisis level. All detention centers and intake probation departments should have referral procedures available for implementing hospitalization for such cases. Attempting to treat active and acute psychotic or major depressive episodes on an outpatient basis or in juvenile detention and corrections facilities runs substantial risks, unless the correctional facility in which the youth resides is specialized to do so.

Other cases of intense emotional distress may not require hospitalization, but need psychiatric or psychological consultation within a day or two. Some detention centers are equipped, staffed, and managed in a way that allows some youths with serious but less disruptive symptoms of depression or anxiety to be treated by a consulting mental health professional, especially when medication may be prescribed and monitored within the detention center.

## *Identification of Crisis Conditions: A Two-Tiered Approach*

Methods to identify crisis conditions should be in place at every initial contact with a youth (e.g., first interview with a new probation officer, admission to a rehabilitation program). But the most critical identification points are at probation intake and detention intake, when youths are entering the system from the general community. These same points, however, are among the most difficult for evaluating adolescents' mental conditions. Often no record of past behavior or past mental health service history is available, and parents frequently are not present to offer reliable information.

*The nature of the obligation requires that every youth be evaluated at this point for the crisis conditions of concern.* The cost of intake evaluation of every youth by psychiatrists or psychologists typically is prohibitive, so whatever methods are used must be employed by intake probation officers and detention intake staff. The volume of cases does not allow them to spend more than a brief time to evaluate every person.

Under these circumstances, a two-tiered standardized intake screening process is suggested for identification of critical mental health problems associated with our crisis conditions. This process is intended to sort youths into progressively smaller groups representing greater risk and therefore the greater potential need for immediate intervention.

FIRST-LEVEL SCREENING. The first level of intake screening should involve a brief screening tool that asks standardized questions about various behaviors, thoughts, and feelings related specifically to suicide and self-injurious behavior, extent of recent substance use, and symptoms relevant for depressed mood, anxiety, and thought disturbance. All of these factors can be assessed with existing screening tools that have some degree of known reliability and validity, as well as a track-record of application in juvenile justice intake settings by nonclinical staff (see chapter 3). These methods use a relatively small number of items to screen for recent thoughts of self-harm and feelings of hopelessness and worthlessness, as well as recent substance use. Items regarding depression, anxiety, and thought disturbance also focus on thoughts and feelings associated with mental disorders, although they do not address all criteria that would be required to establish formal diagnoses.

Large numbers of youths in juvenile justice intake are likely to endorse at least some questions within each or all of these areas. Thus the tool should identify levels of severity or frequency of these symptoms and provide cut-off scores that represent "clinical significant" or "abnormally high" levels of endorsement of the screening questions for a given dimension. Youths scoring "high" are then considered potentially at risk for the related crisis condition.

Some of the available mental health screening instruments do not ask specifically about recent use of medication for a mental or emotional disorder. This could be accomplished, however, with one or two interview items to that effect.

The instrument used in first-level screening should have known reliability and validity. Given the nature of brief symptom screening instruments (chapter 3), however, the first-level screening will at best have good sensitivity—that is, will identify most youths who actually present substantial risks in the crisis conditions in question—while manifesting only modest specificity—that is, will misidentify as "high risk" a significant number of youths who do not actually present substantial risks ("false positive" cases). This raises the need for additional screening.

SECOND-LEVEL SCREENING. The second level of intake screening should be applied to all youths scoring above the cut-off threshold on first-level screening. Its purpose is simply to reduce obvious false positives and maximize the obvious true positives. In this sense, the second-level screening is a "triage" system that separates those youths who are "screened in" during the first-level screening into three categories: (a) those clearly not in need of crisis intervention, (b) those who clearly are in need (and for whom crisis intervention is begun immediately), and (c) those whose status remains questionable.

Second-level screening can be accomplished in different ways for the

various potential crisis conditions, typically involving standardized interview tools that have been developed to screen for specific problems or
disorders. For *suicide, self-injury, and substance use conditions,* one might
suppose that second-level screening would involve examination for formal
diagnoses of mental disorders often associated with these conditions. But
the discussion in chapter 2 suggests that this is not necessarily the most
effective approach in these cases. For example, while mood disorders are
common among youths with self-injurious tendencies, most youths with
mood disorders are not self-injurious, and some without mood disorders
are self-injurious. The objective of second-level screening for self-injury
and substance use risks can be accomplished better with any of a number
of specialized screening tools that establish directly what we want to know,
rather than providing diagnoses from which we have to make inferences
about what we want to know. Several of these tools, described in chapter
3, ask a limited number of standardized interview questions about suicide
potential of substance use requiring only a few minutes. They can be used
in a brief "discussion" format, indicating to the youth that the staff member wants to further explore some issues because of the youth's endorsement of a high number of first-level screening items.

For suicide potential, for example, these tools typically focus on
whether youths were reporting their present feelings in the first-level
screening (versus thoughts and feelings that they have had recently but
not currently), whether the feelings have been momentary or continuous,
whether they themselves believe that they might harm themselves in the
next few days and, if so, whether the youth has a plan and whether there
are means and the opportunity to carry it out. The use of these screening
tools will raise some cases to an "obvious" level of concern and suggest
a low level of concern for others, while some will remain "questionable."

Second-level screening with tools that focus specifically on substance
use can identify conditions that would make the risk of immediate effects
of intoxication or of withdrawal symptoms highly likely or unlikely. For
example, is the youth currently under the influence of a substance that
was ingested in the hours prior to intake (without which the immediate
effects of substance use are unlikely)? Has the youth been under the influence of any substance every day for a period of several days (raising
the likelihood of Substance Dependence and the risk of withdrawal
symptoms)? A number of substance use screens are available that focus
on such questions (chapter 3), allowing one to identify obviously low-risk
cases and obviously high-risk cases with relatively little time commitment.

For youths with high first-level screening scores on *mood, anxiety, or thought disturbance symptoms,* and who have not already been identified for crisis intervention related to imminent self-injury or substance use problems, deciding on the nature of second-level screening is a bit more complex. Let us consider three approaches.

First, one might imagine that second-level screening related to these conditions should involve determining a formal diagnosis, on the theory that a crisis case related to these types of symptoms should at least rise to the level of meeting criteria for a DSM-IV disorder. This could include administration of a structured interview tool (see chapter 3) that determines whether the youth meets DSM-IV criteria for a mood, anxiety, or psychotic disorder. This approach seems important, but what we have learned in chapters 2 and 3 raises concerns about its adequacy. Some youths in crisis may not meet formal criteria for a DSM-IV diagnosis. For example, an adolescent may present with a number of serious symptoms usually associated with Dysthymic Disorder yet fail to meet criteria for the disorder because their condition is newly developed and the complete symptom picture has not yet emerged. Most youths in significant distress associated with a crisis condition will meet criteria for some mental disorder, but some will not. For this reason, using diagnosis as a threshold for crisis intervention runs a risk, whatever its magnitude, of overlooking some of those who need crisis intervention.

Alternatively, second-level screening for youths scoring high on symptoms associated with mood, anxiety, or thought disturbances could focus on discovering the extent and magnitude of impaired functioning that may place them in danger in the community (if screening is occurring at intake) or in pretrial detention. In other words, questions of diagnosis could be set aside, using instead instruments that assess severity of functional impairment (see chapter 3) as our second screen for identifying cases that need attention immediately. This may seem appropriate in light of the limited objectives of crisis intervention, but it has its liabilities. DSM-IV is the language of the mental health system and of mental health professionals from whom the juvenile justice system may be seeking assistance in responding to youths' mental health crises. While an accurate diagnosis under crisis conditions often will not say what to do to respond to the crisis, it does provide important clinical information. Moreover, some evidence that a formal disorder exists may be required before third-party payers will reimburse providers for psychiatric services. In addition, mental health professionals will certainly need a diagnostic impression before they implement treatment. For example, some youths may describe bizarre ideas or apparent hallucinations without having Schizophrenia or other psychotic disorders. Administering antipsychotic medication would not be appropriate in those cases, but could be mistakenly provided if no effort was made to determine whether the youth's report of bizarre ideas was part of a more systematic set of symptoms suggesting a formal psychotic disorder.

The obvious third choice for second screening of these cases is to employ both a structured diagnostic tool and a measure of functional impairment. This, too, is not an easy choice, because it requires more time than either of the other two options alone. But the use of both types of tools clearly creates the best second-level screening to distinguish between youths who create the greatest concern and those about whom there is less pressing worry.

IMPLEMENTING SCREENING. The instruments described for first-level screening typically can be administered and scored by probation officers and front-line detention and juvenile corrections staff with only a few hours of in-service training on the instrument. Second-level screening, however, requires greater experience with interviewing young people. While standardized interview questions can be used for second-level screening (and can even be accomplished by computer with the Voice DISC-IV: see chapter 3), interviewers need practiced skill in communicating with youths to explore their intent when they answered first-level screening questions positively. This process can be taught to a wide range of juvenile justice personnel, but it is best conducted by social workers or bachelor's degree mental health counselors who have had some training in the concepts of mental and emotional disturbances among youths.

Mental health screening is likely to occur in the context of staff members' routine process of gathering a broader range of intake information from each youth. Typically staff must spend some time interviewing a person at intake to obtain information about birth date and place of residence, parents' names and phone numbers, name of school, and information about medical conditions and recent medical contacts.

Precisely when mental health intake screening should occur in detention, however, is a matter of some uncertainty. As described in chapter 3, youths' self-reports may be influenced by momentary emotions, so that screening them within the first hour after admission risks obtaining reports of thoughts and feelings that are very transient. Allowing for at least a brief delay so that youths may become oriented to their new surroundings seems warranted. On the other hand, delaying the screening for many hours might cause one to miss the crisis condition one wishes to identify, risking a suicide attempt or drug-use reaction before the potential is known. The proper time is probably between one and twelve hours after admission, but there is no authoritative answer to the best time within that span. A safe policy would include two administrations of the screening tool, the first one within an hour or two after admission to detention and the second one about twenty-four hours later. For the screening tools identified in chapter 3, there is no reason to believe that a second administration soon after the first would interfere appreciably with the accuracy of the results.

Probation intake and detention facilities employing mental health screening must have in place a set of effective rules to prevent the potential for the unfair use of screening data in subsequent adjudicative processes. Staff must be able to tell youths, at the time of screening, that their answers to mental health screening questions will not be used at their trials. Without this assurance, at least some youths who would otherwise be forthcoming might withhold information, thus defeating the purpose of screening for mental health problems. Jurisdictions that do not have such protections in place should follow the examples of other jurisdictions that have prohibited the use of screening data from use in subsequent legal hearings. Legal mechanisms for ensuring such protections range from legislation to agency regulations or judicial orders pertaining to a specific juvenile court.

OUTCOMES OF SCREENING. Clear-cut cases of high risk may need no further evaluation prior to referral to inpatient mental health or substance-related crisis facilities. Others may present clear risks and require some clinical intervention, but fall short of the need for hospitalization. A request for psychiatric consultation will be appropriate in many of the latter cases, as well as those in which the risk is not clearly apparent but is still questionable after screening.

But what is meant by a "clear-cut case of high risk," or "those in which the risk is not clearly apparent?" While we may be tempted to answer that "we know it when we see it," that is not sufficient for purposes of defining screening outcomes for crisis intervention. The instruments themselves will give us an indication of the degree of severity of various types of symptoms. For example, the Massachusetts Youth Screening Instrument (see chapter 3) provides scores on six types of clinical symptoms, as well as two kinds of cut-off scores for identifying "high" scorers. But instruments will not tell the user specifically which cut-off scores, on what scales, signal the need for hospitalization, referral for psychiatric consultation, or simply close monitoring.

These decisions are matters of policy. Juvenile justice agencies themselves must determine how screening results will be translated into staff directives for the emergency interventions described earlier. Unfortunately, the state of the art provides juvenile justice administrators little structure for deciding how to make policy decisions that turn screening results into staff responses. It would be helpful, of course, if we could tell the administrators that their cut-off criteria for intervention should identify some specific percentage of youths because current evidence tells us that this is approximately the proportion of youths that needs crisis intervention. Were we to attempt this for detention centers, the following sets of data would be relevant.

First, the figure cited earlier regarding suicide attempts and gestures—about one in forty admissions—is our best estimate regarding cases that might need intervention related to self-harm. The ratio would be considerably higher for girls' facilities, perhaps one in twenty admissions. But there are no data with which to make estimates for youths seen at intake probation or during postdisposition probation in the community.

Second, the actual proportion of youths entering juvenile justice detention and corrections facilities who meet criteria for Substance Abuse or Substance Dependence disorders is relatively high (chapter 1)—between one-third and one-half of admissions. But there are no data with which to estimate the proportion that presents crisis conditions.

Third, as observed in chapter 1, it is difficult to estimate the proportion of youths in juvenile justice facilities meeting criteria for disorders with a higher risk of serious mental or emotional disturbance (e.g., Schizophrenia, Bipolar Disorder, Major Depressive Disorder, and more serious anxiety disorders). Conservative estimates might calculate the proportion at about 20 percent (Cocozza & Skowyra, 2000). Recall, however, that only some of these cases will manifest symptoms of sufficient severity to require emergency attention. For example, the Virginia study cited in chapter 2 found that only 9 percent of youths (in a detention center in which 80 percent met criteria for some mental disorder) required immediate intervention.

These data are the best we can offer, but they are not of much value to the juvenile justice administrator who wishes to set a cut-off score at a level that identifies about the "right" proportion of youths as crisis cases. As can be seen, the data barely address this question, much less answer it. Moreover, any estimates are likely to be enormously misleading for some detention centers, because patterns of referral of youthful offenders with and without mental disorders vary greatly from one detention center to another. A particular detention center's actual proportion of youths with serious mental disorders (or crisis conditions) may be far above or far below any estimates based on studies of specific facilities or national averages. Thus juvenile justice administrators have little guidance for deciding that specific screening scores should translate into "positive" cases requiring specific crisis interventions.

## Diversion

The process of diversion typically refers to the juvenile justice system's option not to pursue adjudication of certain youths at intake, but instead to refer them to community programs early in the juvenile justice process. Diversion may be implemented by juvenile courts for various purposes (e.g., to avoid stigmatization of young first-time, minor offenders who might never again offend if they are left alone). In the case of youths with mental disorders, diversion may be employed to maximize the youth's opportunity for obtaining necessary treatment. Adolescents in need of treatment for their mental disorders, it is argued, should be diverted from the juvenile justice system when the system's interest in their treatment, especially for purposes of reducing their future delinquency, outweighs the value of their adjudication. This circumstance is most likely to arise in two types of cases: (a) misdemeanor cases involving first-time offenders with mental disorders, and (b) misdemeanor or felony cases involving youths with serious and chronic mental disorders (see the discussion later in this chapter of youths with "serious emotional disturbances" [SED]). The number of such cases in the average juvenile court is not known, but it is substantial.

The range of methods and programs for diverting youths with mental disorders from ordinary delinquency processing during the intake process has not been documented. In one sense, diversion is probably part of most juvenile intake probation systems, since almost all intake probation officers exercise some discretion (at least in cases involving nonserious charges) in determining whether a youth's case will be filed for adjudication or "adjusted informally"—for example, by an agreement with the parents for the youth to obtain community services. At the other extreme are highly programmatic efforts for the diversion of seriously emotionally disturbed adolescents from traditional delinquency processing. One recent example is the "juvenile mental health court." In Santa Clara County (California), the Court for the Individualized Treatment of Adolescents (CITA: Arredondo et al., 2001), for example, targets the 10–15 percent of delinquency cases involving youths with chronic and serious mental disorders. It uses a screening and assessment process to identify such youths for special legal processing by a team of clinical and legal professionals (including prosecutor and defense counsel), all of whom have special knowledge of and sensitivity to adolescent mental disorders. Cases adjudicated through this process are heard by a specially designated CITA judge. The process fashions case outcomes that hold youths accountable for their offenses while focusing the disposition on the use of community and juvenile justice resources to provide treatment for the offenders and their families.

Special programs for diversion may have the potential to target treatment efforts for young offenders with mental disorders. But it is important to recognize that neither generalized or programmatic diversion efforts can do much good if there are inadequate services awaiting diverted youths. Diversion programs might be helpful when effective community mental health services actually are available to youths, and when there is sufficient follow-through to ensure that young offenders and families actually become involved in those services. But if that part of the diversion process is not given adequate attention, or if the community mental health services are nonexistent, "diversion" simply becomes the juvenile justice system's way of avoiding its responsibility. Diversion without services or follow-through throws youths back on the street without help at a time that is critical for responding to their symptoms and potentially avoiding their development of more chronic delinquency.

## Stabilization Treatment

Beyond treatment for crisis conditions, the juvenile justice system should *identify youths in need of clinical interventions because of mental disorders that seriously impair their future functioning, and the system should make clinical interventions available, consistent with legal limits, to the extent that they have known efficacy for improving functioning sufficiently to facilitate rehabilitative objectives.* The complexity of this definition is related to a number of issues reviewed in previous chapters, and they need to be further explained here.

### What Stabilization Treatment Means

"MENTAL DISORDERS THAT SERIOUSLY IMPAIR FUTURE FUNCTIONING." This definition identifies stabilization treatment not as treatment for every youth with a mental disorder, but as treatment in cases in which symptoms of disorder seriously impair functioning in a way that matters for overall rehabilitative objectives. This proposition recognizes that not all youths with mental disorders need treatment insofar as symptom severity and its functional consequences vary among those with any given mental disorder (chapter 2). Meeting criteria for a mental disorder is a threshold prerequisite, and the definition does not limit the obligation to any particular subset of DSM-IV disorders. But the definition does not necessarily obligate the juvenile justice system to provide treatment for all of the 60–70 percent of youths who meet criteria for a mental disorder. It limits the obligation to those whose functioning is seriously impaired by the symptoms of their disorders. The degree of impairment that may be called "serious," however, is not limited to the acute, crisis conditions reviewed earlier.

"IMPROVING FUNCTIONING SUFFICIENTLY TO FACILITATE REHABILITATIVE OBJECTIVES." This concept defines the objective of stabilization treatment in the juvenile justice system. The goal of clinical intervention of this type is *not* the remission of disorders or even "adequate functioning" in general. The objective is to improve functioning incrementally by reducing the severity of symptoms of mental disorder, so that other rehabilitation efforts have a better chance of succeeding.

"KNOWN EFFICACY." The system should provide treatment that evidence has shown to be of benefit when applied to youths with psychiatric and demographic characteristics similar to those of the youth in question. This requirement is two-pronged. The system is obligated to provide treatments for which there is evidence of efficacy. By the same token, the system is not obligated to provide—indeed, should be *required not* to provide—treatments for which there is no known efficacy for the type of youths in question. To do otherwise is wasteful of resources and potentially detrimental to youths, caretakers, and the interests of society (see the first section of this chapter, as well as chapter 4).

By implication, this concept also requires that when the juvenile justice system seeks to meet its obligation to implement a treatment for which efficacy is known, it must do so in accordance with the specifications associated with the evidence for the treatment's efficacy. For example, if evidence of efficacy was established with procedures administered by mental health professionals with a certain level or type of training, the treatment must be provided by that type of professional. If evidence for efficacy was established with youths who were seen on an outpatient basis, then the treatment must be implemented in that context, not with youths in secure juvenile justice facilities.

"MAKE CLINICAL TREATMENTS AVAILABLE." The juvenile justice system's custodial obligation should not hold the system responsible for treating youths, but for providing the opportunity for treatment to occur. Two qualifying points are embedded in this concept. First, while the juvenile justice system might implement treatments for a variety of disorders, it might instead find ways to provide access to some treatments provided by other agencies, such as a state's mental health system for children and adolescents. Thus the juvenile justice system's obligation to make certain treatments "available" does not require that it administer all of those treatments.

Second, the "availability" concept recognizes that *youths and their caretakers should have the opportunity to accept or forgo treatment* that is made available *as a custodial obligation* of the juvenile justice system. The system does not neglect its obligation by not providing treatment if youths and their caretakers choose not to take advantage of the appropriate treatment that the system offers. As we shall see later, this does not mean that the system must receive consent from caretakers in all cases. For example, chapter 7 proposes that when clinical treatment will be beneficial for the youth and is *necessary in order to ensure public safety,* the system may have an independent authority to engage the youth in that treatment. But when potential beneficial clinical treatment is not essential to reduce risk of harm to others (and is not covered under the system's crisis-related treatment obligations), the system should obtain caretaker's or guardian's consent. Note that the same is not true for the broad range of methods employed in *rehabilitation* efforts of the juvenile justice system, which may be implemented without parental consent. It applies to psychopharmacological and psychotherapeutic activities that are designed to alter impaired functioning associated with the symptoms of mental disorder.

"IDENTIFY YOUTHS IN NEED." The system must discover which youths are in need of stabilization treatment (as defined in the foregoing paragraphs). This implies that there be in place a system of assessment, which will be discussed later.

"CONSISTENT WITH LEGAL LIMITS." This qualifier recognizes that law might prohibit certain types of interventions at certain stages of juvenile justice processing. For example, some states (or courts) will allow defense attorneys to bar pre-adjudication psychological assessment or treatment of their young clients (except for purposes of mandated screening and crisis intervention). This practice is based on due process considerations that protect one against providing self-incriminating evidence during the adjudicative process.

## What Treatments Are Required for Which Youths?

PSYCHOPHARMACOLOGIC INTERVENTION. There is considerable evidence (chapter 4) for the efficacy of medication for youths with ADHD and youths with mood disorders, and more equivocally for those with anxiety disorders. Some of these youths will not have received psychopharmacological interventions—indeed, will not have been diagnosed—prior to their entrance into the juvenile justice system. The system should make medications for these disorders available to those in juvenile justice custody.

Our definition of stabilization treatment, however, suggests some limits to the use of medications. First, medication should be confined to cases in which the symptoms of the disorders seriously impair functioning in ways that produce an impediment to rehabilitative objectives. All youths with ADHD manifest impulsiveness or attention problems to some degree, and all adolescents with mood disorders manifest problems in motivation, self-esteem, and irritability. But their effects in terms of functional impairment vary across cases, so that not all persons with these diagnoses will require medication.

Second, caretaker (e.g., parental) consent should be required for pharmacological interventions related to stabilization treatment. There are legal and moral reasons to impose this limit on the use of medications by the justice system. A compelling clinical reason, however, is the importance of involving parents in the treatment of their children. Youths' compliance with medication while they are being rehabilitated in the community, or after they return to the community from secure rehabilitation programs, often depends heavily on their parents' efforts. Failing to engage parents in the treatment process decreases the likelihood that they will play this role.

PSYCHOTHERAPIES AND PSYCHOSOCIAL INTERVENTIONS. Juvenile justice planners might suppose that the custodial treatment obligation includes the need to provide a different type of psychotherapy or psychosocial intervention for each different type of mental disorder encountered among youths. But our review of treatment efficacy in chapter 4 does not suggest this. Certainly there are diagnosis-specific psychotherapies, and sometimes they are important to provide. But many of the methods with known efficacy are not designed for one diagnostic type alone. Cognitive-behavioral therapies, family therapies, and Multisystemic Therapy focus on building skills, problem-solving, and learning new cognitive and social responses, or on modifying the relations between youths and others in their world, especially family members. Their intent is to alter conditions that underlie or exacerbate the symptoms of mental disorder, and many of these conditions apply across various mood and anxiety disorders, as well as substance use disorders (chapter 4). Given that this is so, it suggests that the juvenile justice system is not necessarily obligated to arrange for specific types of psychotherapies for specific types of disorders.

Indeed, almost all youths in juvenile justice custody might benefit from these methods, and ideally they would be widely available to delinquent youths. In the present context, however, our definition of stabilization treatment creates a special obligation to make them available to youths with mental disorders, when their disorders are responsible for serious functional impairments that must be remedied to meet the system's rehabilitative objectives.

Some of the more efficacious psychosocial treatment methods described in chapter 4 involve the family in therapy or work with youths to develop new behavioral and social patterns within various systems in the community (e.g., school, work, and peer groups). Depending on the specific method, these forms of therapy typically are difficult to implement in secure juvenile facilities, because the youth's incarceration restricts access to the psychosocial interactions that are needed in order to implement the therapy. If the obligation to provide these treatments to youths with mental disorders is taken seriously, it means that the juvenile justice system must not only make these methods available, but it must also reduce to a minimum the mentally disordered youths it incarcerates and therefore deprives of the opportunity to benefit from the methods.

SPECIAL NEEDS YOUTHS. In this review of treatment methods, I have thus far not mentioned specifically the need for certain treatment services that do not fall neatly into either psychopharmacological or psychosocial therapy categories. These special services pertain to (a) young offenders with Schizophrenia and SEDs—a special category of youths with "serious emotional disturbances" (described in chapters 2 and 4)—and (b) youths with developmental disabilities. Their needs require not merely discrete forms of therapy, but broader and more complex systems of care.

Youths with Schizophrenia rarely are seen in the juvenile justice system, partly because Schizophrenia itself is rare in adolescence. When they are encountered, typically their treatment requires expert psychiatric care, often involving periodic inpatient services, transitional services, and continuity of outpatient services. Similarly, the category of youths called SEDs typically have chronic, multiple, and serious emotional disorders that require special care. Among clients of child mental health services outside the juvenile justice system, approximately 10 percent are SED youths who require nearly one-half or more of the resources of the child mental health system (Davis & Vander Stoep, 1997). Young offenders in these categories need specialized treatment, transitional services, and continuity of care after community reentry that the juvenile justice system not only cannot provide but also should not attempt on its own. Its obligation to these youths is to ensure that the mental health system, ideally in collaboration with the juvenile justice system (as discussed later in this chapter), provides the treatment and continuity of care that they need.

Youths with *developmental disabilities,* especially those with mental retardation, have a variety of special educational needs that fall outside our definition of clinical treatment. When they also have other types of mental disorders, though, the system's obligation to treat those disorders applies to them as to other youths. Having said this, one must recognize that the efficacy of the psychotherapies and psychosocial interventions reviewed earlier often is not known when applied to youths with mental retardation. Youths with intelligence test scores well below 70 and whose everyday functioning is seriously compromised by their intellectual deficits typically are not included in research studies of the efficacy of treatments for other mental disorders (e.g., mood or anxiety disorders). While cognitive-behavioral modes of therapy often are helpful for youths with these disorders, those with mental retardation frequently do not bring to therapy the necessary cognitive abilities to engage in this type of therapy process. Their treatment is best managed by public or private agencies charged with treating those with mental retardation, which have the specialized professionals and programs necessary to meet the needs of developmentally disabled youths.

## Assessment for Stabilization Treatment

The obligation to provide stabilization treatment to youths whose symptoms of mental disorder seriously impair their functioning includes an obligation to identify those youths. How is this best accomplished?

THE ASSESSMENT PROCESS. The screening procedures described earlier provide a reasonable way to identify the minority of youths who may be in need of more comprehensive assessment in order to determine their specific stabilization treatment needs. Screening methods, however, will almost never provide the necessary information to formulate stabilization treatment needs and objectives. That requires a more careful, individualized, and extensive assessment.

There are two points in the juvenile justice process where comprehensive assessments to plan stabilization treatment are especially important. One is during the process of intake, and involves youths for whom it is unclear whether they will be processed for adjudication or will instead be referred to community services. The other is for youths during adjudicative processing, involving those who are scheduled for court hearings to adjudicate their charges, which usually will be followed by a dispositional hearing to determine their placement and the type of rehabilitative and clinical services they will be provided. In both circumstances, when screening suggests the possibility of serious mental and emotional problems, the system should be able to provide to this relatively select group of youths a comprehensive assessment by a child psychologist or child psychiatrist. This assessment can be of critical assistance to probation and the court in identifying the nature of a youth's mental disorder and stabilization treatment needs. The assessment should produce the following:

- A developmental and psychological profile of the youth
- A diagnosis if disorder is present
- If disorder is present, an indication of the severity of symptoms and their actual effects on the youth's functioning
- A treatment recommendation
- An explanation concerning how the treatment is expected to improve the youth's functioning in ways that are important for the court's overall rehabilitative objectives

A formal diagnosis, as well as a measure of the level of impairment of functioning, typically is necessary not only to guide the treatment recommendation, but also because treatment may require reimbursement from third-party payers who will not pay without this information.

The nature of assessments for juvenile courts regarding the need for treatment and rehabilitation has been described elsewhere (e.g., Grisso, 1998). Typically such an assessment requires clinical interviews with the youth and the youth's parents, and obtaining detailed information from past records regarding the youth's functioning in various settings throughout his or her development (especially school records, past medical and mental health records, and law enforcement and court records). Psychological testing may be required, especially in complex cases (e.g., when there are substantial difficulties in determining among several psychiatric diagnoses), as well as special medical tests in some circumstances (e.g., when a youth's difficulties suggest the possibility of medical disease or neurological impairment).

IMPLEMENTING THE ASSESSMENT FOR STABILIZATION TREAT- MENT NEEDS. For cases involving youths with serious mental disorders, some juvenile courts obtain their treatment-planning assessments from mental health professionals who are employed full-time or part-time in "juvenile court clinics." Other juvenile courts obtain these assessments from public mental health agencies or professionals in private practice (Grisso, 1998), and psychopharmacological assessments may sometimes be provided by general physicians rather than mental health professionals.

Whatever arrangement is used, the system should rely on professionals who have training and experience in working with young people. Psychological or psychiatric examiners charged with making assessments for stabilization treatment must understand, for example, the concepts of developmental psychopathology described in chapter 2, such as age-relativity of symptoms, comorbidity, and continuity/discontinuity of mental disorders among children and adolescents. Most clinical psychologists and psychiatrists have had some exposure to developmental concepts, as well as assessment and treatment of adolescents, sometime during their training. Only some of them, however, subsequently go on to specialize in the area. Some juvenile justice systems face a dilemma in this regard, in that child-specialized clinicians are few or nonexistent in some jurisdictions (especially in some rural areas). Thus, while professionals who specialize in child and adolescent development issues are preferred when they are available, to require them would risk some jurisdictions having no services at all. Nevertheless, the risk of inappropriate assessment and treatment when employing non-child-specialized professionals must be recognized.

Juvenile courts should have in place policies and practices that restrict the use of information from assessments during adjudicative processing, allowing it to be used only after the youth has been found delinquent and the court is ready to consider the disposition—that is, the youth's placement and the nature of services that are deemed to be needed. Results of assessments for treatment planning should not be available during the adjudicative hearing at which allegations of delinquency are tried. Whether a youth has a mental disorder is usually irrelevant for determining whether he or she did what was charged. Moreover, the availability of information at trial based on a compulsory evaluation could constitute a violation of the right to avoid self-incrimination.

One way to ensure this protection is to require that all assessments for treatment planning be conducted after adjudication. But the delay that this creates between adjudication and disposition has prompted many jurisdictions to allow examiners to perform their assessments prior to adjudication, so that the results will be readily available at the time of the dispositional hearing (which usually occurs very soon—ranging from minutes to a few days—after adjudication of the charges). When this is so, pertinent state law or regulations must be in place to prevent the use of the results as evidence at trial.

## Maintenance Treatment

The term "maintenance treatment" refers to clinical services that are provided after the objectives of crisis and stabilization treatment have been accomplished. The goal of maintenance treatment is to prevent the recurrence of serious functional impairment as a result of relapse. In the context of juvenile justice custody, maintenance treatment typically involves care that continues beyond the time that the system has custody of the youth. Its objective in that regard is "preventive," insofar as it seeks to decrease the likelihood that youths will return to the juvenile justice system at some future time as a consequence of behaviors related to recurrent symptoms of mental disorder. Examples include the youth with ADHD who needs to continue stimulant medication, SED adolescents with chronic and multiple mental disorders that make them especially prone to relapse, and those whose functioning is especially associated with family dysfunctions that may need continued attention beyond the juvenile justice system's period of custody.

The system's responsibility for maintenance treatment, of course, does not require direct provision of clinical services after custody has been relinquished. Its obligation is to take reasonable steps to facilitate youths' and families' continued access to mental health services outside the juvenile justice system, as needed in order to maintain the youths' adequate functioning. (One might also argue that the system has an obligation to exercise influence on mental health agencies to provide the types of maintenance treatment that young offenders with mental disorders require.) Continued access to services typically begins by ensuring that referral to appropriate community mental health resources routinely occurs at termination of juvenile justice custody. In most cases it will not be sufficient merely to "inform" youths and parents of potential sources of services. The referral process usually should be deliberate and systematic—for example, arranging for initial appointments and providing relevant information to the service provider regarding the youth's and family's needs.

## Unanswered Questions for Policy and Research

This perspective on the juvenile justice system's obligations to provide custodial treatment raises several challenges for which there are no ready answers. Some of them could be addressed if adequate empirical information were available. Others will never be answered with better data, because they are essentially matters of policy that require weighing competing values. They can be described as (a) *issues of measurement and criteria,* (b) *dilemmas associated with the "efficacy" of treatment,* and (c) *systemic and intersystemic modes of service delivery.*

### Can Our Measures of Psychopathology Be Improved?

Our ability to identify youths with significant functional impairments due to mental disorders relies heavily on the quality of our screening and assessment methods. How well those instruments can do their jobs is seriously limited by problems in conceptualizing and defining mental disorders of children and adolescents (chapter 2). The field of developmental psychopathology does not appear to be on the verge of finding better ways to define discrete disorders among adolescents or to project their course. Indeed, the fact that youths are still developing biologically and psychologically suggests that the comorbidity, symptom overlap, and discontinuity seen in youths' mental disturbances are not due to our inability to find the true order hidden beneath the chaos, but rather constitute the true, chaotic nature of psychopathology in adolescence.

If this is so, we can never expect our screening and diagnostic tools to be highly efficient in identifying various types of mental disorders or discrete symptoms among adolescents; they cannot find what is not there. Our current tools may be doing as well as can be expected. But three issues need special attention.

THE VALIDITY OF SCREENING INSTRUMENTS. A very significant part of the system's custodial treatment obligation lies in its screening of every young offender for symptoms associated with mental disorder. The best screening tools we now have for this purpose in juvenile justice settings (see chapter 3: the BSI, CAFAS, MAYSI-2, and POSIT) provide adequate standardization and good evidence of reliability, as does the

Voice DISC-IV for diagnoses. But evidence for their validity—their ability to measure what they say they measure—is barely sufficient to support their use. This is not because current research challenges their validity, but because not enough research has been done. This research must receive high priority, because almost everything else in the juvenile justice system's mandate for treatment flows from this starting point.

THE UTILITY OF SCREENING INSTRUMENTS. Good screening and assessment methods are useful to the extent that they are implemented and used competently, and they are useless if they are not. If they are not administered and used appropriately by juvenile justice staff, screening tools are little more than window dressing implemented only for purposes of meeting requirements rather than trying to accomplish the purposes that those requirements represent. Yet we know little about the actual use of screening tools in detention centers and intake probation offices. Moreover, there is no literature that systematically guides the juvenile justice system in developing and maintaining the quality of mental health screening.

The type of research that is needed to provide this guidance is not likely to be done by researchers who develop screening tools. Their interests and skills are focused on the fine points of translating psychological concepts into test items and refining them psychometrically. Studying real-world uses and consequences of those tools requires special research methods associated with the field of evaluation research, aimed at describing the performance, outcome, costs, and benefits of programs as they use the tools that psychometrists have produced. In part, the difference between these research endeavors is captured in terms we have encountered earlier when discussing the value of treatment methods. Test developers study the "efficacy" of tools to measure what was intended when they were designed. But evaluation research is required to determine whether those tools are "effective" when used in actual practice. Moreover, evaluation research can help us determine whether a program's use of tools to identify youths who need mental health services has an impact on the actual provision of services.

THE INTERPRETATION OF SCREENING AND ASSESSMENT RESULTS. The purpose of screening and assessment is to provide reliable case-by-case data that can express a youth's degree of symptoms, diagnoses, or functional impairments. Tools can also provide cut-off scores that signal when a case manifests critically high degrees of these characteristics compared to other youths. But none of the instruments can tell juvenile justice personnel how high is "high enough" to warrant the need for crisis intervention or special stabilization treatment. When are symptoms *severe,* and how much is required to make a mental disorder *serious?* Is it sufficient for the youth's level of depression to be higher than for 70 percent of her peers? 85 percent? 90 percent? There are no empirical answers to these questions. Their answers lie primarily in judgments about the degree of suffering we are not willing to tolerate.

This question is of enormous importance, because it goes to the heart of the definition for our custodial obligation to provide treatment. Where the cut-off is set will determine which youths, and how many youths, we must provide clinical care. Without policies that offer guidance for setting a standard, juvenile justice systems may set the level for "seriousness" so high that many of those who should receive treatment will not, or so low that the large number of adolescents referred for treatment will abuse our resources and reduce the quality of care for the ones who are truly in need.

## How Can We Best Apply the "Known Efficacy" Requirement?

The system's obligation to implement only treatments with known efficacy presents certain dilemmas for stabilization treatment that must be recognized, but for which no ideal resolution is immediately apparent. These include (a) questions about the generalizability of efficacy, and (b) costs of the obligation to implement efficacious treatments with fidelity.

EFFICACY, GENDER, AND ETHNICITY. Girls in the juvenile justice system have special needs compared to boys in the system and to girls outside it. As noted in chapter 2, a greater proportion of girls than boys in juvenile justice facilities meet criteria for mental disorders, and the severity and comorbidity of their disorders on average are greater than for boys. Girls often have been included in the studies that established the efficacy of various types of treatment, but few of those studies focused on juvenile justice samples of girls. As a consequence, we are less certain that the efficacy of certain psychotherapies and psychosocial interventions extends to girls in juvenile justice custody.

Minority youths often have been included in tests of the efficacy of various treatments for adolescents. Unfortunately, treatment efficacy studies rarely report separate outcome data by ethnicity, and some of the psychopharmacological studies have been in clinical settings in which the majority were not ethnic minority youths. More encouraging, efficacy studies of several of the psychosocial interventions have been performed with samples containing substantial proportions of ethnic minority youths.

Where there are questions about the efficacy of treatments by gender and ethnicity, our mandate to provide treatments with known efficacy presents a dilemma. Failure to provide those interventions for girls and ethnic minority youths seems clearly and unfairly discriminatory. Yet when we include them in treatment, we do so with some degree of uncertainty regarding the value of the treatment for them.

The proper empirical approach to this dilemma is to stimulate a great deal more research on the efficacy of various treatments for girls and ethnic minority youths, and if necessary, to develop special treatment methods for girls who are young offenders with mental disorders. The proper policy while we wait for those results is less certain, but on balance it would seem to require that we apply treatments with known efficacy without distinction for gender or ethnicity, while taking extra care to monitor the potential risks and value of treatment for those categories of youths as treatment proceeds.

MAKING EFFICACIOUS TREATMENTS EFFECTIVE. In chapter 4 we noted that few treatments with efficacy have been studied for their effectiveness when implemented in real-world settings—that is, with self-referred cases in ordinary practice, outside of clinical research studies that controlled the samples and conditions of treatment experimentally. Therefore, were we to require that treatments must have known efficacy *and* effectiveness before using them to fulfill obligations to provide treatment, the system would have little to offer youths with mental disorders. Under these circumstances, providing efficacious treatments without evidence for their effectiveness seems the best course, rather than denying services until researchers can provide the information.

The ultimate answer to this dilemma, of course, is to engage in as much research as possible to test the effectiveness of treatments while they are being provided to young offenders with mental disorders. In the meantime, policy should require that efficacious treatments of unknown effectiveness must be implemented with fidelity. The manner in which a treatment is executed must be true to the fundamentals that were employed when the treatment was tested and found to be of value. For example, the treatment must be administered according to the manualized directions for the method. The level of training of therapists who administer a particular type of treatment must be the same as the training of therapists in the efficacy studies that demonstrated the treatment's potential. Moreover, that level of expertise must be maintained over time to avoid changes in the procedure as a consequence of staff turnover or the tendency for therapists to "drift" away from the method's specific procedures. This attention to quality will justify the use of efficacious treatments for which actual effectiveness in practice is uncertain.

## What Systemic Arrangements Can Best Fulfill the Mandate?

As noted earlier, the juvenile justice system is not a mental health system. It has a variety of responsibilities that may conflict with the provision of diverse methods of clinical care that are needed by youths with mental disorders. But the system need not always administer the treatments that it is obligated to make available. Some things it must do itself, especially the identification of youths who should be receiving treatment. Some of that treatment can be provided by the system, but as noted earlier in this chapter, much of it probably must be obtained from other sources.

Exactly how that can best be accomplished is a complex and unresolved question. Barnum and Keilitz (1992) offered one of the better descriptions of some of the options for "models of service delivery" involving various degrees and types of interaction between the juvenile justice system and other child welfare agencies. In brief, they described four models, three of which are relevant for our consideration:

- *Agency-Centered Interaction:* The juvenile justice system provides as much clinical service as it can, then purchases services in the community from local providers (child mental health centers, independent clinicians) when a youth's clinical service needs are beyond the system's capacity.
- *Collaborative Interaction:* The juvenile justice system and the child mental health system together operate specific programs, facilities, or community services for young offenders who need mental health services. The two systems recognize their joint responsibility for subsets of youths whose behaviors and needs are associated with the responsibilities of both systems, and their funds are pooled for purposes of providing the specific programs or running the special facilities for these "overlap" youths.
- *Child-Centered Interaction:* Instead of developing specific intersystem programs or facilities, the juvenile justice and mental health systems take joint responsibility for obtaining whatever broad range of services a youth might need. Typically cases are managed by multi-agency teams, so that system boundaries are almost invisible, at least for purposes of finding clinical and rehabilitative services for young offenders with mental disorders.

In the years since this formulation of models of delivery of mental health services to young offenders, a number of communities have implemented variations on these three themes (e.g., Cocozza & Skowyra, in press), and research is underway to evaluate their effectiveness. There is no reason to believe that any one of these models is inherently superior to the others. What works for a particular community may depend on complex factors associated with its systems' budgets, histories, flexibility, and particular constellation of service providers.

Juvenile justice and mental health system interactions have a chance to work well in meeting the juvenile justice system's custodial treatment obligations, because the youths in question and the traditional objectives of both systems present a maximum opportunity for alignment of their interests. This does not necessarily mean, however, that the same will be true with regard to the juvenile justice system's obligations in the other two sociolegal contexts. Due process for adolescent defendants with mental disorders, and the management of public safety risks associated with them, are more closely aligned to juvenile justice objectives than those of the mental health system. We will confront those issues in the two chapters that follow.

*Chapter 6*

# Locating the Due Process Obligation

As the juvenile justice system of the 1990s moved progressively toward a model of just deserts patterned after the criminal justice system, it was necessary that juvenile courts pay increasing attention to due process in the adjudication of youths (chapter 1). Moreover, increases in the transfer (waiver) of youths to criminal court for trial "as adults" put the spotlight on developmental factors and mental disorders that might place them in special jeopardy in the adjudicative process. Special due process concerns focusing on adolescents and mental disorder have been raised regarding the following:

- Competence to waive *Miranda* rights "voluntarily, knowingly and intelligently"
- Capacities to participate meaningfully in their trials (competence to stand trial)
- Criminal responsibility (questions of "not guilty by reason of insanity")

What is the juvenile justice system's obligation to protect youths from unfair adjudicative consequences associated with their mental disorders? The legal, procedural, and clinical circumstances of each of these three due process issues are so different that they must be considered individually. Therefore, they form the three primary sections of this chapter, followed by a summary of policy and research questions that must be answered in order to fulfill the system's due process obligations to youths with mental disorders.

## Mental Disorder and the Waiver of *Miranda* Rights

### Context

Recall that the legal question about the waiver of *Miranda* rights is whether a youth, when making a statement to police officers, has waived the rights "voluntarily, knowingly and intelligently." When courts are required to weigh the validity of such prior waivers of *Miranda* rights, they are instructed to consider the "totality of the circumstances" (*Fare v. Michael C.*, 442 U.S. 707 [1979]). This includes (a) the circumstances surrounding police questioning, such as the actions of police officers when giving the *Miranda* warnings or eliciting a confession, as well as (b) characteristics of the youth that might have reduced his or her capacities to understand and weigh the nature of the waiver decision. An invalid waiver excludes the youth's statement (usually a confession) as evidence at trial. This applies in juvenile court and in criminal court if the youth is to be tried as an adult.

Although our focus is on the capacities of adolescents to make decisions about the waiver of their legal rights, a second question often raised regarding police interrogations of youths is the reliability or truthfulness of their confessions after they have waived their *Miranda* rights. There is mounting evidence of cases in which youths have confessed to police officers things that they did not do (e.g., Drizin, 2003). Whereas immaturity may increase the risks of false confessions (e.g., Gudjonsson, 1992), there is no systematic evidence about the relation of mental disorders to the truthfulness of youths' confessions, and theories that would provide a foundation for discussing the relation have yet to be explored. So our focus here is exclusively on the validity of waiver of rights, not the reliability of statements made thereafter.

At the time of *Miranda* waiver, some police officers might be concerned that a youth's waiver could be invalid due to his immaturity or mental disorder. After all, they have a prosecutorial interest in obtaining a confession that will stick. Little is known empirically, however, about whether or how often police officers consider these matters, and how it may affect their behavior.

A youth's obvious intoxication at the time of questioning probably suggests to some officers that they should delay the process if they want to use the confession in court. And in some jurisdictions suspects of a certain young age may not be asked to waive rights and make statements without parental involvement (Grisso, 1981). (Even so, parents may not waive or assert the rights for youths; only defendants may waive their constitutional rights in delinquency or criminal proceedings.) But in most jurisdictions, no particular procedures or requirements are in place urging police officers to investigate whether a youth might have a mental disorder that could invalidate the youth's waiver of *Miranda* rights.

Questions about the validity of waiver typically occur long after the period of police interrogation, several weeks or months into the adjudicative process. The question arises as a motion to the court by the youth's attorney for excluding the confession on the grounds that it was obtained improperly. In principle, the question could be raised by the judge, but in practice it arises only if the defense decides to make it an issue. No one has studied the practices of defense lawyers in this regard, but experience suggests that there are a number of factors that influence whether a youth's attorney will raise the *Miranda* waiver question:

- The attorney's competence, awareness of the legal issue, and assertiveness
- The nature of other evidence in the case (for example, other facts that substantiate the charges even without the youth's confession, reducing the importance of a challenge on the basis of invalid waiver)
- The seriousness of the charges and the costs of challenging the validity of the waiver (for example, whether the process and time required to argue the motion—sometimes prolonging pretrial detention—might not be in the best interest of the youth in a case involving very minor charges)
- Attorney, judicial, and legal uncertainty regarding the relevance of non-psychotic mental disorders for abilities associated with the invalidation of waiver of rights

If the waiver is challenged due to a youth's mental disorder (or on any other basis such as immaturity), typically defense counsel will need a forensic mental health evaluation by a clinical psychologist or psychiatrist to provide evidence regarding the youth's mental or emotional state at the time the police interrogation, as well as the effects this may have had on the youth's abilities to provide a valid waiver of rights. A few studies have provided procedural guidance for clinicians when performing these evaluations (e.g., Frumkin, 2000; Fulero & Everington, 1995; Grisso, 1998, 2003; Oberlander & Goldstein, 2001; Oberlander, Goldstein, & Goldstein, 2003), although little is known about typical practices. In general, the evaluation requires paying attention to the specific circumstances of the interrogation and to the characteristics of the youth (including mental disorder), and obtaining information to address whether and to what degree those characteristics are likely to have had a negative influence on the youth's understanding and reasoning at the time of the waiver. Most important for our purposes, this evaluation will require an examination of (a) the youth's relevant cognitive abilities and developmental status, (b) the presence of mental disorder and, if it is found, (c) the nature and degree to which it existed at the time of police questioning and, if it did, (d) the degree to which it might have impaired the youth's functioning in a way that is relevant for the legal question.

The forensic mental health evaluation may be sought independently by defense counsel or ordered by the court (on petition by defense counsel) and paid for with public funds. In the latter case, the evaluation may be performed by a mental health professional who typically performs court-ordered evaluations, or the courts in some jurisdictions allow defense counsel to use public funds to obtain an "independent" examiner.

Given this general context, our interest in the juvenile justice system's obligations to protect youths from the consequences of invalid waiver of *Miranda* rights boils down to two questions:

- Does the juvenile justice system have an obligation to impose special due process protections for youths with mental disorders *at the time of police questioning?*
- What are the system's obligations to youths with mental disorders to ensure that the question of the validity of the waiver is *properly raised during the adjudicative process* and, when raised, results in a proper clinical assessment and adjudication of the question?

The analysis here focuses primarily on special protections for adolescents with mental disorders. But it cannot be divorced from the broader issue of special protections that may be due to youths simply because of their developmental immaturity compared to adults.

## Police Interrogation

Law and policy concerning the need for special protections for youths in general at the time of police interrogation (Feld, 2000; Grisso, 1981) have focused primarily on the questioning of those under the age of fourteen, calling for a requirement to provide parental or attorney assistance prior to any request for a waiver of rights. Many jurisdictions have adopted rules of this type, and some of them require adult assistance for youths ages fourteen and older as well. But none go beyond age or intoxication when specifying any other characteristics requiring special caution.

Should police officers be required to delay interrogation of youths with mental disorders until legal counsel or parents are present to advise the youth? If so, two approaches to implementing the requirement are possible. Under the first approach, the assumption is made that most youths interrogated for suspected crimes have a mental disorder (based on current data on the prevalence of mental disorders among young offenders: chapter 1). Thus legal counsel or parental assistance would be required in the questioning of *every* juvenile suspect, with possible exceptions (e.g., questioning to stop crimes in progress). This approach is neither practically nor clinically satisfying. It could create considerable interference with effective law enforcement, prosecution, and public safety interests. It also presumes that we know the prevalence of mental disorders among youths questioned by police officers, which we do not since our data are based on the smaller proportion of youths who penetrate to the detained and adjudicated level of the system. Even if the prevalence rates could be applied, this approach presumes that all youths who meet criteria for mental disorders are sufficiently impaired in their functioning to warrant this protection. This probably is not the case (chapter 2), although in fact we simply do not know (chapter 4).

The second approach requires pre-interrogation judgments in each case regarding the presence and seriousness of mental disorder. But there is no reasonable way to fulfill this requirement. Given the circumstances, police officers could not obtain mental health records on the spot. Expecting them to administer a screening instrument for mental health needs to provide a reliable index of mental disorder would be absurd in such a high-stress context, as would inferences based on an interview by a mental health examiner (even provided that some system could be devised to make examiners available routinely for "prewaiver evaluations").

The only interrogation-level protection for youths with mental disorders that makes sense is to enhance the review of cases later in the adjudicative process. If the system is to exercise a special obligation to protect mentally disordered youths from invalid waiver of rights, that can best be done by focusing on postinterrogation review—the process whereby the validity of waivers is challenged—rather than on attempts to control the interrogation process itself.

*Postinterrogation Review*

The juvenile justice system should offer special protections to ensure that the potential for an invalid waiver due to the effects of mental disorder is reviewed early in the adjudication process. Two approaches can be taken for special protections with this purpose.

First, the system might require that judges review the waivers of all youths with mental disorders as they approach their trial dates. This could begin with some mechanism for identifying that a youth has a serious mental disorder with symptoms of sufficient severity that they seriously impair the youth's cognitive or social functioning. Mental health screening in intake probation and pretrial detention programs (see chapter 5) might provide a starting point for identifying such youths. When identified as potentially meeting some criterion for degree of disorder, youths who have waived rights and made confessions without assistance of parents or legal counsel could be scheduled automatically for forensic mental health evaluation and judicial review. The difficulty with this approach is deciding whether the costs are warranted by the protections it provides. For example, putting a youth through the ordeal of an additional forensic evaluation, and consuming valuable court evaluation resources, may be insensitive and wasteful when the prosecution's case is heavily based on evidence other than the youth's confession. In other cases it may actually be in the youth's interest to plead delinquent rather than challenge the allegation.

A good argument, therefore, can be made for a second approach that relies on defense counsel's discretion concerning whether to refer the question to the court. That request would trigger an assessment by a forensic mental health professional for an opinion about the nature of the youth's disorder and what effect, if any, it is likely to have had on his of her capacities to understand and decide at the time of waiver of the rights. In addition to allowing defense counsel to avoid *Miranda* evaluations where they are not in the youth's legal interest, it encourages counsel to raise the question in some cases that would not have met the "serious mental disorder" screen-in criteria of an automatic review approach. For example, attorneys might have an obligation to make every possible challenge in cases in which youths' might be transferred for trial in criminal court, where their confessions could be used to obtain substantial sentences "as adults." Thus, the judgment about whether to set in motion an assessment and a complete review of the validity of waiver is so closely tied to the task of building a defense that it is best left to defense counsel, not to automatic rules for routine review.

If this approach is accepted, then the system's obligation is twofold. *First*, it should develop a mechanism for routinely providing relevant information to defense counsel—for example, data from mental health screening, intake probation officer's knowledge of past mental health history—for purposes of considering the potential invalidity of *Miranda* waiver due to symptoms of mental disorder. *Second*, the court should make available adequate forensic mental health assessment services on the question of mental disorder and the youth's waiver when reasonably requested by defense counsel.

This approach hinges heavily on the quality of defense counsel. The system has an obligation to provide youths with attorneys who are aware of the importance of the question of waiver of *Miranda* rights, as well as the potential relation of mental disorder to abilities that are relevant for rights waiver decisions. Toward the end of this chapter I further explore the problem of ensuring the quality of forensic assessments and legal counsel for youths with mental disorders.

## Mental Disorder and Youths' Competence to Stand Trial

The legal label for this due process question can be misleading because it suggests that we are concerned about defendants' abilities to participate in the hearing at which they "stand trial." In fact, however, at issue is the defendant's ability to participate in the *process of adjudication,* which extends from arraignment through the hearings at which guilt or innocence and disposition are decided. In some jurisdictions, many youths— probably 80 percent or more—plead guilty and never actually have to participate in a formal courtroom argument about their cases. The adjudication process may go on for several weeks or months, and it includes the youth's participation with legal counsel in building a defense and considering options about pleading and plea bargaining. In some cases the amount of time during which they must participate in the adjudicative process can be quite long—one or two years for youths who are charged in juvenile court, participate in hearings regarding their transfer to criminal court and, if transferred, participate in the process of criminal adjudication. So our concern is not merely with the effects of mental disorder on adolescents' understanding and participation in the courtroom (although those are relevant). Our concern extends also to their understanding and decisionmaking throughout the process as they work with counsel in the development of a defense and consideration of legal options. Abilities relevant for these purposes are described in chapter 4.

*Context*

As noted in chapter 1, about two-thirds of the states have laws explicitly acknowledging that the protections of competence to stand trial apply in delinquency hearings, and only one state (Oklahoma) has rejected the application of the concept in juvenile court (Bonnie & Grisso, 2000). Judges are required to address the question of competence whenever it is raised, even if the evidence for concern is slight (*Drope v. Missouri*, 420 U.S. 162 [1975]; Grisso, 2003). In virtually every jurisdiction, any party—defense, prosecution, or the judge—may raise the question of the defendant's competence to stand trial at any time during the adjudication process (Melton et al., 1997). Nevertheless, in practice it will almost always be defense counsel that raises the question.

We have little information to suggest when or why defense counsel raises the question of competence to stand trial for their juvenile clients, but we know that they do not raise it in most cases involving youths with mental disorders. This is borne out by qualitative evidence (case examples) (Tobey, Grisso, & Schwartz, 2000), although it is easily inferred when one compares the small number of competence cases to the prevalence of mental disorder in studies of juvenile defendants. (This observation does *not* imply that the question should be raised for all youths with mental disorders; that question is addressed later.)

Many factors might influence whether defense counsel will raise the question in cases involving youths with mental disorders. They are similar to those suggested in the previous discussion of waiver of *Miranda* rights: (a) attorney competence and awareness of the legal issue; (b) clarity or uncertainty about the standard for competence when applied to youths, especially the degree to which the variety of mental disorders among them are legally and clinically relevant for questions of trial-relevant abilities; and (c) costs of raising the question weighed against the consequences.

The cost-benefit analysis is particularly pertinent in deciding whether to raise the question of competence to stand trial. Some attorneys will petition the court to address the question not so much because they are concerned about their clients' incompetence as because they believe the consequences may have secondary benefits for them (Barnum, 2000; Grisso, Miller, & Sales, 1987). For example, pretrial treatment or mental health evaluations for mentally disordered youths may be very hard to obtain in some jurisdictions. If those jurisdictions also provide for inpatient hospitalization during evaluation of a youth's competence to stand trial, this motivates some attorneys to raise the competency question, without actual concern about competence, primarily to obtain a mental health evaluation and immediate inpatient treatment that they believe their clients need.

Conversely, some attorneys will decide *not* to raise the question even if they believe their mentally disordered clients lack substantial abilities associated with competence to stand trial, because they wish to protect them from the secondary consequences. Will a hearing on the competency question itself require a delay in the process so that my client, already burdened with a mental disorder, must endure the stresses of pretrial detention even longer? If she is found incompetent to stand trial, might the disposition—treatment to restore competence so that the trial process can be resumed—involve a secure facility, where she will be further deprived of family contact and educational or mental health services she might otherwise have received in the community? Might it be better for her to avoid the competency question, plead guilty, and get things over with so that she can start the process of longer-range treatment?

Attorneys in these situations walk a tightrope between two ethical obligations. In the first instance (calling for a forensic evaluation without an interest in its intended purpose), they misuse the legal process in order to fulfill their obligation to meet the mental health needs of their clients. In the second instance, they choose to go forward at trial with potentially incompetent clients who may not be able to make decisions with the autonomy that due process requires, in order to fulfill their obligation to protect their clients from the consequences of a competency inquiry that may be detrimental to their longer-term welfare.

Jurisdictions vary regarding the procedures they employ for obtaining forensic mental health evaluations when the question of a youth's competence is raised. Some require evaluations in inpatient child psychiatric hospital units, while others allow for evaluations wherever the youth is residing (pretrial detention or at home). Models for the clinical process for evaluating an adolescent's competence to stand trial have been created (e.g., Barnum, 2000; Grisso, 1998). Typically they include a psychological description of the youth, an evaluation of type and severity of mental disorder, the youth's actual understanding and reasoning abilities relevant for participation (as defined in legal standards for competence), and the relation between the mental disorder and deficits in those abilities. The degree to which forensic examiners actually assess and provide information related to all of these conditions in juvenile cases is not known.

As noted in chapter 4, we have little empirical evidence regarding the actual relation between youths' mental disorders and their abilities associated with competence to stand trial. Moreover, case law itself has not yet provided appellate decisions that clearly define the ways in which immaturity or specific mental disorders of youths should be interpreted when applying the concept of competence to stand trial in juvenile court (Bonnie & Grisso, 2000; Redding & Frost, 2002).

When youths are found incompetent to stand trial due to the effects of mental disorders, the law typically provides that the trials be placed on hold while they receive treatment for "restoration of competence." Little is known about the nature of this treatment in most jurisdictions, although a few states have developed special competency restoration programs for juveniles (e.g., inpatient in Florida: McGaha et al., 2001; outpatient in Virginia: Virginia Department of Mental Health, Mental Retardation, and Substance Abuse Services, 2001). A juvenile's treatment progress must be assessed periodically to determine whether he or she has achieved competence (e.g., every three months or six months in some jurisdictions), and the trial process resumes whenever they have attained competence. Following well-established legal requirements in the criminal courts, the charges against juvenile defendants typically must be dismissed if competency is deemed incapable of being accomplished or if they do not attain competence within a specific period of time (within one year in some jurisdictions).

The circumstances of evaluations for youths' competence to stand trial if they are being tried in *criminal* court have never been described. Law provides them the same protections as for any other criminal defendant, of course. But the relevance of immaturity or specific developmental forms of psychopathology for competence to stand trial in criminal court is almost entirely unexplored and unspecified in most jurisdictions (Bonnie & Grisso, 2000; Redding & Frost, 2002). Moreover, forensic mental health examiners in criminal courts may or may not have an adequate knowledge of developmental psychopathology and special expertise in evaluating youths.

Given this context, a number of points in the adjudicative process warrant concern in view of the juvenile justice system's obligation to protect the right of youths with mental disorders to be competent to stand trial:

- Does the system have a special obligation to identify youths with mental disorders for whom the question of competence should be raised?
- What are the system's obligations regarding the assessment of mentally disordered youths for whom the question is raised?

- What are the system's obligations for treatment in cases in which youths with mental disorders are found incompetent?

## Raising the Question of Competence

As in criminal proceedings, all parties in delinquency proceedings are charged with ensuring the fairness of the trial process. This means that all bear some responsibility for raising the issue of a youth's potential incompetence to stand trial when they have evidence to suggest it. It is reasonable, however, to let most of that responsibility rest on defense counsel, who has the greatest opportunity to observe and interact with the youth while beginning the process of building a defense. Ideally there would be screening guidelines to assist counsel in identifying youths who are at greater risk of incompetence due to mental disorder. Grisso, Miller, and Sales (1987), for example, suggested that attorneys at least should consider the competence question for youths who have any one of the following characteristics:

- Twelve years of age or younger (more recent evidence suggests fourteen or younger: Grisso et al., 2003)
- Past mental health records indicate earlier diagnosis and/or treatment for a serious mental illness or mental retardation
- Past educational records suggest very low IQ or indicate that schools have identified a "learning disability"
- Pretrial behaviors suggest deficits in memory, attention, or interpretation of reality when compared to other youths of similar age in similar legal circumstances

These sorts of guidelines, however, should not be used to infer incompetence, nor should attorneys necessarily be required to raise the issue in every case in which these criteria are met. Not all youths with mental disorders of the type suggested in these guidelines manifest important deficits in competency abilities. The system should rely on the attorney's own observations of a youth who meets any of these criteria to suggest whether the question needs to be raised—for example, the attorney's own experience of talking to a youth who is so distracted that he does not seem to be able to grasp what the attorney is saying, or the suicidal youth who seems to have no interest in working with her attorney. Of course, this presumes a level of competence among juvenile defense attorneys to actually make such observations and recognize their potential importance. I further explore this issue in the final section of this chapter.

Bonnie and Grisso (2000) have suggested an exception to attorney discretion for one circumstance. They propose that the juvenile justice system consider a requirement to obtain an assessment and a judicial decision about competence to stand trial in *all* cases in which youths are being considered for transfer to criminal court for trial, and for all youths in criminal court in states that automatically charge juveniles as adults for certain offenses. This obligation rests on evidence that the risk of incompetence is greater for youths in general than for adults (see studies in chapter 4), and that the potential consequences of criminal prosecution warrant added protection. Its importance is even greater for youths with serious mental disorders. The proposal is not without difficulties. States that automatically transfer large numbers of youths (e.g., Florida, with several thousand a year) would find this number of competence evaluations a considerable burden. Moreover, in some states, the consequences of criminal court conviction after transfer are not necessarily substantially different from those in juvenile court, with many youths simply being placed on adult probation. So a desire to protect youths from unfair adjudications is only a starting point for deciding whether a state should require competency evaluations for all youths facing transfer. The decision must also be based on costs (to the state and to youths) and on the degree to which the protection seems to be needed in light of actual dispositions facing transferred youths in various types of transferred cases (e.g., seriousness of offenses) in the state in question.

## Assessments for Competence to Stand Trial

The system has an obligation to provide forensic mental health evaluations for competence to stand trial upon counsel's request. Evaluations should be timely and should not require inpatient hospitalization except in cases in which this is necessary for the youth's welfare. Evaluations related to trial competence require intimate knowledge of the developmental context for mental disorders that might impair the capacities of juveniles for trial participation (chapter 4). Thus competency evaluations should be performed by clinicians with specialization in both child/adolescent clinical conditions and a clear knowledge of the forensic issues involved. To avoid the possibility of providing information that would assist in prosecution, the evaluation should focus fairly narrowly on questions of competence to participate in future legal proceedings, not on matters pertaining to reasons for the juvenile's past or present offending. Laws or regulations should be in place—as they are in almost all criminal courts for adult defendants (Melton et al., 1997)—to prohibit the use of any information from this evaluation in adjudication hearings.

## Treatment for Incompetence

Laws of most jurisdictions will require that youths found incompetent due to mental disorder must be provided treatment in order to remediate their deficits. The specific purpose of treatment in such cases is to reduce symptoms sufficiently to allow competence abilities to improve (Barnum, 2000). When the symptoms responsible for those impairments are related to disorders such as depression, psychotic conditions, Posttraumatic Stress Disorder (PTSD) or Attention-Deficit/Hyperactivity Disorder (ADHD), treatment should include psychopharmacological or psychosocial methods that have been shown to have efficacy for those disorders (chapter 4). The system's primary obligation at this point is not only to provide effective treatment, but to do so in a context that avoids unnecessary restriction of liberty. Hospitalization should be avoided in favor of treatment in the community whenever possible, and reevaluation should be frequent and result in quick notification of the court when substantial gains have been made.

The system must recognize that the relevant abilities of some youths with mental disorders will not improve within a reasonable period of time—for example, cases that simply do not respond to otherwise effective treatments, youths whose mental disorders are comorbid with mental retardation that limits the cognitive gains that can be made, or those who manifest some improvement but who are limited by their immaturity associated with their very young age or developmental delays. When treatment does not achieve competence within a reasonable period of time (one year in the criminal laws of many states), the juvenile justice system must dismiss the charges and ensure that the youth continues to obtain necessary treatment services within the broader context of the state's child welfare system. While dismissing charges in such cases may seem insensitive to values associated with victim empathy and just deserts, the rule has been applied routinely in all jurisdictions in criminal courts for many decades (Melton et al., 1997). It is based on the principle that one may not use criminal charges as a justification for continued treatment and confinement in order to "restore" competence when there is little or no prospect that restoration can ever occur (*Jackson v. Indiana*, 406 U.S. 715 [1972]).

## An Insanity Defense in Juvenile Court?

The insanity defense constitutes admission to the alleged illegal act but a claim that the mental state that is required to hold an individual responsible for a criminal act was absent due to mental disorder, rendering the defendant "not guilty by reason of insanity" (NGRI). Among the more common definitions of the mental states in question is whether the defendant, due to mental disorder, was unable to "appreciate the wrongfulness" of the act or to "conform his conduct to the requirements of law" (Melton et al., 1997).

The relevance of the insanity defense as a legal concept in juvenile court is highly questionable. Even the most zealous juvenile advocates almost never raise the insanity defense in states that provide it for delinquency cases. Cases are rare in criminal court as well, where the defense is raised in less than 1 percent of adult felony cases (and is unsuccessful in three out of four) (for a review, see Borum, 2003b). But most juvenile justice jurisdictions have never seen an insanity defense raised in juvenile court, and many others may have seen only one or two in recent history. Either the relevance of the insanity defense has not been discovered by the juvenile court, or it has simply been deemed unnecessary.

One can offer reasons why the insanity defense *could* apply to delinquency cases as well as criminal cases. United States constitutional law has extended most of the protections of criminal court to defendants in juvenile court, and adolescents may sometimes have serious mental disorders that, at the time of the alleged offense, severely impair their "appreciation" of what they are doing or the type of self-control to which the insanity definition refers.

But from a clinical perspective, it is difficult to argue that the juvenile justice system should be obligated to consider the insanity defense in delinquency cases in juvenile court except in exceptional circumstances. In most delinquency cases, the outcome of a finding of not guilty by reason of insanity for a youth with serious mental disorder has no different consequence than if the youth were found delinquent. In either case, the system would be obligated to ensure the provision of whatever mental health treatment was needed in light of the youth's mental disorder and level of impairment. The only time that an NGRI defense in juvenile court might be of any different consequence would be in cases involving potential penalties that extended beyond the juvenile court's usual jurisdictional age. For example, for some of the most serious offenses, some states allow juvenile courts to retain custody of delinquent youths well beyond age eighteen, and some may sentence youths to periods of time extending to their twenty-fifth birthdays. In these cases, one might consider the juvenile justice system's obligation to provide the insanity defense for this small minority of youths with serious mental disorders, in that it is provided for adult defendants who face similar punitive consequences.

Having said this, it is difficult to imagine how the concept would be applied. After 150 years of experience with the insanity defense in criminal court, neither the law nor legal and mental health scholars have been able to agree on just what is meant by a "substantial lack of appreciation of the wrongfulness of one's act" or an "inability to conform one's conduct to the requirements of law" (Finkel, 1988; Melton et al., 1997). Some experts in forensic psychiatry have concluded that there is no way for mental health professionals to determine whether people, with or without mental disorder, were able to control their behavior at the time of an alleged offense, and law expressly forbids clinicians to offer such conclusions in federal cases (American Bar Association, 1989). In contrast to the concept of competence to stand trial, no empirical evidence exists to show that forensic psychiatrists or psychologists can make reliable judgments about the relation between defendants' mental disorders and these legal concepts. Given this history of the insanity defense, one can only imagine the chaos that would ensue if it were applied to youths with mental disorders that are far more complex, comorbid, fluid, and idiosyncratic than adult Schizophrenia, the disorder that has most commonly been involved in adult insanity cases.

In summary, the juvenile justice system should not be obligated to "protect" youths with mental disorders by offering them the insanity defense in delinquency cases, except in rare circumstances in which youths with mental disorders are being considered for transfer to criminal court. The meaning of the NGRI concept is vague, its application to adolescents with developmental forms of mental disorders is completely uncharted, and its legal and clinical consequences are of dubious value.

## Unanswered Questions for Policy and Research

Several challenges stand between the juvenile justice system's due process obligations to youths with mental disorders and its ability to meet those obligations. They include the need for (a) *legal clarity* regarding the system's application of due process concepts to cases involving youths with mental disorders, and (b) *competent professionals* to recognize and handle cases involving adolescents whose mental disorders require special attention.

## Discovering How Due Process Concepts Should Apply in Juvenile Cases

The legal concepts of trial competence and valid waiver of rights have developed in the context of criminal law applied to adults. As a consequence, the relation of mental disorders to these concepts has been heavily influenced by the nature of psychopathology in adults. For example, disorders such as Schizophrenia, Major Depression, and profound Mental Retardation are typical of almost all adult cases in which the question of competence to stand trial is raised. It can be argued that a wider range of disorders is relevant for questions of legal competence among adolescents. Many mood, anxiety, and attention deficit disorders create cognitive and emotional impairments in youths that are the equivalent of those seen in more serious disorders of adulthood (chapter 2), especially when they add to already deficient abilities associated with "normal" immaturity of adolescents.

It is imperative that the system make substantial efforts to clarify the application of competence criteria to mentally disordered youths in delinquency cases, as well as youths who are tried in criminal court. Those clarifications should not require the specific types of disorders that have dominated the application of the concepts in criminal law. In fact, they should not even define specific childhood disorders that "qualify" for meeting the legal criteria. They should focus instead on the nature of a youth's actual functional impairments—due to mental disorder—that are relevant for the competency concept. The focus should be on identifying the abilities that are relevant for defining a "competent defendant" in juvenile court, allowing for a broad recognition of the types of mental disorders that might impair those abilities.

This approach will be more easily adopted in juvenile courts than in criminal courts that try adolescents as adults. For example, few criminal courts will ever have seen cases in which the question of competence to stand trial was raised because of the adult defendant's ADHD or anxiety disorder. But those disorders in adolescents should not be considered irrelevant for the question of competence. (Of course, they should not be considered dispositive either; usually ADHD will not create disabilities that are so serious as to require a finding of incompetence.) Imagine an extreme case in which ADHD is responsible for an adolescent's inability to focus on decisions or the trial process. This consequence is as relevant for the legal question as if the same inability was due to the distractions of psychotic delusions. And it may be more relevant for an adolescent than for an adult, given the youth's lesser maturity (chapter 4).

Clarifying the application of legal standards requires either the modification of statutes or the establishment of new interpretations through case law. The justice system has a long way to go in modifying its laws regarding mental disorder and due process for adolescents through either of these mechanisms. For example, the laws of most states have yet to recognize "immaturity" as a potential reason for incompetence to stand trial, much less the implications of child and adolescent forms of psychopathology or severe learning disabilities for applying the concept in juvenile or criminal court.

## Can We Improve the Quality of Legal and Clinical Professionals?

If there is a single most important obligation of the system for protecting the legal interests of youths with mental disorders, it is *the obligation to provide them competent defense attorneys and competent forensic mental health professionals who perform evaluations related to waiver of rights and competence to stand trial.* Fulfilling this obligation requires solving problems related to both availability and competence of these professionals.

DEFENSE COUNSEL. The story regarding legal representation of youths in delinquency proceedings is told candidly and painfully by an American Bar Association document entitled "A Call for Justice" (Puritz et al., 1995: for all quotations in this paragraph). The vast majority of youths must rely on defense attorneys appointed by the court and paid by public funds. While many excellent and dedicated juvenile defense attorneys accept this role, juvenile bar advocates say that this is not the norm. Many public defenders for youths are "neophytes who receive less training than their prosecutorial counterparts" and who are "more concerned with maintaining ongoing relationships with the judges who appoint them than with protecting interests of their clients" (p. 22). Too frequent are views like that of one attorney who, when talking about representing youths, suggested that "It's better for my clients if I don't make a stink about their cases . . . judges don't like it when you file motions" (p. 32). In one study reviewed by Puritz et al. (1995), over one-half of public defenders of youths said they had little interest in juvenile law itself, most had no special preparation for representing youths, and only 15 percent thought of their role as being like that of a true defense attorney. It is the norm—not the exception—for youths in our nation's juvenile courts to have spoken to their defense attorneys only for a few minutes prior to trial, often in the hallway or holding cell just before entering the courtroom to offer their "defense" (which is often a guilty plea).

If these prospects for youths' representation are not sufficiently disturbing, one must recognize that in some jurisdictions adolescents in delinquency cases are not represented by counsel at all. They are guaranteed the constitutional right to legal representation by U.S. Supreme Court cases such as *In re Gault,* 387 U.S. 1 (1967). But in some juvenile courts they are asked to waive their right to counsel early in the pretrial process, and many youths do so before a defense attorney has ever been appointed (and thus, of course, without advice of counsel). This practice is particularly troubling in light of evidence that many youths are not competent to know what they are waiving (chapter 4). And their waiver of counsel typically means that no one will raise the question of their incompetence.

Thus it is clearly naïve to believe that our obligations to protect the rights of due process for youths with mental disorders are resolved by assigning the task to defense counsel. Ultimately something must be done to improve the average quality of lawyering for juveniles before we can expect any meaningful improvement in legal protections for young defendants with mental disorders. Puritz et al. (1995) prescribed a wide range of initiatives to begin to remedy the situation, including changes in law, comprehensive training efforts, certification standards, and monitoring of practice. An important part of this effort must include in-service training that improves juvenile defense attorneys' understanding of youths' developmental capacities, mental disorders, and their relation to legal questions about their competence and waiver of rights (e.g., Schwartz & Rosado, 2001).

Defense attorneys are not the only ones who need this education. Indeed, their heightened awareness of competency issues among juveniles may only increase their frustration if juvenile prosecutors and juvenile court judges with whom they work are unclear about the issues. Judges who are well informed about issues of juveniles' competency can communicate to defense attorneys the expectation that counsel attend to their clients' legal interests, and they can promote judicial education for attorneys and other juvenile court judges within their jurisdictions. Moreover, a fair use of criteria for competence in juvenile court will depend substantially on prosecutors' abilities to address the issues that defense attorneys raise in juvenile competence cases. Prosecutors and chief juvenile court judges can also have a significant influence on juvenile justice policy at a state or national level. But education of the defense bar is key to the solution, because it is up to defense counsel to know when to raise the issue of juveniles' competence.

FORENSIC MENTAL HEALTH PROFESSIONALS. Very little is known about the mental health professionals who are asked to perform evaluations for the courts in juvenile *Miranda* waiver and competence-to-stand-trial cases (Grisso, 1998). Examination of early data from a study in progress in urban areas of the United States (Grisso, Quinlan, & Vincent, 2003) indicates that most examiners who perform these evaluations are clinical psychologists, and most of them have some child and adolescent clinical training. Fewer, however, have specialized training in evaluations for forensic issues like competence to stand trial or *Miranda* waiver. Requests for competency evaluations in delinquency cases are rare (zero to ten per year) in about one-half of large juvenile courts and are frequent (over fifty per year) in a minority of them. One suspects that requests are far less frequent, and the assessment abilities of the examiners less forensically specialized, in smaller jurisdictions where the courts rely primarily on local child mental health agencies or private practitioners for occasional evaluations rather than on clinicians whose primary, everyday practice is service to the court. Currently little information is available, though, on the quality of competence evaluations in juvenile courts, either nationally or in specific jurisdictions.

The good news is that the issue of forensic evaluations for youthful offenders recently has gained national attention in the professional organizations and literature to which court examiners turn for guidance (chapter 4). Most clinicians whose practice substantially involves forensic evaluations for juvenile courts probably are at least aware of the fundamental issues involved in these evaluations. But they have not yet been provided reliable information with which to address those issues. They have not yet been given specialized tools and strategies for assessing competence in juvenile cases, and no national standards for those evaluations have emerged. Developmental psychology has provided *some* information on the development of decisionmaking abilities among adolescents compared to adults (see chapter 4), *a little* information about their decisionmaking in specific legal contexts (e.g., participation in one's trial: Grisso et al., 2003), and *almost no* information on the relevance of mental disorders for decisionmaking among adolescents in any context. These are priority areas for future research and development, and the field will be limited in its ability to improve due process protections for youths until researchers can provide information of this type.

## Chapter 7

# Fulfilling the Public Safety Obligation

Chapter 1 identified the juvenile justice system's mandate to reduce the likelihood of harm to others by youths in its custody. This creates three types of obligations: (a) to assess and identify youths who pose significant risk to the public in order to provide necessary security, (b) to reduce the risk through proper management to avoid current harm to others, and (c) through rehabilitation to reduce the risk of future violence by youths. Assessment, security, and rehabilitation issues arise at various points in juvenile case processing, and the relevant questions are asked (in principle) about every juvenile who passes through the system.

This chapter does not seek to develop comprehensive standards or strategies with which the juvenile justice system can fulfill these obligations in general. It addresses a narrower question. What role should *mental disorder* play in the system's process of assessing and identifying youths with high risks of violence, and thus in exercising greater security (e.g., pretrial detention, long-term secure rehabilitation) and special interventions when high-risk adolescents are encountered? Is mental disorder relevant and, if so, how is it relevant and what is the proper response?

This chapter first examines the various points in juvenile justice case processing where the assessment of risk arises, and reviews briefly some of the important lessons of chapter 4 regarding the relation between youths' mental disorders and their aggressive and violent behavior. Then these lessons are used to chart the system's public safety obligations regarding *short-range, medium-range,* and *long-range* risks of violence.

## When Does the Public Safety Obligation Arise?

There are three general points in the processing of delinquency cases when the identification of potentially violent juvenile behavior is most critical. One is at the *point of entry* soon after arrest and referral to the juvenile court. The second is at the *dispositional stage* of the process, when judgments are made about the placement of delinquent youths. The third is at the *point of exit from secure facilities or juvenile justice custody,* often requiring a judgment about the degree to which it is safe to release youths to the community.

### Judging Aggression Risk Going In

Soon after an adolescent is taken into custody by police officers, a decision must be made whether to allow the youth to live at home during further processing of the referral or whether he or she needs the security of a pretrial juvenile detention facility. Typically youths may be held in "emergency detention" at the discretion of police or probation officers and detention staff for a day or two (jurisdictions vary regarding the allowable time), but judicial review is required in most states to hold them beyond that brief period. The review decides in each case whether criteria (usually statutory) are met that justify continued detention. These legal criteria typically focus on the likelihood that the youth otherwise will be endangered, is likely to run away from home, or will endanger others in the community if not detained (Grisso, Tomkins, & Casey, 1988). Thus, while our discussion here is on the potential for harmful acts committed by juveniles against others, some youths will be held in detention because they themselves need protection—for example, when there is no parent or guardian available to provide the youth a place of residence. Once a juvenile offender is in detention, staff are expected to make judgments concerning whether he or she is likely to present a risk of harm to other youths or staff, so that they can exercise appropriate precautions to safeguard residents and themselves.

At this point in the process, the focus is on estimating the "short-range" risk of harm to others (or harm to the youth)—whether the person would be likely to harm others within the next few days, weeks, or months if not detained. Continued pretrial detention because of risk of harm to others is almost *pro forma* in many jurisdictions for youths charged with serious assaultive offenses. In other cases the judgment is often based on past offenses, observations of present behavior, and home conditions, as judged by the intake or supervisory probation officer. Many jurisdictions have developed their own sets of checklists and rating forms to assist in this judgment, typically employing "risk factors" that are believed to be important in identifying high-risk youths. Occasionally clinicians are asked to do brief evaluations to assist the court in the detention decision.

## Judging Aggression Risk at Disposition

There are three decision points at which the question of the risk of future harm to others affects disposition decisions: judicial transfer hearings, postadjudication disposition hearings, and state youth authority decisions about placement after commitment.

JUDICIAL TRANSFER (WAIVER) TO CRIMINAL COURT. Sending youths to criminal court for trial occurs in two broad ways. (Some states use both mechanisms, while some use one or the other: see Snyder & Sickmund, 1995; Fagan & Zimring, 2000). One approach requires that certain serious offenses by youths above a particular age (most often twelve or fourteen) are filed in criminal court automatically (typically called "statutory exclusion") or at the prosecutor's discretion. Many states have added this approach to their statutes during the past twenty years. The second approach, employed in most states since the earliest days of juvenile courts, makes youths' trial in criminal court a matter of juvenile court discretion, rather than automatic on the basis of the offense alone. In those states, prosecutors may petition the juvenile court for a judicial hearing to consider the transfer of a youth to the jurisdiction of the criminal court for trial as an adult (in some states, "waiver of jurisdiction," "certification," or "bindover").

These two general forms of transfer appear to have different motivations and purposes. The use of statutory exclusion—that is, automatic transfer based on the nature of the offense—is primarily a statement about the public's desire to "teach kids a lesson," or to make sure that youths get what the public perceives as appropriate punishment for serious offenses, or to deter them from committing transferable offenses in the first place. Transfer by judicial discretion, on the other hand, is governed by criteria that judges are supposed to weigh to determine whether the *youth*—not only the youth's offense—is of a "type" that should be tried under criminal law applied to adults.

In this second form of transfer, the "real" factors that go into judicial decisions to transfer youths are difficult to identify. Cases involving sensational or particularly heinous offenses sometimes create considerable public pressure on judges to transfer youths simply for retributive reasons. The legal criteria, however, specify that transfer requires evidence at a special hearing supporting the conclusion that the youth is "not amenable to rehabilitation" in the juvenile justice system and presents a significant "danger to others" (Grisso, Tomkins, & Casey, 1988). Paraphrased, these criteria are aimed at identifying those about whom the juvenile justice system concludes, "This is a youth who is a serious danger to others, and will continue to be a danger to others beyond adolescence, because there is a very low likelihood that this adolescent will respond to any rehabilitation or treatment efforts available to the juvenile justice system." In effect, the juvenile justice system is giving up on the youth, who is believed to be dangerous, unsalvageable, and a continuing threat to public safety.

The focus of these judicial transfer criteria is on estimating "long-range" risk of harm to others, in that the transfer question asks about risk not only during adolescence but also into adulthood. Forensic clinicians often are asked to evaluate adolescents scheduled for transfer hearings, so they can advise the court about the youth's characteristics that bear on the "amenability" and "dangerousness" criteria.

POSTADJUDICATION DISPOSITION HEARINGS. Disposition hearings follow courts' findings of delinquency. They focus in large part on whether a youth can be rehabilitated in the community while on juvenile court probation or should be committed to the state's youth authority (the juvenile equivalent of a state's department of corrections for adults). Most states' youth authorities have a range of program options, including greater levels of security than can be provided by most juvenile court probation departments. Thus the court's disposition decision is in part a judgment about the degree of security a youth is likely to need in order to ensure public safety during the period of rehabilitation or correction.

This requires an estimate of "middle-range" risk of harm to others— the likelihood of serious aggression during a period of months or years between the adjudication and the time that the youth will reach the end of a prescribed period of custody associated with the offense that was committed or the state's maximum age for juvenile justice custody. Typically judicial decisions are based on information provided by intake probation officers, and sometimes clinicians, who make rehabilitation and security recommendations to the court at the disposition hearing.

STATE YOUTH AUTHORITY PLACEMENT. In many states, when a juvenile court commits a juveniles to the state's youth authority, the youth authority itself decides whether it will work with them on probation in the community (at home, at community residential facilities) or in juvenile corrections facilities with varying degrees of security. That decision is based in part on judgments about the adolescent's likelihood of harm to others in the community if he or she were not incarcerated. These, too, are "middle-range" judgments about risk of harm to others during the person's remaining adolescent years. Often such decisions are made on the basis of prior offense record and other historical variables that locate the youth on a multidimensional table (sometimes called a "grid"). This assigns a level of risk to the youth, with the level itself determining his or her eligibility for community services or correctional facility placements with various degrees of security.

### Judging Aggression Risk Going Out

Finally, the system is obligated to make judgments about level of risk of harm to others when it considers transitioning the youth from more to less secure placements, and when it considers terminating probation or juvenile justice custody. One particularly important judgment may be made for some adolescents when they reach the age limit of the juvenile justice system (sixteen, seventeen, or eighteen, depending on the state). Many states have laws that allow the juvenile justice system to extend its jurisdiction over a youth beyond the maximum age under certain circumstances, sometimes to the age of twenty-one. Some states provide for this on the basis of a finding of continued danger to the community, while others require a finding of danger as well as continued need for treatment services that the system has been providing, or the need for a period of transition from a secure facility to the community in which the youth must establish contacts for the future.

These judgments generally focus on "short-range" and "middle-range" risks of harm, since they are concerned with transition and stabilization after custody. Judgments about long-range risk (likelihood of engaging in violent behavior during adulthood) usually are not relevant, because at this point the juvenile justice system typically would have no authority to retain jurisdiction beyond age seventeen or eighteen (or beyond age twenty-one if jurisdiction were extended), even if the youth were a high risk to society in the long run.

### A Summary of What We Know

These are the contexts in which the system might consider an adolescent's mental disorder to be a factor related to short-range, middle-range, or long-range risk of aggression. But, as reviewed in chapter 4, our actual use of mental disorders as factors in judging and responding to youths' aggressive behaviors is promoted and limited in the following ways.

There is evidence that adolescents' mental disorders may have some influence on their future aggression. When measured at a given point in time, some symptoms of mental disorders increase the likelihood of aggression in the short-range sense. But data on mental disorders often will not be of great use for longer-range judgments of risk. Symptom states may change considerably in response to further maturation or changes in stressful conditions in a youth's life, and because of the general discontinuity of some disorders during the adolescent years. Estimates of longer-range risk require evidence that a disorder (as well as aggressive tendencies) has persisted for some time—for example, that it began earlier in the youth's development and has continued across several years. Even so, the relation is not strong enough to be predictive. For example, youths with persistent symptoms of Attention-Deficit/Hyperactivity Disorder (ADHD) and Conduct Disorder (CD) are at greater risk of aggression in the long-range sense than youths with other mental disorders, yet only some of them actually continue to be aggressive threats beyond adolescence. The norm of desistance from aggression as adolescents age into adulthood holds even for this group.

The literature on mental disorders and aggression in youth (chapter 4) provides a number of other cautions to keep in mind:

- Research is discovering a number of "pathways" to (and out of) aggressive patterns of behavior, creating complexity in efforts to estimate or predict continuity of aggression in individual cases.
- The few "principles" that are arising in research cannot necessarily be applied to girls and to ethnic minority youths, whose patterns of development and relations between mental disorder and aggression might be different than for boys and non-Hispanic white youths.
- The fact of comorbidity of disorders among adolescents complicates the relation between mental disorder and aggression (as when Substance Use Disorders are related to increased aggression when comorbid with ADHD or CD but far less so when comorbid with internalizing disorders)
- Adolescents with mental disorders are more likely to have juvenile justice system involvement than youths without them, but mental disorder is far less helpful in distinguishing between more or less aggressive youths *within* the juvenile justice system.

Regarding the relation between treatment of mental disorders and aggression, there is evidence (chapter 4) that some forms of treatment reduce symptoms of mental disorder and reduce both aggression and delinquency recidivism. However, most of these studies assess outcomes over a relatively short-range or medium-range period of time. Little research has addressed whether treatment creates a longer-range benefit—for example, whether aggressive youths with mental disorders who obtain treatment during adolescence are less likely to engage in violent behaviors as they mature into adulthood than similar youths who do not receive treatment.

Given what is currently known about these matters, what are the juvenile justice system's obligations to identify and respond to youths' mental disorders in the interest of public safety? Separate analyses are needed for measuring the short-range risks at intake, the medium-range risks during treatment, and the long-range risks to society as adolescents age into adulthood.

## Mental Disorders and Risks of Harm at Intake

### Assessing Mental State at Intake

Mental and emotional states that may be symptoms of mental disorders should be identified for public safety purposes at probation and detention intake, and should be available when decisions are made regarding the need to continue detention beyond an emergency period. There is sufficient theoretical and empirical evidence (chapter 4) to believe that certain symptoms of some mental disorders among youths warrant an increase in concern about their short-range potential for aggression. When current mental states of adolescents are assessed at the detention decision point and found to include potentially important symptoms of mental disorder associated with aggression—for example, anger associated with depression, anxiety associated with trauma, or hyperactive impulsiveness—these conditions do not "predict" imminent aggression. But they increase the risk of it, especially if the youth is expected to be in an environment that may include provocation or stressful situations if not detained.

*More than the mere "existence" of anger or anxiety would be necessary, of course, even to warrant short-range concern.* Many youths are angry or anxious from time to time without posing a risk of harm. And the period of time involving arrest and detention is likely to engender some degree of these emotions for most adolescents. As measured, the mental or emotional states in question would need to be high or intense in relation to one's peers in order to warrant increased concern—that is, high in comparison to other same-age youths (consistent with a developmental perspective on psychopathology: chapter 2) under similar circumstances (for example, at time of arrest).

This assessment obligation can be met with mental health screening measures (see chapter 3) that provide triage regarding mental and emotional states, including anger or hostility. None of these methods can predict aggression, of course, but they are capable of indicating the presence and severity of various thought, emotional, and behavioral symptoms of mental disorder associated with risk of aggression.

Across time, however, the value of a single moment-in-time measurement of a youth's symptoms will decrease. Changes in mood and affect are more the rule than the exception for most adolescents. And evidence in chapter 4 suggested that a majority of youths who manifest mental health problems at one point in time do not manifest them persistently across a year or two. A single measure does not help us to distinguish whether a persons anger, sadness, anxiety, or impulsiveness (or the lack of them) is transient or whether it is characteristic of that person across time. A symptom may be relevant for short-range concerns even if it is transient. But brief measures alone cannot tell us whether it will have continued significance as the time since the measurement increases by several weeks or months.

This suggests two cautions. First, to ensure the safety of other juveniles and the public, *evaluation for mental states related to aggression should be repeated periodically* while youths are in detention. This would, in fact, be routine for youths who initially showed severe symptoms, if detention centers sought more comprehensive assessments for them as recommended under the custodial treatment obligation outlined in chapter 5. Second, the information obtained from brief screening instruments at this point *should not be used to make any guesses about middle-range or long-range risk.* Information from front-door assessments of depression, anger, or impulsiveness should not follow youths into the courtroom several weeks or months later. The information often will be obsolete or irrelevant regarding middle-range concerns at the disposition hearing. Moreover, pretrial screening and assessment data should be prohibited from use in adjudication hearings (see chapter 5).

Of course, symptom information when determining whether a youth needs secure pretrial detention for public safety should be only one piece of information among several. Typically some information is available regarding any aggressive incidents in the adolescent's immediate past (that is, the past few days), and sometimes detention staff or probation officers are aware of family, community, and peer stressors (or positive family support) that represent the environment to which the youth would be returning if not detained. Many of these factors are used in the Structured Assessment of Violence Risk in Youth (SAVRY: Borum, Bartel, & Forth, 2002), a tool that offers good potential as a second screen for youths whose characteristics raise concern on the first brief screening of mental and emotional states. Symptoms of mental disorders may take on more or less significance in light of these additional observations (Grisso, 1998).

## Managing Risks of Harm at Intake

The system also has an obligation, of course, to do something to reduce the risk of harm to others when a youth's symptoms suggest a substantial risk. Placement in pretrial detention is one response, but it is not the end of the system's obligation. Once detained, some juveniles manifest conditions that threaten other adolescents or staff in the detention facility itself. When these conditions are potentially related to symptoms of serious mental disorders, merely exercising staff members' usual disciplinary options to control youths' behavior often will not reduce the risk. Anger resulting from depression, irritability associated with anxiety, and delusional thinking that includes the notion that other people are a threat to oneself usually cannot be "disciplined away." As in the custodial treatment obligation at the pretrial detention stage, the public safety obligation also requires that the juvenile justice system seek psychiatric consultation in such cases, and emergency inpatient mental health services when necessary, in order to reduce the severity of the symptoms that are behind the risk to others in the immediate environment. Psychopharmacological interventions that have been found efficacious in reducing symptoms associated with aggression (chapter 4) will often play some role in this response.

Detention, however, is not the only response to a risk of harm to the public. Other possible responses include allowing the youth to return home with arrangements for accepting voluntary services from community mental health programs while awaiting trial, finding the youth a temporary community placement (e.g., temporary foster home), or foregoing detention altogether in favor of immediate treatment in an adolescent inpatient psychiatric program.

But why would a juvenile justice system even consider nondetention options when youths present a risk of harm to others? The answer lies in two considerations. First, *there is no absolute level of risk that determines whether youths should be placed in secure detention prior to trial.* "Risk" is encountered in degrees across cases. No bright-line of risk clearly defines when adolescents should be detained and when they should not. Some clearly are high risk, some are little or no risk, and some present more equivocal degrees of risk for which the need for detention is less certain. And courts themselves will differ in the degree of risk that they are willing to tolerate when making the detention decision. Thus some youths may not be detained although they present a "moderate" level of risk in relation to their peers. When this is so, and when symptoms of mental disorders are part of the condition creating the risk, the system should be obligated to ensure that youths obtain and accept mental health services in the community to safeguard against the escalation of symptoms—and an increase in risk of harm—during the immediate future.

The second consideration is that *detention may not be the best place to ensure public safety in some cases involving very disruptive mental disorders.* For those with psychotic-like symptoms that seriously impair their functioning and self-control, placing them in detention to determine whether they might "settle down" in a few days not only runs serious risks of increasing their suffering, but also may exacerbate their symptoms, increase the likelihood of violence, and create undue risks of harm to others in the detention facility. In such cases, detention should be bypassed for immediate hospitalization.

## Mental Disorders and Risks of Harm during Treatment

The focus in this section is on the relation of mental disorder to risk of harm at the dispositional stage of legal processing and during the period of time when the juvenile justice system has custody of the youth for rehabilitation and treatment purposes. Two public safety concerns are raised at this point for adolescents with mental disorders: (a) whether their mental disorders contribute to increased risk requiring security measures during their custody, and (b) the degree to which their mental disorders require special treatment that will reduce future risk of aggression. Both of these are issues for medium-range judgments about risk of aggression. Does the youth's mental disorder contribute to increased risk during the expected period of custody (typically several months to a year or two)? And should the dispositional plan, and the ensuing period of custody, include treatment for the youth's disorder because of a prospect for decreased risk of aggression at least during the adolescent years? Because attending to medium-range risk is also involved in deciding whether to release youths from secure placements or from custody itself, I examine special obligations associated with those decisions as well.

## Making Dispositional Recommendations about Risk of Harm

Chapter 5 identified the system's obligation to perform comprehensive mental health evaluations for use in disposition hearings, when information from mental health screening or other sources suggests that the youth's functioning may be impaired by symptoms of mental disorder. Chapter 5 also described the process and content of those disposition evaluations. The public safety obligation simply adds to that recommendation the need for the evaluation to include data and careful interpretation regarding the implications of the youth's mental disorder for risk of harm to others during the future custody and rehabilitation, as well as the role that treatment for mental disorder should play in reducing the postcustodial risk of aggression.

Such an evaluation obviously will require a thorough diagnostic assessment, involving both structured methods and clinical interviewing by a professional with child clinical expertise. But our limited ability to make estimates of the risk of aggression beyond a few weeks or months suggests that the evaluation cannot rely solely on a clear picture of the youth's *current* status. As judgments about risk of harm focus on periods of time increasingly removed from the present, they require ever more detailed historical information about the past—about the youth's course of development, both normal and pathological, as well as information about the family and environmental context in which that development has occurred.

This information must also include data to build a picture of the adolescent's pattern of past aggressive behavior. This requires going far beyond "arrest records" and general descriptions of "unruliness." For example, some aggressive youths are aggressive wherever they go, but most are more or less aggressive depending on the social contexts they encounter. Thus one youth may get into fights while on the street, but show few signs of aggression in structured, supervised settings like school. Another may only exhibit aggression when confronted by authority. Some aggressive adolescents frequently exhibit aggressive behavior, while others are usually quiet until they suddenly "explode." (For a more detailed discussion of these variables in child clinical assessments of risk of harm, see Borum, 2000; Grisso, 1998.) As a consequence, examiners have an obligation to obtain information from past school and mental health records, as well interviews with parents and other third parties with frequent contact with the youth.

Only in this way can they acquire the types of information that will augment diagnostic results when trying to describe levels, types, and probable conditions of future risk.

This needs to be stressed because it must be taken into consideration when juvenile courts construct their expectancies for disposition assessments involving youths with serious mental disorders. Courts cannot expect examiners to perform these evaluations adequately by giving the youth a paper-and-pencil test and asking a few diagnostic questions. At least two to three weeks are required—sometimes more—to request and obtain relevant records from various agencies, arrange and conduct interviews, give and score various tests, process the information, and write a report for the court. Part of the juvenile justice system's obligation is to provide the resources and time to allow this process to happen in a manner that fulfills the public safety objective with integrity.

Having said this, we must acknowledge that even dispositional assessments of the best quality cannot be expected to provide courts with empirically validated probability statements regarding the degree of risk if a youth were not placed in a secure facility. Instruments designed to approximate that level of certainty for juvenile offenders are only now being developed (chapter 3). In the meantime, the obligation is fulfilled if courts are provided reliable and complete information about adolescents' mental disorders, as well as logical interpretation that characterizes youths as presenting lower, higher, or similar levels of risk compared to their peers who come before the court. Even if this is all that is achieved, it will be more than is normally found in current juvenile court practices.

## Deciding to Provide Treatment to Reduce Risk

Disposition assessments should describe, and the juvenile justice system should make available, treatment that will reduce the risk of future harm associated with mental disorders of aggressive youths. Typically the treatments identified in chapter 4 and discussed for the custodial treatment obligation in chapter 5 are those that are needed to satisfy the public safety obligation. By and large, treatments that have been found to reduce symptoms of mental disorder in aggressive youths have also reduced aggression and recidivism (chapter 4), at least for periods that might be called middle range (during adolescent years). Whether they reduce the long-range risk of aggression (behavior later in adulthood) has not been determined for most treatments.

Clinical debates about the treatment of aggression in delinquent youths sometimes ask whether treatment for mental disorders can actually be expected to make a dent in the public safety issue, given that youths with mental disorders may have underlying antisocial personalities—represented, for example, by comorbid Conduct Disorder—that are the "real" source of their aggression. If this is so, isn't treating symptoms of mental disorder irrelevant for many youths from a public safety perspective?

Undoubtedly, adolescents with both antisocial characteristics and mental disorders do exist, and for them, treatment of their disorder might not provide the ultimate "success" that we seek. But two considerations suggest that the treatment of Conduct Disorder youths for their comorbid psychiatric disorders is worth the effort. First, even in antisocial youths, it is likely that reducing symptoms of anxiety- or depression-related anger also reduces the risk of short-range and medium-range aggressive incidents, in that it lessens the likelihood that they will react emotionally to potential triggering events. Second, diagnosis of Conduct Disorder is made on the basis of repetitive and illegal behavior over a significant period of time (chapter 2). It is likely that in many youths, the diagnosis itself was made on the basis of behavior that was the consequence of their other mental disorders. In other words, the label "Conduct Disorder" is not necessarily a sign that a youth has an "antisocial personality" that will continue to threaten society even if other symptoms are successfully reduced. In this light, it would seem unwise to forgo treatment of young Conduct Disorder offenders to reduce their aggression risk, based solely on the notion that "treatment might change symptoms, but it won't change their underlying antisocial character."

## Mental Disorders and Long-Range Risks of Harm

As noted earlier in this chapter, all states provide for the transfer (waiver) of some young offenders to be tried in criminal court. Statutes typically require that the offense charged must be serious (often assaultive), and that the youth must be above a certain minimum age (typically twelve, thirteen, or fourteen). We reviewed two types of transfer. One of these—judicial transfer—requires a court hearing and a judgment about the youth's "dangerousness" and "amenability to treatment," both of which focus primarily on the risk of long-range (adulthood) aggression if the youth is retained in the juvenile justice system. Two other mechanisms—statutory exclusion and prosecutor discretion—transfer youths based primarily on their age and the nature or frequency of their offenses, without a judicial consideration regarding their psychological characteristics or mental conditions. What is the juvenile justice system's obligation to consider adolescents' mental disorders in relation to these two types of transfer, given the system's interest in reducing long-range risks of harm to others when youths reach their adult years?

## Judicial Transfer

In cases in which juvenile courts are considering the transfer of young offenders to criminal court for trial, the system should be obligated to provide the court a thorough and comprehensive developmental and mental health evaluation. This follows from the presumption that the history and course of some mental disorders of adolescence bear some relation to the risk of long-range aggression. In addition, the prospect for treatment of those disorders is relevant for the question of their long-range risk of aggression, and thus relevant for the "danger" and "amenability to rehabilitation" questions that drive the judicial transfer decision.

But can mental health professionals actually provide that information? Standards recently have been proposed for performing mental health evaluations specifically to address the questions raised in transfer hearings (Grisso, 1998, 2000a), as well as questions of future aggression (e.g., Borum, 2000). But can mental health examiners determine whether an adolescent's prior offending has been in part a function of his mental disorder? And can they project which youths with mental disorders are more and less likely to respond to treatment for their disorders, thus reducing or augmenting the long-range risk of danger to others in their adult years?

These questions are extraordinarily complex. From the general literature on prediction of future violent behavior (chapter 4), we know that the mere presence of current symptoms or aggressive behaviors at a point in time in adolescence has little value for long-range predictions of risk of violence during adulthood. From the field of juvenile criminology (chapter 4), we know that (a) most youths who engage in delinquent behaviors in adolescence desist from serious illegal behaviors as they age into adulthood, and that (b) youths with certain patterns of development of mental disorders and aggressive behavior are less likely to desist in the long run. Yet even among those in the latter "high-risk" group, only a minority manifest serious aggression persisting into adulthood, and we have yet to develop good ways to distinguish among them in a predictive sense. From the field of developmental psychopathology (chapter 2), we know that the continuity of youths' mental disorders—whether they will persist throughout adolescence and into adulthood—differs from one disorder to another and is difficult to predict from case to case. There are some treatments that will decrease the persistence of their disorders (chapter 4). But there is little information to distinguish between youths for whom this is more or less likely to happen given that they are provided treatment—that is, which of them are more or less "amenable" to efficacious treatments that the system might offer them. In short, our current state of knowledge based on empirical research about adolescent offenders' mental disorders provides only very limited guidance for projecting their long-range risk of harm to others.

Why, then, should a mental health evaluation be mandatory for transfer hearings involving the question of treatment responsiveness and long-range risk of harm? If clinicians cannot provide courts with opinions—based on sound research evidence—regarding the relation of youths' current mental disorders to their long-range risk of harm, should they be providing any judicial input at all? The answer is yes, but the answer itself reveals a serious risk in the use of clinical information in transfer cases.

The legal criteria for transfer mandates that a judge must decide whether a youth will be a danger to others beyond the adolescent years. Neither law nor science provides any clear guidance for judges in making this decision. But few would deny that the decision, however it is to be made, requires knowledge of the life circumstances of the youth thus far. If those circumstances include a mental disorder, it would be strange to conclude that information about it should go undiscovered or ignored by the court, even if its relation to future, long-range violence is empirically uncertain. In many cases the information at least helps provide a context for the youth's past and current aggressive behavior, and it is reasonable to expect judges to want to make inferences about the nature of a youth's current aggression when attempting the task of estimating the risk of future aggression. Moreover, imagine that a youth has a particular mental disorder for which there is a psychopharmacological or psychosocial treatment with known efficacy, he has yet to receive that treatment, and his characteristics are similar to those of youths who have benefited from it in the past. Would one wish to exclude that information from judicial consideration because (a) one is not sure that the mental disorder caused the youth's past aggression, and (b) there is no evidence that this would necessarily reduce this particular youth's likelihood of future aggression in adulthood?

From this perspective, it seems clear that mental health evaluations should be a part of the process of transfer hearings. The information they can provide about the past and current status of adolescents with mental disorders would seem to be necessary for any logical consideration of their future treatment response and long-range aggression, even if there is little scientific evidence to make those predictions.

But note that this explanation for the relevance of mental health evaluations in transfer cases also identifies their risks. The judge is required to make a decision with great uncertainties and little guidance. The clinician can provide information that is relevant for the decision, but without a scientific basis for reducing the uncertainties about how the information should be used. In these circumstances, judges often want more from clinicians than they can provide—an "answer" to the questions of long-range aggression and amenability—and clinicians will want to be helpful. This dynamic can draw clinicians well beyond the boundaries within which they can legitimately provide information about an adolescent's disorder, its relation to current and past offending, and the potential value of particular types of treatment. They often expect—and are expected—to conclude their evaluations by offering opinions and testimony about the "answer" to the "future dangerousness" and "amenability to treatment" criteria, the very conclusions for which they do not have an empirical foundation.

One might say that clinicians are in no poorer position than judges, and are possibly in a better one, to draw such conclusions (an argument the U.S. Supreme Court itself made for admitting mental health experts' predictions of future aggression as evidence: *Barefoot v. Estelle*, 463 U.S. 880 [1983]). But that very status as "expert" means that judges are likely to place more weight on clinicians' opinions than their science can support. The better use of mental health evaluations in transfer cases is to ensure that judges understand the role of mental disorder in a youth's offending, as well as the treatment prospects, without expecting that clinicians have a scientific basis for answering the bottom-line questions with which the court is faced.

## Nonjudicial Transfer (Statutory Exclusion, Prosecutor Discretion)

When charges against juvenile offenders are filed in criminal court by statutory exclusion or prosecutor discretion (based largely on offense and age), one would think that little could be said about the juvenile justice system's obligations to those youths. After all, after transfer they are not in the juvenile justice system's jurisdiction, and no juvenile court had any hand in transferring them. *But the juvenile court is not only a system for processing youths. It is also a political force with some influence in the making of laws that affect them.* Therefore, it is worthwhile to consider what obligation the juvenile court might have regarding youths with mental disorders whose charges are automatically filed in criminal court.

A majority of young people who offend meet criteria for at least one mental disorder, and in some of those cases their mental disorders seriously impair their functioning and play some role in their offending. Only some of the latter cases present a substantial risk of long-range persistence of either mental illness or aggressive behavior in adulthood. Yet statutory exclusion brings all of these youths into criminal court as long as they are over a certain age and are charged with a serious offense. Statutory exclusion makes no distinction among adolescents regarding those who have mental disorders, those who have persistent patterns of development of disorders and aggressive behaviors, or those whose mental disorders may respond to treatment that would reduce long-range risks to public safety.

What happens when these disordered adolescents arrive at the doorstep of the criminal justice system? We have virtually no reliable information describing young defendants with mental disorders who appear in criminal courts, much less reliable information about their fate. But on its face, the nature of most criminal courts offers no reason to believe that they are equipped to identify adolescents' mental disorders. Many adult defendants have mental disorders, but this does not prepare criminal courts to recognize developmental forms of psychopathology, given their many differences and complexities compared to adult psychopathology (chapter 2). Even if a criminal court were to call for a mental health evaluation (and there is no evidence concerning whether or how often this is done for adolescents in criminal court), the criminal justice system's forensic mental health examiners often are not qualified to evaluate children, and the court itself is unprepared to grasp the significance of youths' disorders for their offending. Moreover, if youths' mental disorders are identified while they are in the criminal justice system, the system's laws and procedures do not ensure that careful attention will be paid to them. And even if they did, the likelihood that the system could provide or arrange for appropriate mental health treatment of adolescents is probably small.

Therefore, transferring youths with mental disorders to the criminal justice system is almost certain to produce some volume of cases in which the justice system fails to provide treatment in the interest of long-range public safety. The risk is compounded by the fact that many youths tried in criminal court will not receive lengthy sentences, but will be returned to the community on probation, usually under the loose supervision of criminal court probation officers who have no knowledge of adolescent development, developmental psychopathology, or community mental health resources for adolescents.

Not all young offenders with mental disorders need treatment for public safety purposes, and not all young offenders with mental disorders should necessarily be retained in the juvenile justice system. But statutory exclusion as a mechanism for transfer provides no way to potentially identify those youths for whom the long-range risk might be reduced with treatment—adolescents for whom public safety interests would be better served by retaining them in the juvenile justice system where they might be provided treatment.

Given these circumstances, one might propose that the juvenile justice system, as part of its public safety obligation, should actively seek the development of laws and procedures that make special provisions for avoiding inappropriate prosecution of youths with mental disorders who are charged with offenses in criminal court. The proposal would urge this obligation because of the risk to public safety when the criminal justice system does not provide treatment to youths whose further development of aggressive patterns of behavior might be avoided. This obligation can be advanced even though we do not know specifically which adolescents, with what types of mental disorders and aggression histories, will be long-range risks. The fact that statutory exclusion is indiscriminate means that the criminal justice system is receiving but failing to respond to at least some youths with mental disorders whose treatment could enhance public safety.

If the juvenile justice system has a public safety obligation to attend to this issue, what alternatives could it seek in the form of "special provisions for avoiding inappropriate criminal court prosecution of youths with mental disorders?" Two broad options are possible, but both meet with substantial objections.

One option is to provide for hearings prior to arraignment for those transferred to criminal court through statutory exclusion. In each case, the hearing would determine whether criminal court prosecution is appropriate in light of the adolescent's developmental and mental health status. Mental health evaluations would be performed in preparation for the hearing. A variation on this theme would create routine assessment, perhaps including a diagnostic tool like the Voice DISC-IV (see chapter 3) that could determine the need for a more comprehensive evaluation.

Some states already provide for a "reverse transfer" hearing of this type (Snyder & Sickmund, 1995), although little is known about the nature of the hearings or the criteria that criminal courts apply to make their decisions. There is no evidence that the identification and consideration of mental disorders receive any special attention in current reverse transfer hearings.

A proposal for the routine evaluation and judicial review of mental disorders for statutorily transferred youths raises many questions and problems:

- Who would perform the evaluations? The criminal courts' usual mental health examiners typically would not be competent to diagnose and describe the consequences of adolescents' mental disorders.
- What would be the consequences of procedural delay? The proposed evaluations would further prolong the adjudication of youths, with some consequence for their development and the courts' dockets.
- What would be the costs? They would be negligible in some states (statutory exclusion transfers a few cases annually in Massachusetts, where it is limited to first-degree murder charges) and enormous in others (Florida transfers for a wide range of offenses, resulting in 2,000 transferred youths annually in recent years).
- What legal standards would be applied? Various standards are possible, requiring a focus on medium-range or long-range risks, definitions of applicable mental disorders, and standards and burdens of proof.
- What empirical guidance could be offered? As noted earlier, the state of knowledge regarding the relation between youths' mental disorders, aggressive behaviors, predictions and trajectories for future aggression, and effects of treatment on those trajectories is frustratingly limited.

Many of these obstacles are created by society's decision to subject children to a system of criminal law designed for adults. But adolescents are not adults. The criminal justice system cannot provide a meaningful solution to public safety questions pertaining to youths with mental disorders any more than clinical diagnostic systems developed for adult psychopathology can provide a meaningful structure for understanding child psychopathology (chapter 2). Legal, social, diagnostic, forensic, and treatment systems developed for adults do not work for young offenders with mental disorders. Attempts to "fix" the criminal justice process so that it can better respond to adolescents with mental disorders probably would be a wasted effort.

The second alternative, therefore, is to abolish statutory exclusion laws, providing for transfers to criminal court only by juvenile court discretion based on evidence provided at judicial transfer hearings. This would offer the best review of cases to determine those in which treatment for mental disorders in the juvenile justice system, rather than incarceration in adult prisons, might best serve the public's long-range safety interest, as well as those cases in which patterns of development suggest little benefit of continued care by the juvenile justice system.

This proposal would meet with substantial resistance from those who argue that statutory exclusion is an important tool in dealing with juvenile crime. Moreover, an argument can be made for retention of statutory exclusion laws by asserting that intentions to abolish it in the interests of youths with mental disorders are bogus. The sentiment against statutory exclusion presumes that those persons retained in the juvenile justice system for treatment to reduce the risk of future aggression will actually receive that treatment, and that the treatment they receive will have known efficacy. As matters stand today, few if any juvenile courts can make that claim. Better solutions for ensuring public safety through treatment of young offenders with mental disorders will first require that the system live up to the proposed custodial treatment mandate.

## Unanswered Questions for Policy and Research

The juvenile justice system's public safety obligation raises some of the most pressing and difficult questions one encounters when addressing the problems associated with young offenders and their mental disorders. A few of the more salient issues include (a) the need for research to provide information relevant to public safety decisions about young offenders with mental disorders, (b) the need to resolve a conflict between the objectives of short-range and long-range public safety, and (c) the absence in the juvenile justice system of an adequate response to young offenders with chronic and persistent mental disorders.

### *Research to Improve Decisionmaking about Risk of Harm*

Cautions about what we do not know regarding the relation of mental disorders and future aggression among adolescents have been offered at every turn in this chapter. Glancing back over the section in chapter 4 that explores issues related to the public safety context will bring into focus a host of unanswered questions in this area that require attention by researchers. Among these, a few are especially pressing in light of the juvenile justice system's policy and practice needs:

• *Developing Risk Assessment Tools and Strategies.* Clinicians are greatly in need of empirically validated measures and strategies for assessing risk of future aggression among youths. Prototypes are now available (e.g., EARL-20B and SAVRY: see chapter 3), and current research to develop their validity should also provide new information on the relation between mental disorders and future aggression among young offenders.

- *"Pathway" Research on Aggression and Mental Disorders.* Some of the most important studies of delinquency in the past ten years have investigated developmental pathways to persistent delinquency and to desistance in aggression during the transition from adolescence to adulthood (chapter 4). Parallel to these studies, the field of developmental psychopathology has increased its investigation of continuity and discontinuity in the development and course of various types of mental disorders in children and adolescents. The field needs a marriage of these two strands of research, examining the developmental trajectories of aggressive behavior in the context of the development of mental disorders (not merely Conduct Disorder and ADHD) across childhood and adolescence.
- *Variations in Principles for Girls and Ethnic Minorities.* Research on adolescents' mental disorders and aggression must address the relative lack of information on variations in general principles associated with gender and ethnicity. There is a small but growing literature for girls, but separate data for various ethnic minority groups in juvenile justice settings is more the exception than routine practice.
- *Discovering Whether Treatment Matters.* This chapter frequently acknowledges that policy and practice regarding public safety are difficult to determine in the absence of actual evidence that treating young offenders' mental disorders alters their long-range trajectory—for example, reduces the likelihood that their aggression would continue into adulthood. Addressing this question is an ambitious research undertaking, but it is necessary if we ever want to advance the ultimate public-safety justification for providing treatment to young and aggressive offenders with mental disorders.

The research that we need most urgently often requires the most time to carry out. Such is the case here, but it is some consolation that studies have already begun in each of these areas.

## A Conflict between Short-Range and Long-Range Obligations

There are a number of difficult policy issues to resolve if juvenile court dispositions are to make available worthwhile treatment for adolescents' mental disorders in the interest of reducing future aggression. One of these issues deserves special discussion, because it is created by a conflict between two obligations that are both part of the public safety mandate.

The juvenile justice system has an obligation to identify youths who need secure residential placement to protect the public. Having identified the risk and the disorder in a particular case, the system also has an obligation to make available treatment that will reduce the risk of aggression when the youth is released from secure custody. Yet satisfying one of these obligations often frustrates the system's ability to satisfy the other. The secure facility that is required often will not be the best place for the youth to receive the treatment that is required. Psychopharmacological treatments, as well as some individual and peer group methods, can be employed in secure facilities. But as noted in chapter 4, the known efficacy of treatments for young offenders is almost in inverse relation to their capacity to be administered in secure youth authority programs. The two most promising treatments, Functional Family Therapy and Multisystemic Therapy, both require intervention with the youth in conjunction with entities—the family, and the community—to which youths in secure facilities typically have little or no access. The latest authoritative reviews aimed at maximizing the system's ability to reduce future aggression among high-risk delinquent youths clearly point to community interventions (e.g., Borum, 2003a).

There is little that can be done about this dilemma if the public truly needs to be protected from the immediate risk of violent behavior. But "truly needs to be protected" may be the key to reducing the weight of the dilemma. Given that the most efficacious treatments for reducing aggression related to mental disorders must be implemented outside secure facilities, might the system be obligated to avoid secure incarceration of youths with mental disorders whenever possible?

How could this be done? One way is to employ a realistic and responsible threshold for risk in discretionary decisions about secure placement. There will always be some whose risk of harm to others is so great that it cannot be tolerated without secure placement. There are others, however, for whom the risk is modest, vague, or questionable, yet who are sent to secure placements simply because it is "safer" for the immediate future. Erring on the side of safety cannot be faulted. But it can be challenged when there are competing social interests in reducing medium-range and longer-range risks. *The advantage of efficacious community-based treatment to reduce later risk might outweigh incarcerating youths in order to err on the side of caution, in cases involving ambiguous or only moderate risk*. Moreover, the fact that a youth might be receiving a treatment such as Multisystemic Therapy reduces the immediate risk because of the high degree of structure and support provided by this form of treatment.

A second way to deal with the dilemma is to ensure that youths placed in secure facilities do not remain there longer than is necessary to reduce risk sufficiently to warrant community reentry. This requires a twist in policy perspective for some juvenile justice programs. Typically community release is predicated on evidence that a youth has been "rehabilitated" or "successfully treated." The policy perspective I propose here is that community release should sometimes occur when risk has been sufficiently lowered to *begin* the system's primary intervention—occurring after the youth's release—to reduce middle- and long-range risk.

This perspective, of course, flies in the face of determinate sentences, just deserts, and "holding kids responsible." That is a conflict with which the system should struggle. It was a rather one-sided argument when everyone knew that "nothing" was the answer to questions about what worked in the treatment of aggressive behaviors, and "very little" described what was known about the value of treatments for mental disorders among youths. These circumstances have somewhat improved (chapter 4). It is time to talk about modifying sentencing policies that deprive youths of community-based treatments that might better serve the public safety mandate.

For those who would take up this struggle, be forewarned that your armor is thin and your swords are not yet well honed. When arguing for discretionary and often "early" release from secure facilities in order to allow community treatment of mental disorders, here are some of the thrusts that you will have to parry:

- "So, in your system, when two boys rob a woman at gunpoint, the one who has a mental disorder would do less hard time?"
- "Does the victim of an assault by a neighborhood boy feel more safe knowing that the boy—who's next door again getting his community-based Multisystemic Therapy—might be less harmful in a year or two?"
- "Since mental disorders are more frequent among white than minority kids in juvenile secure facilities, doesn't your proposal mean that white kids will tend to get community treatment while black kids will more often be locked up?"
- "Do you remember *why* the juvenile justice system turned to determinate sentencing in the 1980s? It was because juvenile *advocates* thought it was better than the inconsistent, biased discretion of courts whose dis-

position decisions often resulted in disproportionately long confinement for minorities. How will you protect against abuses of discretion when the system is deciding who will be released for community treatment and who will not?"

- "That book, *Double Jeopardy,* says it over and over again—things related to development in childhood and adolescence make diagnoses and risk estimates far more difficult in young offender cases than in adult cases. Given that state of the art, how are you going to weigh the costs of potential misdiagnoses and miscalculations of risk against the potential value of the treatment that will be provided?"

These questions are not unanswerable, but they deserve more than a superficial, ideological response. They represent real and important problems that need to be resolved regarding the risks the system can take in moving toward better community-based treatment for young offenders with mental disorders.

## A Basis for Collaboration

Surfacing from time to time throughout this book has been a group of youths that constitute an important but relatively small minority within the juvenile justice system. They are the "seriously emotionally disturbed"—SED youths with chronic, persistent, and multiple mental disorders who constitute a small proportion of the consumers of public mental health services but who consume an extraordinary proportion of its resources. As described by Davis and Vander Stoep (1997), their mental health needs are extreme and continue through their adolescent years into adulthood. They experience episodic, acute distress periodically, often in response to stressful life circumstances that push them beyond their fragile capacities to cope. In those moments, if their reaction includes aggressive behavior, their destination—a psychiatric or a correctional facility—often will depend on a police officer's interpretation of the momentary act as "crazy" or criminal.

When SED youths arrive at detention centers or juvenile correctional facilities, staff typically feel ill-equipped to deal with the depth and complexity of their disorders and their degree of functional impairment. Their occasional acute episodes of disorder while in detention or secure corrections often require their repeated transportation to inpatient mental health units, where they are treated for a few days until their episode begins to subside, allowing them to be returned to the juvenile justice facility.

Eventually they return to the community for some period of time, where the juvenile justice system again places them in the hands of community mental health programs that often feel ill-equipped to deal with their needs. For example, in most communities, acceptance of mental health services is voluntary. Individuals may not be coerced into taking medications that stabilize their conditions or engaging in psychosocial therapies. Given many SED youths' limited capacities to recognize their own needs, together with motivations that are driven by "normal" adolescent impulses and oppositional tendencies and, too often, with parents who fail to guide them, often these youths avail themselves of mental health services inconsistently or lose touch with them altogether. When SED youths with serious problems with aggression require psychiatric hospitalization, often their behaviors stretch the capacities of hospital staff to ensure the safety of others in the unit.

The needs and behaviors of many SED youths are such that they belong to both the mental health and the juvenile justice system. But neither system is equipped to provide what they need in order to manage their disorders and protect them and society from their occasionally dangerous behaviors. The irony of this situation is that both systems embody some of the parts that are needed for effective functioning. Broken as it is in some communities, the child public health system is the primary mechanism for appropriate mental health services for youths. The juvenile justice system, in turn, has the legal authority to provide the structure that can ensure that SED youths with problems of aggression use those services in the consistent manner that is necessary for their welfare and public safety interests.

These objectives would best be served by collaboration on the parts of the two systems. By collaboration I mean a joint venture in which the systems share specially trained personnel and joint-agency funding for specific programs, targeting youths whose lives typically require the attention of both agencies (such as SED youths with frequent delinquent behaviors). An outpatient program of this type would use the legal authority of probation and the clinical skill of mental health professionals and child welfare managers to ensure continuity of care for the youths involved. Most states of moderate size would benefit also from a collaborative secure inpatient psychiatric unit, devoted exclusively to SED youths with frequent juvenile justice system involvement, and accessible from both the community and the juvenile justice system's detention and corrections facilities.

The notion of collaborative programs involving state mental health and juvenile justice agencies is not new (see Barnum & Keilitz, 1992; chapter 5). But it has been slow to develop, despite the recent emergence of models for mental health service delivery that try in part to overcome difficulties created by boundaries between various child public welfare agencies (for example, "wraparound" programs: Burchard, Bruns, & Burchard, 2002).

Collaborations that are less comprehensive than the type that I have suggested have begun to appear. For example, "treatment foster care" programs have experienced the values of close collaboration with juvenile probation officers "as team members . . . to provide a law enforcement presence," "assist in problem situations," and serve as "a backup if the youth becomes highly noncompliant" (Chamberlain, 2002, p. 132). Another example is offered by the new "juvenile mental health courts" (see discussion of "diversion" in chapter 5 in the section on crisis-related treatment; Arredondo et al., 2001), in which multidisciplinary teams of mental health professionals and attorneys fashion special dispositions for SED delinquent youths that integrate community mental health services and the juvenile court's public safety concerns. These descriptions of innovative, collaborative programs have the feel of the benefits that might accrue if mental health and juvenile justice systems engaged in limited, joint-agency ventures targeted for specific subsamples of youths that currently "belong" to both agencies.

Chapter 1 reviewed evidence for the substantial proportion of youths in juvenile justice custody meeting criteria for mental disorders, as well as recent calls for greater attention to their needs. It then posed the question "Are we calling for the juvenile justice system to become the nation's mental health system for troubled adolescents?" The answer throughout this volume is "no." But almost every obligation we have encountered has pointed to the need for the juvenile justice system to consider more effective collaborations with the child mental health system. And some conceptual tools to guide the invention of innovative policies and agency structures are available (e.g., Barnum & Kielitz, 1992; Friedman, 2003).

The most extreme collaboration, of course, would entail that the juvenile justice system lose its identity in a total restructuring of state agencies, creating one child welfare agency that responds to youths' mental health needs as well as their aggressive and other illegal behaviors. There are many reasons why this "ultimate" collaboration probably is not desirable. But cosmetic fixes at the other end of the spectrum weakly proposing "better communication between agencies" will fall far short of what is needed. Somewhere between these extremes are the creative collaborations that the two systems must develop if the juvenile justice system is ever to fulfill its public safety, adjudicative, and custodial treatment obligations to society and to young offenders with mental disorders.

# References

Abramovitch, R., Peterson-Badali, J., & Rohan, M. (1995). Young people's understanding and assertion of their rights to silence and legal counsel. *Canadian Journal of Criminology, 37,* 1–18.

Achenbach, T. (1991a). *Manual for the Youth Self-Report and 1991 profile.* Burlington, VT: University of Vermont, Department of Psychiatry.

Achenbach, T. (1991b). *Manual for the Child Behavior Checklist/4-18 and 1991 profiles.* Burlington, VT: University of Vermont, Department of Psychiatry.

Achenbach, T. (1991c). *Manual for the Teacher's Report Form and 1991 profile.* Burlington, VT: University of Vermont, Department of Psychiatry.

Achenbach, T. (1993). *Empirically based taxonomy: How to use syndromes and profile types derived from the CHCL/4-18, TRF, and YSR.* Burlington, VT: University of Vermont, Department of Psychiatry.

Achenbach T. (1995). Diagnosis, assessment, and comorbidity in psychosocial treatment research. *Journal of Abnormal Psychology, 23,* 45–65.

Achenbach, T. (1999). The Child Behavior Checklist and related instruments. In M. Maruish (Ed.), *The use of psychological testing for treatment planning and outcomes assessment* (2nd ed., pp. 429–466). Mahwah, NJ: Lawrence Earlbaum.

Achenbach, T., & Edelbrock, C. (1984). Psychopathology of childhood. *Annual Review of Psychology, 35,* 227–256.

Achenbach, T., & Edelbrock, C. (1989). Diagnostic, taxonomic, and assessment issues. In T. Ollendick & M. Hersen (Eds.), *Handbook of child psychopathology* (pp. 53–73). New York: Plenum Press.

Achenbach, T., & McConaughy, S. (1997). *Empirically based assessment of child and adolescent psychopathology: Practical applications* (2nd ed.). Thousand Oaks, CA: Sage.

Albano, A., DiBartolo, P., Heimberg, R., & Barlow, D. (1995). Children and adolescents: Assessment and treatment. In R. Heimberg, M. Liebowitz, D. Hope, & F. Schneier (Eds.), *Social phobia: Diagnosis, assessment, and treatment* (pp. 387–425). New York: Guilford.

Alexander, J., Waldron, H., Newberry, A., & Liddle, N. (1988). Family approaches to treating delinquents. In E. Nunnally, C. Chilman, & F. Cox (Eds.), *Mental illness, delinquency, addictions, and neglect* (pp. 128–146). Newbury Park, CA: Sage.

American Academy of Child and Adolescent Psychiatry. (2001). Practice parameter for the assessment and treatment of children and adolescents with suicidal behavior. *Journal of the American Academy of Child and Adolescent Psychiatry,* 40, 24/S-51/S.

American Association for Correctional Psychology. (2000). Standards for psychological services in jails, prisons, correctional facilities, and agencies. *Criminal Justice and Behavior,* 27, 433–494.

American Bar Association. (1989). ABA *criminal justice mental health standards.* Washington, DC: American Bar Association.

American Bar Association. (2001). *Youth in the criminal justice system: Guidelines for policymakers and practitioners.* Washington, DC: ABA.

American Correctional Association. (1991). *Standards for juvenile detention facilities.* Lanham, MD.

American Law Institute. (1962). *Model penal code.* Washington, DC: ALI.

American Psychiatric Association. (1994). *Diagnostic and statistical manual of mental disorders* (4th ed.). Washington, DC: American Psychiatric Association.

Anastasi, A. (1988). *Psychological testing* (6th ed.). New York: Macmillan.

Angold, A., & Costello, E. (1993). Depressive comorbidity in children and adolescents: Empirical, theoretical, and methodological issues. *American Journal of Psychiatry,* 150, 1779–1791.

Angold, A., Costello, E., & Erkanli, A. (1999). Comorbidity. *Journal of Child Psychology and Psychiatry,* 40, 57–87.

Angold, A., Costello, E., Farmer, E., Burns, B., & Erkanli, A. (1999). Impaired but undiagnosed. *Journal of the American Academy of Child and Adolescent Psychiatry,* 38, 129–137.

Angold, A., Erkanli, A., Farmer, E., Fairbank, J., Burns, B., Keeler, G., & Costello, E. (2002). Psychiatric disorder, impairment, and service use in rural African American and white youth. *Archives of General Psychiatry,* 59, 893–901.

Angold, A., Weissman, J., John, K., Merikangas, K., Prusoff, B., & Wickramaratne, P. (1987). Parent and child reports of depressive symptoms in children at low and high risk for depression. *Journal of Child Psychology and Psychiatry,* 28, 901–915.

Appelbaum, P., & Grisso, T. (1988). Assessing patients' capacities to consent to treatment. *New England Journal of Medicine,* 319, 1635–1638.

Appelbaum, P. S., & Grisso, T. (1995). The MacArthur Treatment Competence Study, I: Mental illness and competence to consent to treatment. *Law and Human Behavior,* 19, 105–126.

Archer, R. (1999). Overview of the Minnesota Multiphasic Personality Inventory—Adolescent (MMPI-A). In M. Maruish (Ed.), *The use of psychological testing for treatment planning and outcomes assessment* (2nd ed., pp. 341–380). Mahwah, NJ: Lawrence Earlbaum.

*Arizona Daily Star* (2000, November 13). "Mental Health Care: Too Many Teens, Too Few Beds: Financial Woes Have Forced Nearly All Long-Term Residential Facilities in Tucson to Close."

Arredondo, M., Kumli, J., Soto, L., Colin, E., Ornellas, J., Davilla, R., Edwards, L., & Hymn, E. (2001). Juvenile mental health court: Rationale and protocols. *Juvenile and Family Court Journal,* 52, 1–20.

Atkins, D., Pumariega, W., & Rogers, K. (1999). Mental health and incarcerated youth, I: Prevalence and nature of psychopathology. *Journal of Child and Family Studies,* 8, 193–204.

Augimeri, L., Koegl, C., Webster, C., & Levene, K. (2001). *Early Assessment Risk List for Boys (EARL-20B): Version 2.* Toronto, Canada: Earlscourt Child and Family Centre.

Barkley, R. (1996). Attention-Deficit/Hyperactivity disorder. In E. Mash & R. Barkley (Eds.), *Child psychopathology* (pp. 63–112). New York: Guilford.

Barkley, R. (1997). *Defiant children: A clinician's manual for assessment and parent training* (2nd ed.). New York: Guilford.

Barkley, R. (1990). *Attention-deficit hyperactivity disorder: A handbook for diagnosis and treatment.* New York: Guilford.

Barnum, R. (2000). Clinical and forensic evaluation of competence to stand trial in juvenile defendants. In T. Grisso & R. Schwartz (Eds.), *Youth on trial: A developmental perspective on juvenile justice* (pp. 193–224). Chicago: University of Chicago Press.

Barnum, R., & Keilitz, I. (1992 ). Issues in systems interactions affecting mentally disordered juvenile offenders. In J. Cocozza (Ed.), *Responding to the mental health needs of youth in the juvenile justice system* (pp. 49–87). Seattle, WA: National Coalition for the Mentally Ill in the Criminal Justice System.

Bates, M. (2001). The Child and Adolescent Functional Assessment Scale (CA-FAS): Review and current status. *Clinical Child and Family Psychology Review,* 4, 63–84.

Bazelon Center for Mental Health Law. (1993). *Federal definitions of children with emotional disorders.* Washington, DC: Bazelon Center for Mental Health Law.

Benedek, L., & Cornell, D. (Eds.). (1989). *Juvenile homicide.* Washington, DC: American Psychiatric Press.

Benthin, A., Slovic, P., & Severson, H. (1993). A psychometric study of adolescent risk perception. *Journal of Adolescence,* 16, 153–168.

Bickman, L. (1996). A continuum of care: More is not always better. *American Psychologist,* 51, 689–701.

Bickman, L., & Rog, D. (Eds.). (1995). *Creating a children's mental health service system: Policy, research and evaluation.* Beverly Hills, CA: Sage.

Biederman, J., Mick, E., Faraone, S., & Burback, M. (2001). Patterns of remission and symptom decline in conduct disorder: A four-year prospective study of an ADHD sample. *Journal of the American Academy of Child and Adolescent Psychiatry,* 40, 290–298.

Biederman, J., Newcorn, J., & Sprich, S. (1991). Comorbidity of attention deficit hyperactivity disorder with conduct, depressive, anxiety, and other disorders. *American Journal of Psychiatry,* 148, 564–577.

Biederman, J., & Spencer, T. (1999). Depressive disorders in childhood and adolescence: A clinical perspective. *Journal of Child and Adolescent Psychopharmacology,* 9, 233–237.

Bird, H., Canino, G., Rubio-Stipec, M., Gould, M., Ribera, J., Sesman, M., Woodbury, J., Huertas-Goldman, S., Pagan, A., Sanchez-Lacay, A., & Moscoso, M., (1988). Estimates of the prevalence of childhood maladjustment in a community survey of Puerto Rico: The use of combined measures. *Archives of General Psychiatry,* 45, 1120–1126.

Blumstein, A. (1995). Youth violence, guns, and the illicit drug industry. *Journal of Criminal Law and Criminology,* 86, 10–36.

Blumstein, A., & Wallman, J. (Eds.). (2000). *The crime drop in America.* Cambridge: Cambridge University Press.

Bonnie, R. (1992). The competence of criminal defendants: A theoretical reformulation. *Behavioral Sciences and the Law,* 10, 291–316.

Bonnie, R., & Grisso, T. (2000). Adjudicative competence and youthful offenders. In T. Grisso & R. Schwartz (Eds.), *Youth on trial: A developmental perspective on juvenile justice* (pp. 73–103). Chicago: University of Chicago Press.

Borduin, C., Mann, H., Cone, L., Hengeller, S., Fucci, B., Blaske, D., & Williams, R. (1995). Multisystemic treatment of serious juvenile offenders: Long-term prevention of criminality and violence. *Journal of Consulting and Clinical Psychology,* 63, 569–578.

Borum, R. (2000). Assessing violence risk among youth. *Journal of Clinical Psychology,* 56, 1263–1288.

Borum, R. (2003a). Managing at-risk juvenile offenders in the community. *Journal of Contemporary Criminal Justice,* 19, 114–137.

Borum, R. (2003b). Not guilty by reason of insanity. In T. Grisso, *Evaluating competencies: Forensic assessments and instruments* (2nd ed., pp. 193–227). New York: Kluwer Academic/Plenum Publishers.

Borum, R., Bartel, P., & Forth, A. (2002). *Manual for the Structured Assessment of Violence Risk in Youth (SAVRY): Version I, Consultation Edition.* Tampa, FL: Florida Mental Health Institute, University of South Florida. Online information available at http://www.fmhi.usf.edu/mhlp/savry/statement.htm.

Brady, K., Myrick, H., & McElroy, S. (1998). The relationship between substance use disorders, impulse control disorders, and pathological aggression. *American Journal on Addictions,* 7, 221–230.

Brandt, J., Kennedy, W., Patrick, C., & Curtin, J. (1997). Assessment of psychopathy in a population of incarcerated adolescent offenders. *Psychological Assessment,* 9, 429–435.

Broday, S., & Mason, J. (1991). Internal consistency of the Brief Symptom Inventory. *Psychological Reports,* 68, 94–101.

Burchard, J., Bruns, E., & Burchard, S. (2002). The wraparound approach. In B. Burns & K. Hoagwood (Eds.), *Community treatment for youth* (pp. 69–90). New York: Oxford University Press.

Burns, B. (1999). A call for a mental health services research agenda for youth with serious emotional disturbance. *Mental Health Services Research,* 1, 5–20.

Burns, B., & Hoagwood, K. (Eds.). (2002). *Community treatment for youth: Evidence-based interventions for severe emotional and behavioral disorders.* New York: Oxford University Press.

Burns, B., Hoagwood, K., & Mrazek, P. (1999). Effective treatment for mental disorders in children and adolescents. *Clinical Child and Family Psychology Review,* 2, 199–254.

Butcher, J., Williams, C., Graham, J., Archer, R., Tellegen, A., Ben-Porath, Y., & Kaemmer, B. (1992). *Minnesota Multiphasic Personality Inventory—Adolescent (MMPI-A): Manual for administration, scoring and interpretation.* Minneapolis, MN: University of Minnesota Press.

Campbell, M., Rapoport, J., & Simpson, G. (1999). Antipsychotics in children and adolescents. *Journal of the American Academy of Child and Adolescent Psychiatry, 38,* 537–545.

Canino, G., Costello, E., & Angold, A. (1999). Assessing functional impairment and social adaptation for child mental health services research: A review of measures. *Mental Health Services Research,* 1, 93–108.

Caron, C., & Rutter, M. (1991). Comorbidity in child psychopathology: Concepts, issues and research strategies. *Journal of Child Psychology and Psychiatry,* 32, 1063–1080.

Casey, H., Trainor, R., Orendi, J., Schubert, A., Nystrom, L., Giedd, J., Astellanos, F., Haxby, J., Noll, D., Cohen, J., Forman, S., Dahl, R., & Rapaport, J. (1997). A developmental functional MRI study of prefrontal activation during performance of a go-no-go task. *Journal of Cognitive Neuroscience,* 9, 835–847.

Cauffman, E. (2002, October). *Development and diagnosis: Developmental considerations for mentally ill juvenile offenders.* Paper presented at the annual meeting of the American Academy of Child & Adolescent Psychiatry, San Francisco, CA.

Cauffman, E., Feldman, S., Waterman, J., & Steiner, H. (1998). Posttraumatic stress disorder among female juvenile offenders. *Journal of the American Academy of Child and Adolescent Psychiatry,* 37, 1209–1216.

Cauffman, E., & Grisso, T. (in press). Mental health issues among minority offenders in the juvenile justice system. In D. Hawkins and K. Leonard (Eds.), *Our children, their children: Confronting race and ethnic differences in American criminal justice.* Chicago: University of Chicago Press.

Cauffman, E., & MacIntosh, R. (in press). The measurement validity of the Massachusetts Youth Screening Instrument (MAYSI-2): An assessment of race and gender item bias among juvenile offenders. *Journal of Personality and Social Psychology.*

Cauffman, E., & Steinberg, L. (2000). (Im)maturity of judgment in adolescence: Why adolescents may be less culpable than adults. *Behavioral Sciences & the Law,* 18, 741–760.

Center for the Study and Prevention of Violence. (2002). *Blueprints for Violence Prevention: Blueprints model programs overview.* Boulder, CO: University of Colorado. Available at http://www.colorado.edu/cspv/blueprints.html.

Center for Substance Abuse Treatment. (1999). *Screening and assessing adolescents for substance use disorders.* Rockville, MD: Substance Abuse Mental Health Services Administration.

Centers for Disease Control and Prevention. (1998). *Youth risk behavior surveil-*

*lance—United States,* 1997. CDC Surveillance Summaries, August 14, 1998.

Centers for Disease Control and Prevention. (1999). *Suicide deaths and rates per* 100,000. Available at http://www.cdc.gov/ncipc/data/us9794/suic/htm.

Chamberlain, P. (2002). Treatment foster care. In B. Burns & K. Hoagwood (Eds.), *Community treatment for youth* (pp. 117–138). New York: Oxford University Press.

Charney, D., Deutch, A., Krystal, J., Southwick, S., & Davis, M. (1993). Psychobiological mechanisms of posttraumatic stress disorder. *Archives of General Psychiatry,* 50, 294–305.

Christian, R., Frick, P., Hill, N., Tyler, L., & Frazer, D. (1997). Psychopathy and conduct problems in children: II. Subtyping children with conduct problems based on their interpersonal and affective style. *Journal of the American Academy of Child and Adolescent Psychiatry,* 36, 233–241.

Cicchetti, D. (1984). The emergence of developmental psychopathology. *Child Development,* 55, 1–7.

Cicchetti, D. (1990). An historical perspective on the discipline of developmental psychopathology. In J. Rolf, A. Master, D. Cicchetti, K. Nuechterlien, & S. Weintraub (Eds.), *Risk and protective factors in the development of psychopathology* (pp. 2–28). New York: Cambridge University Press.

Cicchetti, D., & Cohen, D. (1995). *Developmental psychopathology.* New York: Wiley.

Cicchetti, D., & Rogosch, F. (2002 ). A developmental psychopathology perspective on adolescence. *Journal of Consulting and Clinical Psychology,* 70, 6–20.

Cirincione, C., Steadman, H., & McGreevy, M. (1995). Rates of insanity acquittals and the factors associated with successful insanity please. *Bulletin of the American Academy of Psychiatry and Law,* 23, 399–409.

Clarke, G., Rohde, P., Lewinson, P., Hops, H., & Seeley, J. (1999). Cognitive-behavioral treatment of adolescent depression: Efficacy of acute group treatment and booster sessions. *Journal of the American Academy of Child and Adolescent Psychiatry,* 38, 272–279.

Cocozza, J. (Ed.). (1992). *Responding to the mental health needs of youth in the juvenile justice system.* Seattle, WA: National Coalition for the Mentally Ill in the Criminal Justice System.

Cocozza, J., & Skowyra, K. (2000). Youth with mental health disorders: Issues and emerging responses. *Juvenile Justice Journal,* 8(1), Washington, DC: U.S. Department of Justice, Office of Justice Programs, Office of Juvenile Justice and Delinquency Prevention.

Cocozza, J., & Skowyra, K. (Eds.) (in press). *Mental health needs of juvenile offenders: A comprehensive review.* Washington, DC: U.S. Department of Justice, Office of Justice Programs, Office of Juvenile Justice and Delinquency Prevention.

Cohen, P., Cohen, J., & Brook, J. (1993). An epidemiological study of disorders in late childhood and adolescence: II. Persistence of disorders. *Journal of Child Psychology and Psychiatry, 34,* 869–877.

Columbus Dispatch (2001, April 8). "Broken System: Latest Closing Weakens an Overwhelmed Mental Health Network" (reporting the closing of adolescent and children's psychiatric care at Riverside Methodist Hospitals).

Columbus Dispatch (2002, July 28). "Families Face Torturous Trade-off: Parents Give Up Children to Ensure Treatment for Mental Illnesses."

Connor, D. (2002). *Aggression and antisocial behavior in children and adolescents: Research and treatment.* New York: Guilford.

Connor, D., Glatt, S., Lopez, I., Jackson, D., & Melloni, R. (2002). Psychopharmacology and aggression. I: A meta-analysis of stimulant effects on overt/covert aggression-related behaviors in ADHD. *Journal of the American Academy of Child and Adolescent Psychiatry, 41,* 253–261.

Costello, E., Angold, A., Burns, H., Stangle, D., Tweed, D., Erkanli, A., & Worthman, C. (1996). The Great Smoky Mountains Study of Youth: Goals, design, methods and the prevalence of DSM-III-R disorders. *Archives of General Psychiatry, 53,* 1129–1136.

Council of Juvenile Correctional Administrators. (2001). *Performance-based standards for juvenile correction and detention facilities.* Available at http://www.performance.standards.org.

Council of State Governments. (2002). *Criminal justice/mental health consensus project.* Washington, DC: Council of State Governments

Cowden, V., & McKee, G. (1995). Competency to stand trial in juvenile delinquency proceedings: Cognitive maturity and the attorney-client relationship. *Journal of Family Law, 33,* 629–660.

Davis, M., & Vander Stoep, A. (1997). The transition to adulthood for youth who have serious emotional disturbance: Developmental transition and young adult outcomes. *Journal of Mental Health Administration, 24,* 400–427.

Dawson, R. (2000). Judicial waiver in theory and practice. In J. Fagan & F. Zimring (Eds.), *The changing borders of juvenile justice: Transfer of adolescents to the criminal court* (pp. 45–81). Chicago: University of Chicago Press.

Dembo, R., Schmeidler, J., Borden, P., Turner, G., Sue, C., & Manning, D. (1996). Examination of the reliability of the Problem Oriented Screening

Instrument for Teenagers (POSIT) among arrested youths entering a juvenile assessment center. *Substance Use and Misuse, 31,* 785–824.

Dembo, R., Schmeidler, J., Sue, C., Borden, P., Manning, D., & Rollie, M. (1998). Psychosocial, substance use, and delinquency differences among Anglo, Hispanic White, and African-American male youths entering a juvenile assessment center. *Substance Use and Misuse, 33,* 1481–1510.

Derogatis, L. (1993). *Brief Symptom Inventory: Administration, scoring and procedures manual.* Minneapolis, MN: National Computer Systems.

Derogatis, L., & Melisaratos, N. (1983). The Brief Symptom Inventory: An introductory report. *Psychological Medicine, 13,* 595–605.

DiIulio, J. (1995, November 27). The coming of the super-predators. *Weekly Standard,* p. 23.

Dishion, T., McCord, J., & Poulin, F. (1999). When interventions harm: Peer groups and problem behavior. *American Psychologist, 54,* 755–764.

Drizin, S. (2003). The problem of false confessions in Illinois: A report of the Northwestern University Legal Clinic's Children and Family Justice Center. Available at http://www.law.nwu.edu/depts/clinic/news/index.htm.

Durlak, J., Furman, T., & Lampman, C. (1991). Effectiveness of cognitive-behavior therapy for maladapting children: A meta-analysis. *Psychological Bulletin, 110,* 204 –214.

Edens, J., Skeem, J., Cruise, K., & Cauffman, E. (2001). Assessment of "juvenile psychopathy" and its association with violence: A critical review. *Behavioral Sciences and the Law, 19,* 53–80.

Elia, J., Borcherding, B., Rapoport, J., & Keysor, C. (1991). Methylphenidate and dextroamphetamine treatments of hyperactivity: Are there true responders? *Psychiatry Research, 36,* 141–155.

Elliott, D. (1994). Serious, violent offenders: Onset, developmental course, and termination—The American Society of Criminology 1993 Presidential Address. *Criminology, 32,* 1–21.

Elliott, D., Huizinga, D., & Morse, B. (1986). Self-reported violent offending. *Journal of Interpersonal Violence, 1,* 472–514.

Emslie, G., Walkup, J., Pliszka, S., & Ernst, M. (1999). Nontricyclic antidepressants: Current trends in children and adolescents. *Journal of the American Academy of Child and Adolescent Psychiatry, 38,* 517–528.

Faenza, M., Siegfried, C., & Wood, J. (2000). *Community perspectives: On the mental health and substance abuse treatment needs of youth involved in the juvenile justice system.* Washington DC: National Mental Health Association and Office of Juvenile Justice and Delinquency Prevention.

Fagan, J., & Zimring, F. (eds.) (2000). *The changing borders of juvenile justice.* Chicago: University of Chicago Press.

Feld, B. (2000). Juveniles' waiver of legal rights: Confessions, *Miranda,* and the right to counsel. In T. Grisso & R. Schwartz (Eds.), *Youth on trial: A developmental perspective on juvenile justice* (pp. 105–138). Chicago: University of Chicago Press.

Ferris, C., & Grisso, T. (Eds.). (1996). *Understanding aggressive behavior in children.* New York: New York Academy of Sciences.

Finkel, N. (1988). *Insanity on trial.* New York: Plenum.

Fischer, M., Barkley, R., Fletcher, K., & Smallish, L. (1993). The stability of dimensions of behavior in ADHD and normal children over an 8-year follow-up. *Journal of Abnormal Child Psychology,* 21, 315–337.

Fletcher, K. (1996). Childhood posttraumatic stress disorder. In E. Mash & R. Barkley (Eds.), *Child psychopathology* (pp. 242–276). New York: Guilford.

Fombonne, E. (1998). Increased rates of psychosocial disorders in youth. *European Archives of Psychiatry and Clinical Neuroscience,* 248, 14–21.

Forbey, J., & Ben-Porath, Y. (2001). Minnesota Multiphasic Personality Inventory—Adolescent (MMPI-A). In W. Dorfman & M. Hersen (Eds.), *Understanding psychological assessment* (pp. 313–334). New York: Kluwer Academic/Plenum.

Forth, A., Hart, S., & Hare, R. (1990). Assessment of psychopathy in male young offenders. *Psychological Assessment,* 2, 342–344.

Forth, A., Kosson, D., & Hare, R. (1997). *The Hare Psychopathy Checklist: Youth Version (PCL-YV)—Rating Guide.* Toronto, Ontario: Multi-Health Systems.

Foster, J., Eskes, G., & Stuss, D. (1994). The cognitive neuropsychology of attention: A frontal lobe perspective. *Cognitive Neuropsychology,* 11, 133–147.

Fox, J. (1996). *Trends in juvenile violence: A report to the United States Attorney General on current and future rates of juvenile offending.* Boston: Northeastern University Press.

Frick, P. (1998). *Conduct disorders and severe antisocial behavior.* New York: Plenum.

Frick, P., O'Brien, B., Wootton, J., & McBurnett, K. (1994). Psychopathy and conduct problems in children. *Journal of Abnormal Psychology,* 103, 700–707.

Friedman, R. (2003). A conceptual framework for developing and implementing effective policy in children's mental health. *Journal of Emotional and Behavioral Disorders,* 11, 11–18.

Friedman, R., Katz-Levy, J., Manderscheid, R., & Sondheimer, D. (1996). Prevalence of serious emotional disturbance in children and adolescents.

In R. Manderscheid & M. Sonnenschein (Eds.), *Mental health in the United States* (pp. 71–89). Rockville, MD: U.S. Department of Health and Human Services.

Frumkin, H. (2000). Competency to waive *Miranda* rights: Clinical and legal issues. *Mental and Physical Disability Law Reporter,* 24, 326–331.

Fulero, S., & Everington, C. (1995). Assessing competence to waive *Miranda* rights in defendants with mental retardation. *Law and Human Behavior,* 19, 533–543.

Furby, L., & Beyth-Marom, R. (1990). *Risk taking in adolescence: A decision-making perspective.* Washington, DC: Office of Technology Assessment.

Garland, A., Hough, R., McCabe, K., Yeh, M., Wood, P., & Aarons, G. (2001). Prevalence of psychiatric disorders in youths across five sectors of care. *Journal of the American Academy of Child and Adolescent Psychiatry,* 40, 409–418.

Geller, H., Reising, D., Leonard, H., Riddle, M., & Walsh, B. (1999). Critical review of tricyclic antidepressant use in children and adolescents. *Journal of the American Academy of Child and Adolescent Psychiatry,* 38, 513–516.

Giancolo, P., Martin, C., Tarter, R., Pelham, W., & Moss, H. (1996). Executive cognitive functioning and aggressive behavior in preadolescent boys at high risk for substance abuse/dependence. *Journal of Studies on Alcohol,* 57, 352–359.

Giedd, J., Blumenthal, J., Jeffries, N., Castellanos, F., Liu, H., Zikdenbos, A., Paus, T., Evans, A., & Rapaport, J. (1999). Brain development during childhood and adolescence: A longitudinal MRI study. *Nature Neuroscience,* 2, 861–863.

Gittelman, R., Abikoff, H., Pollack, E., Klein, D., Katz, S., & Mattes, J. (1980). A controlled trial of behavior modification and metholphcnidate in hyperactive children. In C. Whalen & B. Henker (Eds.), *Hyperactive children: The social ecology of identification and treatment* (pp. 221–243). New York: Academic Press.

Goodyer, I., & Cooper, P. (1993). A community study of depression in adolescent girls: II. The clinical features of identified disorder. *British Journal of Psychiatry,* 163, 374–380.

Greene, A. (1986). Future-time perspective in adolescence: The present of things future revisited. *Journal of Youth and Adolescence,* 15, 99–113.

Greenhill, L., Halperin, J., & Abikoff, H. (1999). Stimulant medications. *Journal of the American Academy of Child and Adolescent Psychiatry,* 38, 503–512.

Greenwood, P. (1996). Responding to juvenile crime: Lessons learned. *Juvenile Court,* 6, 75–85.

Grills, A., & Ollendick, T. (2002). Issues in parent-child agreement: The case of structured diagnostic interviews. *Clinical Child and Family Psychology Review, 5,* 57–83.

Grisso, T. (1981). *Juveniles' waiver of rights: Legal and psychological competence.* New York: Plenum.

Grisso, T. (1996). Society's retributive response to juvenile violence: A developmental perspective. *Law and Human Behavior, 20,* 229–247.

Grisso, T. (1997). The competence of adolescents as trial defendants. *Psychology, Public Policy, and Law, 3,* 3–32.

Grisso, T. (1998). *Forensic evaluation of juveniles.* Sarasota, FL: Professional Resource Press.

Grisso, T. (2000a). Forensic clinical evaluations related to waiver of jurisdiction. In J. Fagan & F. Zimring (Eds.), *The changing borders of juvenile justice* (pp. 321–352). Chicago: University of Chicago Press.

Grisso, T. (2000b). What we know about youths' capacities as trial defendants. In T. Grisso & R. Schwartz (Eds.), *Youth on trial: A developmental perspective on juvenile justice* (pp. 139–172). Chicago: University of Chicago Press.

Grisso, T. (2003). *Evaluating competencies: Forensic assessments and instruments* (2nd ed.). New York: Kluwer Academic/Plenum Press.

Grisso, T., & Barnum, R. (2003). *Massachusetts Youth Screening Instrument— Second Version: User's manual and technical report.* Sarasota, FL: Professional Resource Press. For information online, see http://www.umassmed.edu/nysap.

Grisso, T., Barnum, R., Fletcher, K., Cauffman, E., & Peuschold, D. (2001). Massachusetts Youth Screening Instrument for mental health needs of juvenile justice youths. *Journal of the American Academy of Child and Adolescent Psychiatry, 40,* 541–548.

Grisso, T., Miller, M., & Sales, B. (1987). Competency to stand trial in juvenile court. *International Journal of Law and Psychiatry, 10,* 1–20.

Grisso, T., Quinlan, J., & Vincent, G. (2003). *Organization, structure and functions of juvenile court forensic evaluation services: A national survey.* Worcester, MA: University of Massachusetts Medical School.

Grisso, T., Steinberg, L., Woolard, J., Cauffman, E., Scott, E., Graham, S., Lexcen, F., Reppucci, N., & Schwartz, R. (2003). Juveniles' competence to stand trial: A comparison of adolescents' and adults' capacities as trial defendants. *Law and Human Behavior, 27,* 333–363.

Grisso, T., & Schwartz, R. (Eds.). (2000). *Youth on trial: A developmental perspective on juvenile justice.* Chicago: University of Chicago Press.

Grisso, T., Tomkins, A., & Casey, P. (1988). Psychosocial concepts in juvenile law. *Law and Human Behavior, 12,* 403–437.

Grisso, T., & Underwood, L. (in press). *Screening and assessing mental health and substance use disorders among youth in the juvenile justice system: A resource guide for practitioners.* Washington, DC: Office of Juvenile Justice and Delinquency Prevention.

Gudjonsson, G. (1992). *The psychology of interrogations, confessions and testimony.* London: Wiley.

Gutheil, T., & Appelbaum, P. (2000). *Clinical handbook of psychiatry and the law* (3rd ed.). Baltimore: Williams and Wilkins.

Haapasalo, J., & Tremblay, R. (1994). Physically aggressive boys from age 6 to 12: Family background, parenting behavior, and prediction of delinquency. *Journal of Consulting and Clinical Psychology, 62,* 1044–1052.

Hammen, C., & Rudolph, K. (1996). Childhood depression. In E. Mash & R. Barkley (Eds.), *Child psychopathology* (pp. 153–195). New York: Guilford.

Hare, R. (1999). Psychopathy as a risk factor for violence. *Psychiatric Quarterly, 70,* 181–197.

Hart, S., & Hare, R. (1997). Psychopathy: Assessment and association with criminal conduct. In D. Stoff, J. Breiling & J. Maser (Eds.), *Handbook of antisocial behavior* (pp. 22–35). New York: Wiley.

Hart, S., Watt, K., & Vincent, G. (2002). Commentary on Seagrave and Grisso: Impressions of the state of the art. *Law and Human Behavior, 26,* 241–245.

Hawkins, D., Laub, J., & Lauritsen, J. (1998). Race, ethnicity, and serious juvenile offending. In R. Loeber & D. Farrington (Eds.), *Serious and violent juvenile offenders* (pp. 30–46). Thousand Oaks, CA: Sage.

Hayes, L. (1999), *Suicide prevention in juvenile correction and detention facilities: A resource guide for performance-based standards for juvenile correction and detention facilities.* Washington, DC: Council of Juvenile Correctional Administrators.

Henggeler, S., Melton, G., & Smith, L. (1992). Family preservation using multisystemic therapy: An effective alternative to incarcerating serious juvenile offenders. *Journal of Consulting and Clinical Psychology, 60,* 953–961.

Henggeler, S., Melton, G., Smith, L., Schoenwald, S., & Hanley, J. (1993). Family preservation using multisystemic treatment: Long-term followup to a clinical trial with serious juvenile offenders. *Journal of Child and Family Studies, 4,* 283–293.

Henggeler, S., Pickrel, S., & Brondino, J. (2000). Multisystemic treatment of substance- abusing and -dependent delinquents: Outcomes, treatment fidelity, and transportability. *Mental health Services Research, 1,* 171–184.

Henggeler, S., Rodick, J., Bordoin, C., Hanson, C., Watson, S., & Urey, J. (1986). Multisystemic treatment of juvenile offenders: Effects on adolescent behavior and family interaction. *Developmental Psychology, 22,* 132–141.

Herjanic, B., & Reich, W. (1983). *Diagnostic Interview for Children and Adolescents: Child version.* St. Louis, MO: Washington University School of Medicine.

Herjanic, H., & Campbell, W. (1977). Differentiating psychiatrically disturbed children on the basis of a structured interview. *Journal of Abnormal Child Psychology, 5,* 127–134.

Hinden, B. R., Compas, B. E., Achenbach, T. M. & Howell, D. (1997). Covariation of the anxious/depressed syndrome: Separating fact from artifact. *Journal of Consulting and Clinical Psychology, 65,* 6–14.

Hinshaw, S., & Anderson, C. (1996). Conduct and oppositional defiant disorders. In E. Mash & R. Barkley (Eds.), *Child psychopathology* (pp. 113–149). New York: Guilford.

Hoagwood, K., Hibbs, E., Brent, D., & Jensen, P. (1995). Introduction to the special section: Efficacy and effectiveness in studies of child and adolescent psychotherapy. *Journal of Consulting and Clinical Psychology, 63,* 683–687.

Hodges, K. (1997). *CAFAS manual for training coordinators, clinical administrators, and data managers.* Ann Arbor, MI: Author.

Hodges, K. (1999). Child and Adolescent Functional Assessment Scale (CAFAS). In M. Maruish (Ed.), *The use of psychological testing for treatment planning and outcomes assessment* (2nd ed., pp. 631–664). Mahwah, NJ: Lawrence Earlbaum.

Hodges, K., & Wong, M. (1996). Psychometric characteristics of a multidimensional measure to assess impairment: The Child and Adolescent Functional Assessment Scale. *Journal of Child and Family Studies, 5,* 445–467.

Hoge, R., & Andrews, D. (1996). *Assessing the youthful offender.* New York: Plenum.

Hoge, S., Bonnie, R., Poythress, N., & Monahan, J. (1992). Attorney-client decision making in criminal cases: Client competence and participation as perceived by their attorneys. *Behavioral Sciences and the Law, 10,* 385–394.

Hollinger, P., Offer, D., Barter, J., & Bell, C. (1994). *Suicide and homicide among adolescents.* New York: Guilford.

Huey, W., & Rank, R. (1994). Effects of counselor and peer-led group assertiveness training on black adolescent aggression. *Journal of Counseling Psychology, 31,* 95–98.

Hughes, J., La Greca, A., & Conoley, J. (Eds.). (2001). *Handbook of psychologi-*

*cal services for children and adolescents.* New York: Oxford University Press.

Huizinga, D. (1995). Developmental sequences in delinquency. In L. Crockett & N. Crowder (Eds.), *Pathways through adolescence: Individual development in context* (pp. 15–34). Hillsdale, NJ: Lawrence Erlbaum Associates.

Huizinga, D., & Jakob-Chien, C. (1998). The contemporaneous co-occurrence of serious and violent juvenile offending and other problem behaviors. In R. Loeber & D. Farrington (Eds.), *Serious and violent juvenile offenders: Risk factors and successful interventions* (pp. 47–67). Thousand Oaks, CA: Sage Publications.

Huizinga, D., Loeber, R., Thornberry, T., & Cothern, L. (2000). *Co-occurrence of delinquency and other problem behaviors.* Washington, DC: Office of Juvenile Justice and Delinquency Prevention.

Huttenlocher, P. (1990). Morphometric study of human cerebral cortex development. *Neuropsychologia, 28,* 517–527.

Inamdar, S., Lewis, D., Siomopoulos, G., Shanok, S., & Lamela, M. (1982). Violent and suicidal behavior in psychotic adolescents. *American Journal of Psychiatry, 139,* 932–935.

Ingram, R., & Price, J. (Eds.). (2001). *Vulnerability to psychopathology: Risk across the lifespan.* New York: Guilford.

Isaacs, M. (1992). Assessing the mental health needs of children and adolescents of color in the juvenile justice system: Overcoming institutionalized perceptions and barriers. In J. Cocozza (Ed.), *Responding to the mental health needs of youth in the juvenile justice system* (pp. 143–163). Seattle, WA: National Coalition for the Mentally Ill in the Criminal Justice System.

Jarvis, T., Tebbutt, J., & Mattick, R. (1995). *Treatment approaches for alcohol and drug dependence: An introductory guide.* Chichester, UK: Wiley.

Jemelka, R., Rahman, S., & Trupin, E. (1993). Prison mental health: An overview. In H. Steadman & J. Cocozza (Eds.), *Mental illness in America's prisons.* Seattle, WA: National Coalition of the Mentally Ill in the Criminal Justice System.

Jensen, P., & Watanabe, H. (1999). Sherlock Holmes and child psychopathology assessment approaches: The case of the false-positive. *Journal of the American Academy of Child and Adolescent Psychiatry, 38,* 138–146.

Johnson, R. (1993). Clinical issues in the use of the DSM-III-R with African American Children: A diagnostic paradigm. *Journal of Black Psychology, 19,* 447–460.

Kagan, J., Resnick, J., Clark, C., Snidman, N., & Garcia-Coll, C. (1984). Behavioral inhibition to the unfamiliar. *Child Development, 55,* 2212–2225.

Kaminar, Y. (2001). Adolescent substance abuse treatment: Where do we go from here? *Psychiatric Services,* 52, 147–149.

Kaminar, Y., Burleson, J., & Goldberger, R. (2000). *Cognitive-behavioral versus psychoeducational therapy: 3- and 9-month treatment outcomes for adolescent substance abusers.* Presented at the Ninth International Conference on Treatment of Addictive Behaviors.

Kaslow, N., & Thompson, M. (1998). Applying the criteria for empirically supported treatments to studies of psychosocial interventions for child and adolescent depression. *Journal of Clinical Child Psychology,* 27, 146–155.

Katz, R., & Marquette, J. (1996). Psychosocial characteristics of young violent offenders: A comparative study. *Criminal Behaviour and Mental Health,* 6, 339–348.

Kazdin, A. (1988). *Child psychotherapy: Developing and identifying effective treatments.* Elmsford, NY: Pergamon.

Kazdin, A. (1996). Problem solving and parent management in treatment for aggressive and antisocial behavior. In E. Hibbs & P. Jensen (Eds.), *Psychological treatments for child and adolescent disorders: Empirically based strategies for clinical practice* (pp. 377–408). Washington, DC: American Psychological Association.

Kazdin, A. (1997). Practitioner review: Psychosocial treatments for conduct disorder in children. *Journal of Child Psychology and Psychiatry,* 38, 161–178.

Kazdin, A. (2000a). Adolescent development, mental disorders, and decision making of delinquent youths. In T. Grisso & R. Schwartz (Eds.), *Youth on trial: A developmental perspective on juvenile justice* (pp. 33–65). Chicago: University of Chicago Press.

Kazdin, A. (2000b). *Psychotherapy for children and adolescents: Directions for research and practice.* New York: Oxford University Press.

Kazdin, A., & Johnson, H. (1994). Advances in psychotherapy for children and adolescents: Interrelations of adjustment, development and intervention. *Journal of School Psychology,* 32, 217–246.

Kendall, P. (1994). Treating anxiety disorders in children: Results of a randomized clinical trial. *Journal of Consulting and Clinical Psychology,* 62, 100–110.

Kendall, P., Reber, J., McLeer, S., Epps, J., & Ronan, K. (1990). Cognitive-behavioral treatment of conduct-disordered children. *Cognitive Therapy and Research,* 14, 279–297.

Knox, M., King, C., Hanna, G., Logan, D., & Ghaziuddin, N. (2000). Aggressive behavior in clinically depressed adolescents. *Journal of the American Academy of Child and Adolescent Psychiatry,* 39, 611–618.

Kovacs, M. (1990). Comorbid anxiety disorders in childhood-onset depressions. In J. Maser & C. Cloninger (Eds.), *Comorbidity of mood and anxiety disorders* (pp. 272–281). Washington, DC: American Psychiatric Press.

Kratzer, L., & Hodgins, S. (1997). Adult outcomes of child conduct problems: A cohort study. *Journal of Abnormal Child Psychology, 25,* 65–81.

Lambert, E., Wahler, R., Andrade, A., & Bickman, L. (2001). Looking for the disorder in conduct disorder. *Journal of Abnormal Psychology, 110,* 110–123.

Lahey, B., Loeber, R., Hart, E., Frick, P., Applegate, B., Zhang, Q., Green, S., & Russo, J. (1995). Four-year longitudinal study of conduct disorder in boys: Patterns of predictors of persistence. *Journal of Abnormal Psychology, 104,* 83–93.

Lapouse, R., & Monk, A. (1958). An epidemiologic study of behavior characteristics of children. *American Journal of Public Health, 48,* 1134–1144.

Lewis, D., Lovely, R., Yeager, C., Ferguson, G., Friedman, M., Sloane, G., Friedman, H., & Pincus, J. (1988). Intrinsic and environmental characteristics of juvenile murderers. *Journal of the American Academy of Child and Adolescent Psychiatry, 27,* 582–587.

Lilienfeld, S., Waldman, I., & Israel, A. (1994). A critical examination of the use of the term and concept of comorbidity in psychopathology research. *Clinical Psychology: Science and Practice, 1,* 71–83.

Link, B., & Steuve, A. (1994). Psychotic symptoms and the violent/illegal behavior of mental patients compared to community controls. In J. Monahan & H. Steadman (Eds.), *Violence and mental disorder: Developments in risk assessment* (pp. 137–159). Chicago: University of Chicago Press.

Lipsey, M. (1992). Juvenile delinquency treatment: A meta-analytic inquiry into the variability of effects. In T. Cook, H. Cooper, & D. Cordray (Eds.), *Meta-analysis for explanation* (pp. 83–126). New York: Russell Sage Foundation.

Lochman, J., Lampron, L., Gemmer, T., & Harris, S. (1987). Anger coping intervention with aggressive children: A guide to implementation in school settings. In P. Keller & S. Heyman (Eds.), *Innovations in clinical practice: A source book* (pp. 339–356). Sarasota, FL: Professional Resource Exchange.

Lochman, J., & Wells, K. (1996). A social-cognitive intervention with aggressive children: Prevention effects and contextual implementation issues. In R. Peters & R. McMahon (Eds.)., *Preventing childhood disorders, substance abuse, and delinquency* (pp. 111–143). Thousand Oaks, CA: Sage.

Loeber, R. (1990). Developmental and risk factors of juvenile antisocial behavior and delinquency. *Clinical Psychology Review, 10,* 1–41.

Loeber, R. (1991). Questions and advances in the study of developmental pathways. In D. Cicchetti & S. Toth (Eds.), *Rochester symposium on developmental psychopathology: Vol. 3. Models and integrations* (pp. 97–116). New York: University of Rochester Press.

Loeber, R., Burke, J., & Lahey, B. (2002). What are adolescent antecedents to an antisocial personality disorder? *Criminal Behavior and Mental Health,* 12, 24–36.

Loeber, R., & Dishion, T. (1983). Early predictors of male delinquency: A review. *Psychological Bulletin,* 94, 68–99.

Loeber, R., Farrington, D., Stouthamer-Loeber, M., & Van Kammen, W. (1998). *Antisocial behavior and mental health problems: Explanatory factors in childhood and adolescence.* Mahwah, NJ: Lawrence Erlbaum Associates.

Loeber, R., & Hay, D. (1994). Developmental approaches to aggression and conduct problems. In M. Rutter & D. Hay (Eds.), *Development through life: A handbook for clinicians* (pp.488–515). Oxford: Blackwell.

Loeber, R., & Hay, D. (1996). Key issues in the development of aggression and violence from childhood to early adulthood. *Annual Review of Psychology,* 48, 371–410.

Loeber, R., & Keenan, K. (1994). Interaction between conduct disorder and its comorbid conditions: Effects of age and gender. *Clinical Psychology Review,* 14, 497–523.

Loeber, R., & Stouthamer-Loeber, M. (1998). Development of juvenile aggression and violence: Some common misconceptions and controversies. *American Psychologist,* 53, 242–259.

Loeber, R., Van Kammen, W., Krohn, M., & Huizinga, D. (1991). The crime-substance use nexus in young people. In D. Huizinga, R. Loeber, & T. Thornberry (Eds.), *Urban delinquency and substance abuse.* Washington, DC: Office of Juvenile Justice and Delinquency Prevention.

*Los Angeles Times* (2000, November 21). "California's Mental Health System Woefully Inadequate, Report Says."

Luna, H., Thulborn, K., Monoz, D., Merriam, E., Garver, K., Minshew, N., Keshavan, M., Genovese, C., Eddy, W., & Sweeney, J. (2001). *Maturation of widely distributed brain function subserves cognitive development.* Available at http://www.idealibrary.com.

Lynam, D. (1997). Pursuing the psychopath: Capturing the fledgling psychopath in a nomological net. *Journal of Abnormal Psychology,* 106, 425–438.

Lynam, D. (1998). Early identification of the fledgling psychopath: Locating the psychopathic child in the current nomenclature. *Journal of Abnormal Psychology,* 107, 566–575.

Magnusson, D., Stattin, H., & Duner, A. (1983). Aggression and criminality in a longitudinal perspective. In K. Van Dusen & S. Mednick (Eds.), *An-*

*tecedents of aggression and antisocial behavior* (pp. 277–301). Boston: Kluwer-Nijhoff.

Mannuzza, S., & Klein, R. (1992). Predictors of outcome of children with attention-deficit hyperactivity disorder. In G. Weiss (Ed.), *Child and adolescent psychiatric clinics of North America: Attention-deficit hyperactivity disorder* (pp. 567–578). Philadelphia: Saunders.

Mannuzza, S., Klein, R., Bessler, A., Mally, P., & LaPadula, M. (1993). Adult outcome of hyperactive boys: Educational achievement, occupational rank, and psychiatric status. *Archives of General Psychiatry, 50*, 565–576.

Marsteller, F., Brogan, D., Smith, I., Ash, P., Daniels, D., Rolka, D., & Falek, A. (1997). *The prevalence of substance use disorders among juveniles admitted to regional youth detention centers operated by the Georgia Department of Children and Youth Services.* Rockville, MD: Department of Health and Human Services, Substance Abuse and Mental health Services Administration, Center for Substance Abuse Treatment.

Martinson, R. (1974). What works? Questions and answers about prison reform. *Public Interest, 10*, 22–54.

Mash, E. (1989). Treatment of child and family disturbance: A behavioral-systems perspective. In E. Mash & R. Barkley (Eds.), *Treatment of childhood disorders* (pp. 3–38). New York: Guilford Press.

Mash, E., & Barkley, R. (Eds.) (1998). *Treatment of childhood disorders* (2nd ed.). New York: Guilford.

Mash, E., & Dozois, D. (1996). Child psychopathology: A developmental-systems perspective. In E. Mash & R. Barkley (Eds.), *Child Psychopathology* (pp. 3–60). New York: Guilford.

McCann, J. (1999). *Assessing adolescents with the MACI: Using the Millon Adolescent Clinical Inventory.* New York: John Wiley.

McGaha, A., Otto, R., McClaren, M., & Petrila, J. (2001). Juveniles adjudicated incompetent to proceed: A descriptive study of Florida's competence restoration program. *Journal of the American Academy of Psychiatry and the Law, 29*, 427–437.

McLaney, M., Del Boca, F., & Babor, T. (1994). A validation study of the Problem Oriented Screening Instrument for Teenagers (POSIT). *Journal of Mental Health, 3*, 363–376.

McMackin, R., & Fulwiler, C. (2001). A public health-juvenile justice collaboration to address the psychiatric needs of incarcerated youth. *Organizational Response to Social Problems, 8*, 335–361.

McMahon, R., & Wells, K. (1998). Conduct problems. In E. Mash & R. Barkley (Eds.), *Treatment of childhood disorders* (2nd ed., pp. 111–207). New York: Guilford.

Mechanic, D. (1973). Some factors in identifying and defining mental illness. In R. Price & B. Denner (Eds.), *The making of a mental patient* (pp. 19–31). New York: Holt, Rinehart and Winston.

Melton, G. (1989). Taking *Gault* seriously: Toward a new juvenile court. *Nebraska Law Review, 68,* 146–181.

Melton, G., Petrila, J., Poythress, N., & Slobogin, C. (1997). *Psychological evaluations for the courts* (2nd ed.). New York: Guilford.

Millon, T., Millon, C., &Davis, R. (1993). *Millon Adolescent Clinical Inventory manual.* Minneapolis, MN: National Computer Systems.

Moffitt, T. (1993). Adolescence-limited and life-course-persistent antisocial behavior: A developmental taxonomy. *Psychological Review, 100,* 674–701.

Moffitt, T., Caspi, A., Dickson, N., Silva, P., & Stanton, W. (1996). Childhood-onset versus adolescent-onset antisocial conduct problems in males: Natural history from ages 3 to 18 years. *Development and Psychopathology, 8,* 399–424.

Moffitt, T., Caspi, A., Rutter, M., & Silva, P. (2001). *Sex differences in antisocial behavior.* Cambridge: Cambridge University Press.

Monahan, J., Steadman, H., Silver, E., Appelbaum, P., Robbins, P., Mulvey, E., Roth, L., Grisso, T., & Banks, S. (2001). *Rethinking risk assessment: The MacArthur study of mental disorder and violence.* New York: Oxford University Press.

Monti, P., Colby, S., & O'Leary, T. (Eds.). (2001). *Adolescents, alcohol, and substance abuse: Reaching teens through brief interventions.* New York: Guilford.

Mulvey, E. (1989). Scenes from a marriage: How can juvenile justice and mental health go on together? *Forensic Reports, 2,* 9–24.

Murray, C., Smith, S., & West, E. (1989). Comparative personality development in adolescence: A critique. In R. Jones (Ed.), *Black adolescents* (pp. 49–62). Berkeley, CA: Cobb and Henry.

Myers, W., Scott, K., & Burgess, A. (1995). Psychopathology, biopsychosocial factors, crime characteristics, and classification of 25 homicidal youths. *Journal of the American Academy of Child and Adolescent Psychiatry, 34,* 1483–1489.

National Commission on Correctional Health Care. (1999). *Standards for health services in juvenile detention and confinement facilities.* Chicago, IL: National Commission on Correctional Health Care.

National Council of Juvenile and Family Court Judges. (2000). *Enhancing the mental health and well being of infants, children and youth in the juvenile and family courts: A judicial challenge.* Reno, NV: National Council of Juvenile and Family Court Judges.

National Mental Health Association. (2000). *Community perspectives on the mental health and substance abuse treatment needs of youth involved in the juvenile justice system.* Washington, DC: Office of Juvenile Justice and Delinquency Prevention.

Neighbors, H., Kempton, T., & Forehand, R. (1992). Co-occurrence of substance abuse with conduct, anxiety and depression disorders in juvenile delinquents. *Addictive Behaviors, 17,* 379–386.

*New York Times* (2001, July 9). "Mentally Ill Children Trapped in Hospitals."

Nicholson, R., & Kugler, K. (1991). Competent and incompetent criminal defendants: A quantitative review of comparative research. *Psychological Bulletin, 109,* 355–370.

Nixon, T., & Northrup, A. (Eds.) (1997). *Children's mental health services: Research, policy and evaluation.* Thousand Oaks, CA: Sage.

Novaco, R. (1994). Anger as a risk factor for violence among the mentally disordered. In J. Monahan & H. Steadman (Eds.), *Violence and mental disorder* (pp. 21–59). Chicago: University of Chicago Press.

Nurmi, J. (1991). How do adolescents see their future? A review of the development of future orientation and planning. *Developmental Review, 11,* 1–59.

Oberlander, L., & Goldstein, N. (2001). A review and update of the practice of evaluating *Miranda* comprehension. *Behavioral Sciences and the Law, 19,* 453–471.

Oberlander, L., Goldstein, N., & Goldstein, A. (2003). Competence to confess. In A. Goldstein (Ed.), *Handbook of psychology: Vol. 11. Forensic psychology* (pp. 335–357). New York: John Wiley.

Office of Juvenile Justice and Delinquency Prevention. (1994). *Conditions of confinement: Juvenile detention and corrections facilities* (Report No. 145793). Washington, DC: Office of Juvenile Justice and Delinquency Prevention.

Office of Juvenile Justice and Delinquency Prevention. (2000). *Juvenile Justice Journal, Vol. VII*(1). Washington, DC: U.S. Department of Justice, Office of Justice Programs, Office of Juvenile Justice and Delinquency Prevention.

Offord, D., Alder, R., & Boyle, M. (1986). Prevalence and sociodemographic correlates of conduct disorder. *American Journal of Social Psychiatry, 4,* 272–278.

Offord, D., Boyle, M., Szatmari, P., Rae-Grant, N., Links, P., Cadman, D., Byles, J., Crawford, J., Blum, C., Thomas, H., & Woodward, C. (1987). Ontario Child Health Study, II: Six-month prevalence of disorder and rates of service utilization. *Archives of General Psychiatry, 44,* 832–836.

*Omaha World-Herald* (2002, January 14). "Nebraska Mental Health System for Children in 'Sorry Condition.'"

Otto, R., Greenstein, J., Johnson, M., & Friedman, R. (1992). Prevalence of mental disorders among youth in the juvenile justice system. In J. Cocozza (Ed.), *Responding to the mental health needs of youth in the juvenile justice system* (pp. 7–48). Seattle, WA: National Coalition for the Mentally Ill in the Criminal Justice System.

Patterson, G. (1975). *Families: Applications of social learning to family life.* Champaign, IL: Research Press.

Paus, T., Zijdenbos, A., Worsley, K., Collins, D., Blumental, J., & Evans, A. (1999). Structural maturation of neural pathways in children and adolescents: In vivo study. *Science, 283,* 1908–1911.

Pennington, B., & Ozonoff, S. (1991). A neuroscientific perspective on continuity and discontinuity in developmental psychopathology. In D. Cicchetti & S. Toth (Eds.), *Rochester symposium on developmental psychopathology: Vol. 3.* Models and integrations (pp. 117–159). New York: University of Rochester Press.

Peterson-Badali, M., & Abramovitch, R. (1993). Grade related changes in young people's reasoning about plea decisions. *Law and Human Behavior, 17,* 537–552.

Peterson-Badali, M., & Abramovitch, R., & Duda, J. (1997). Young children's legal knowledge and reasoning ability. *Canadian Journal of Criminology, 39,* 145–170.

Piersma, H., Boes, J., & Reaume, W. (1994). Unidimensionality of the Brief Symptom Inventory (BSI) in adult and adolescent inpatients. *Journal of Personality Assessment, 63,* 338–344.

Pinta, E. (1999). The prevalence of serious mental disorders among U.S. prisoners. *Correctional Mental Health Report,* 1, 33–34, 44–47.

Pliszka, S., Sherman, J., Barrow, M., & Irick, S. (2000). Affective disorder in juvenile offenders: A preliminary study. *American Journal of Psychiatry, 157,* 130–132.

Price, H., Daffner, K., Stowe, R., & Mesulam, M. (1990). The comportmental learning disabilities of early frontal lobe damage. *Brain,* 113, 1383–1393.

*Progressive* (2001, July). "Arrest My Kid: He Needs Mental Health Care."

Puig-Antich, J., & Chambers, W. (1978). *The Schedule for Affective Disorders and Schizophrenia for School-Aged Children.* New York: State Psychiatric Institute of New York.

Puritz, P., Burrell, S., Schwartz, R., Soler, M., & Warboys, L. (1995). *A call for justice: An assessment of access to counsel and quality of representation in delinquency proceedings.* Washington, DC: American Bar Association Juvenile Justice Center.

Quinsey, V., Harris, G., Rice, M., & Cormier, C. (1998). *Violent offenders: Appraising and managing risk.* Washington, DC: American Psychological Association.

Rahdert, E. (1991). *The Adolescent Assessment/Referral System: Manual.* Rockville, MD: Alcohol, Drug Abuse, and Mental Health Administration.

Raine, A. (1996). Autonomic nervous system factors underlying disinhibited, antisocial and violent behavior: Biosocial perspectives and treatment implications. In C. Ferris & T. Grisso (Eds.), *Understanding aggressive behavior in children* (pp. 46–59). New York: New York Academy of Sciences.

Randall, J., Henggler, S., Pickrel, S., & Brondini, M. (1999). Psychiatric comorbidity and the 16-month trajectory of substance-abusing and substance-dependent juvenile offenders. *Journal of the American Academy of Child and Adolescent Psychiatry, 38,* 1118–1124.

Rapee, R., Barrett, P., Dadds, M., & Evans, L. (1994). Reliability of the DSM-III-R childhood and anxiety disorders using structured interview: Interrater and parent-child agreement. *Journal of the American Academy of child and Adolescent Psychiatry, 33,* 984–992.

Redding, R., & Frost, J. (2002). Adjudicative competence in the modern juvenile court. *Virginia Journal of Social Policy and Law, 9,* 353–410.

Richards, I. (1996). Psychiatric disorder among adolescents in custody. *Australian and New Zealand Journal of Psychiatry, 30,* 788–793.

Richters, J. (1996). Disordered views of aggressive children: A late twentieth century perspective. In C. Ferris & T. Grisso (Eds.), *Understanding aggressive behavior in children* (pp. 208–223). New York: New York Academy of Sciences.

Roberts, R., Attkinson, C., & Rosenblatt, A. (1998). Prevalence of psychopathology among children and adolescents. *American Journal of Psychiatry, 155,* 715–725.

Robertson, A., & Husain, J. (2001). *Prevalence of mental illness and substance abuse disorders among incarcerated juvenile offenders.* Mississippi State, MS: Mississippi State University Social Science Research Center.

Robins, L. (1966). *Deviant children grown up.* Baltimore: Williams & Wilkins.

Rogers, R., Johansen, J., Chang, J., & Salekin, R. (1997). Predictors of adolescent psychopathy: Oppositional and conduct-disordered symptoms. *Journal of the American Academy of Psychiatry and the Law, 25,* 261–271.

Rosenblatt, J., Rosenblatt, A., & Biggs, E. (2000). Criminal behavior and emotional disorder: Comparing youth served by the mental health and juvenile justice systems. *Journal of Behavioral Health Services and Research, 27,* 227–237.

Rutter, M. (1994). Comorbidity: Meanings and mechanisms. *Clinical Psychology: Science and Practice, 1,* 100–103.

Rutter, M., & Garmezy, H. (1983). Developmental psychopathology. In P. Mussen & E. Hetherington (Eds.), *Handbook of child psychology: Vol. 4. Socialization, personality and social development* (pp. 775–911). New York: Wiley.

Rutter, M., & Graham, P. (1968). The reliability and validity of the psychiatric assessment of the child: I. Interview with the child. *British Journal of Psychiatry, 114,* 563–579.

Rutter, M., & Smith, D. (Eds.). (1995). *Psychosocial disorders in young people: Time trends and their cases.* Chichester, UK: Wiley.

Ryan, N., Bhatara, V., & Perel, J. (1999). Mood stabilizers in children and adolescents. *Journal of the American Academy of Child and Adolescent Psychiatry, 38,* 529–536.

Salekin, R., Rogers, R., & Machin, D. (2001). Psychopathy in youth: Pursuing diagnostic clarity. *Journal of Youth and Adolescence, 30,* 173–194.

Scheff, T. (1973). The societal reaction to deviance: Ascriptive elements in psychiatric screening of mental patients in a midwestern state. In R. Price & B. Denner (Eds.), *The making of a mental patient* (pp. 100–119). New York: Holt, Rinehart and Winston.

Schoenwald, S. (1998). *Multisystemic therapy consultation manual.* Charleston, SC: MST Institute.

Schoenwald, S., Scherer, D., & Brondino, M. (1997). Effective community-based treatments for serious juvenile offenders. In S. Henggeler & A. Santos (Eds.), *Innovative approaches for difficult to treat populations* (pp. 65–82). Washington, DC: American Psychiatric Press.

Schwartz, R., & Rosado, L. (Eds.). (2000). *Evaluating youth competence in the justice system.* (Series, "Understanding adolescents: A juvenile court training curriculum.") Washington, DC: American Bar Association Juvenile Justice Center.

Scott, E. (1992). Judgment and reasoning in adolescent decision making. *Villanova Law Review, 37,* 1607–1669).

Scott, E. (2000). Criminal responsibility in adolescence: Lessons from developmental psychology. In T. Grisso & R. Schwartz (Eds.), *Youth on trial: A developmental perspective on juvenile justice* (pp. 291–324). Chicago: University of Chicago Press.

Scott, E., Reppucci, N., & Woolard, J. (1995). Evaluating adolescent decision-making in legal contexts. *Law and Human Behavior, 19,* 221–244.

Scott, E., & Steinberg, L. (2003). Blaming youth. *Texas Law Review, 81,* 799–840.

Seagrave, D., & Grisso, T. (2002). Adolescent development and the measurement of juvenile psychopathy. *Law and Human Behavior, 26,* 219–239.

Shaffer, D., Fisher, P., Dulcan, M., Davies, M., Piacentini, J., Schwab-Stone, M., Lahey, B., Bourdon, K., Jensen, P., Bird, H., Canino, G., & Regier, D. (1996). The NIMH Diagnostic Interview Schedule for Children Version 2.3 (DISC-2.3): Description, acceptability, prevalence rates, and performance in the MECA study. *Journal of the American Academy of Child and Adolescent Psychiatry,* 35, 865–877.

Shaffer, D., Fisher, P., Lucas, C., Dulcan, M., & Schwab-Stone, M. (2000). NIMH Diagnostic Interview Schedule for Children Version IV (NIMH DISC-IV): Description, differences from previous versions, and reliability of some common diagnoses. *Journal of the American Academy of Child and Adolescent Psychiatry,* 39, 28–37.

Shaffer, D., Gould, M., Brasic, J., Ambrosini, P., Fisher, P., Bird, H., & Aluwahlia, S. (1983). A Children's Global Assessment Scale (C-GAS). *Archives of General Psychiatry,* 40, 1228–1231.

Silverthorn, P., & Frick, P. (1999). Developmental pathways to antisocial behavior: The delayed-onset pathway in girls. *Development and Psychopathology,* 11, 101–126.

Simeon, J., Carrey, N., Wiggins, D., Milin, R., & Hosenbocus, S. (1995). Risperidone effects in treatment-resistant adolescents: Preliminary case reports. *Journal of Child and Adolescent Psychopharmacology,* 5, 69–79.

Snyder, H., & Sickmund, M. (1995). *Juvenile offenders and victims: A national report.* Washington, DC: Office of Juvenile Justice and Delinquency Prevention.

Snyder, H., & Sickmund, M. (1999). *Juvenile offenders and victims: 1999 national report.* Washington, DC: Office of Juvenile Justice and Delinquency Prevention.

Sroufe, L., & Rutter, M. (1984). The domain of developmental psychopathology. *Child Development,* 55, 17–29.

Steadman, H., Mulvey, E., Monahan, J., Robbins, P., Appelbaum, P., Grisso, T., Roth, L., & Silver, E. (1998). Violence by people discharged from acute psychiatric facilities and by others in the same neighborhoods. *Archives of General Psychiatry,* 55, 393–401.

Steinberg, L. (2002). Clinical adolescent psychology: What it is, and what it needs to be. *Journal of Consulting and Clinical Psychology,* 70, 124–128.

Steinberg, L., & Cauffman, E. (1996). Maturity of judgment in adolescence: Psychosocial factors in adolescent decision-making. *Law and Human Behavior,* 20, 249–272.

Steiner, H., Garcia, I., & Matthews, X. (1997). Posttraumatic stress disorder in incarcerated juvenile delinquents. *Journal of the American Academy of Child and Adolescent Psychiatry,* 36, 357–365.

Stiffman, A., Chen, Y., Elze, D., & Dore, P. (1997). Adolescents' and providers' perspectives on the need for and use of mental health services. *Journal of Adolescent Health,* 21, 335–342.

Stroul, B. (Ed.). (1996). *Children's mental health: Creating systems of care in a changing society.* Baltimore, MD: Paul H. Brookes Publishing.

Swanson, J., Estroff, S., Swartz, M., Borum, R., Lachicotte, W., Zimmer, C., & Wagner, R. (1997). Violence and severe mental disorder in clinical and community populations: The effects of psychotic symptoms, comorbidity, and lack of treatment. *Psychiatry,* 60, 1–22.

Szatmari, P., Boyle, M.,& Offord, D. (1989). ADHD and CD: Degree of diagnostic overlap and differences among correlates. *Journal of the American Academy of Child and Adolescent Psychiatry,* 31, 1036–1040.

Teplin, L. (1990). The prevalence of severe mental disorder among urban male detainees: Comparison with the Epidemiologic Catchment Area Program. *American Journal of Public Health,* 80, 663–669.

Teplin, L. (1994). Psychiatric and substance abuse disorders among urban male detainees. *American Journal of Public Health,* 84, 290–293.

Teplin, L., Abram, K., McClelland, G., & Dulcan, M. (in press). Comorbid psychiatric disorders in youth in juvenile detention. *Archives of General Psychiatry.*

Teplin, L., Abram, K., McClelland, G., Dulcan, M., & Mericle, A. (2002). Psychiatric disorders in youth in juvenile detention. *Archives of General Psychiatry,* 59, 1133–1143.

Timmons-Mitchell, J., Brown, C., Schulz, C., Webster, S., Underwood, L., & Semple, W. (1997). Comparing the mental health needs of female and male incarcerated juvenile delinquents. *Behavioral Sciences and the Law,* 15, 195–202.

Tobey, A., Grisso, T., & Schwartz, R. (2000). Youths' trial participation as seen by youths and their attorneys: An exploration of competence-based issues. In T. Grisso & R. Schwartz (Eds.), *Youth on trial: A developmental perspective on juvenile justice* (pp. 225–242). Chicago: University of Chicago Press.

Tolan, P., & Gorman-Smith, D. (1998). Development of serious and violent juvenile offending careers. In R. Loeber & D. Farrington (Eds.), *Serious and violent juvenile offenders* (pp. 68–85). Thousand Oaks, CA: Sage.

Torbet, P., Gable, R., Hurst, H., Montgomery, I., Szymanski, L., & Thomas, D. (1996). *State responses to serious and violent juvenile crime.* Washington, DC: Office of Juvenile Justice and Delinquency Prevention.

Tremblay, R. (2002). *Patterns of development of aggression in childhood.* Paper presented at the convention of the Society for Research on Adolescence, New Orleans, LA.

U.S. Department of Justice, Federal Bureau of Investigation. (1976–1993, 1994a, 1995–1996). *Crime in the United States.* Washington, DC: Government Printing Office.

U.S. General Accounting Office. (1995). *Juvenile justice: Juveniles processed in criminal court and case dispositions.* Washington, DC: U.S. General Accounting Office (Document # GAO/VVD-95-170).

U.S. Surgeon General. (1999). *Mental health: A report of the Surgeon General.* Rockville, MD: U.S. Public Health Service.

Vander Stoep, A., Evens, C., & Taub, J. (1997). Risk of juvenile justice system referral among children in a public mental health system. *Journal of Mental Health Administration, 24,* 428–441.

Virginia Department of Mental Health, Mental Retardation, and Substance Abuse Services. (2001, September 17). *Memorandum: New contract for the provision of restoration services to juveniles pursuant to the Code of Virginia 16.1-356 through 16.1-361.* Availability: J. Duval, Director of Juvenile Competency Services, DMHMRSAS, Richmond, VA.

Virginia Policy Design Team. (1994). *Mental health needs of youth in Virginia's juvenile detention center.* Richmond, VA: Virginia Policy Design Team.

Vitiello, B., Hill, J., Elia, J., Cuningham, E., McLeer, S., & Behar, D. (1991). P.R.N. medications in child psychiatric patients: A pilot placebo-controlled study. *Journal of Clinical Psychiatry, 52,* 499–501.

Vitiello, B., Ricciuti, A., & Behar, D. (1987). P.R.N. medications in child state hospital inpatients. *Journal of Clinical Psychiatry, 48,* 351–354.

Wakefield, J. (1992). The concept of mental disorder: On the boundary between biological facts and social values. *American Psychologist, 47,* 373–388.

Waldron, H., Brody, J., & Slesnick, N. (2001). Integrative behavioral and family therapy for adolescent substance abuse. In P. Monti, S. Colby, & T. O'Leary (Eds.), *Adolescents, alcohol, and substance abuse: Reaching teens through brief interventions* (pp. 216–243). New York: Guilford.

Walker, J., Lahey, B., Russo, M., Frick, P., Christ, M., McBurnett, K., Loeher, R., Stouthamer-Loeber, M., & Green, S. (1991). Anxiety, inhibition, and conduct disorder in children: I. Relations to social impairment. *Journal of the American Academy of Child and Adolescent Psychiatry, 30,* 187–191.

Warner, L., Kessler, R., Hughes, M., Anthony, J., & Nelson, C. (1995). Relevance and correlates of drug use and dependence in the United States:

Results from the National Comorbidity Survey. *Archives of General Psychiatry*, 52, 219–229.

Wasserman, G., McReynolds, L., Lucas, C., Fisher, P., & Santos, L. (2002). The Voice DISC-IV with incarcerated male youths: Prevalence of disorder. *Journal of the American Academy of Child and Adolescent Psychiatry*, 41, 314–321.

Weiss, B., Catron, T., Harris, V., & Phung, T. (1999). The effectiveness of traditional child psychotherapy. *Journal of Consulting and Clinical Psychology*, 67, 82–94.

Weisz, J., & Jensen, P. (1999). Efficacy and effectiveness of child and adolescent psychotherapy and pharmacotherapy. *Mental Health Services Research*, 1, 125–157.

Weisz, J., Weiss, B., Alicke, M., & Klotz, M. (1987). Effectiveness of psychotherapy with children and adolescents: A meta-analysis for clinicians. *Journal of Consulting and Clinical Psychology*, 55, 542–549.

Weisz, J., Weiss, B., Han, S., Granger, D., & Morton, T. (1995). Effects of psychotherapy with children and adolescents revisited: A meta-analysis of treatment outcome studies. *Psychological Bulletin*, 117, 450–468.

Westendorp, F., Brink, K., Roberson, M., & Ortiz, I. (1986). Variables which differentiate placement of adolescents in juvenile justice or mental health systems. *Adolescence*, 21, 23–37.

Wierson, M., & Forehand, R. (1995). Predicting recidivism in juvenile delinquents: The role of mental health diagnoses and the qualification of conclusions by race. *Behavioral Research and Therapy*, 33, 63–67.

Winters, K. (2001). Assessing adolescent substance use problems and other areas of functioning: State of the art. In P. Monti, S. Colby, & T. O'Leary (Eds.), *Adolescents, alcohol, and substance abuse* (pp. 80–108). New York: Guilford.

Winters, K., Stinchfield, R., & Opland, E. (2000). The effectiveness of the Minnesota model approach in the treatment of adolescent drug abusers. *Addiction*, 95, 601–612.

Woolard, J., Fried, C., & Reppucci, N. (2001). Toward an expanded definition of adolescent competence in legal situations. In R. Roesch, R. Corrado, & R. Dempster (Eds.), *Psychology in the courts: International advances in knowledge* (pp. 21–40). London: Routledge.

Woolard, J., Reppucci, N., & Redding, R. (1996). Theoretical and methodological issues in studying children's capacities in legal contexts. *Law and Human Behavior*, 20, 219–228.

Yates, B. (1996). *Analyzing costs, procedures, processes, and outcomes in human services*. Thousand Oaks, CA: Sage.

Young, J. (1998). Trends in cost management for healthcare services: Managed care in the 1990s. In J. Young & P. Ferrari (Eds.), *Designing mental health services and systems for children and adolescents: A shrewd investment* (pp. 25–41). Philadelphia: Brunner/Mazel.

Zimring, F. (1998). *American youth violence.* New York: Oxford University Press.

Zoccolillo, M. (1993). Gender and the development of conduct disorder. *Development and Psychopathology, 5,* 65–78.

# Index